Crises in the Caribbean Basin

POLITICAL ECONOMY OF THE WORLD-SYSTEM ANNUALS

Series Editor: IMMANUEL WALLERSTEIN

Published in cooperation with the Section on the Political Economy of the World-System of the American Sociological Association

About the Series

The intent of this series of annuals is to reflect and inform the intense theoretical and empirical debates about the "political economy of the world-system." These debates assume that the phenomena of the real world cannot be separated into three (or more) categories—political, economic, and social—which can be studied by different methods and in closed spheres. The economy is "institutionally" rooted; the polity is the expression of socioeconomic forces; and "societal" structures are a consequence of politico-economic pressures. The phrase "world-system" also tells us that we believe there is a working social system larger than any state whose operations are themselves a focus of social analysis. How states and parties, firms and classes, status groups and social institutions operate within the framework and constraints of the world-system is precisely what is debated.

Volumes in this series:

Volume 1: *Social Change in the Capitalist World Economy* (1978)
        Barbara Hockey Kaplan, *Editor*

Volume 2: *The World-System of Capitalism: Past and Present* (1979)
        Walter L. Goldfrank, *Editor*

Volume 3: *Processes of the World-System* (1980)
        Terence K. Hopkins and Immanuel Wallerstein, *Editors*

Volume 4: *Dynamics of World Development* (1981)
        Richard Rubinson, *Editor*

Volume 5: *Ascent and Decline in the World-System* (1982)
        Edward Friedman, *Editor*

Volume 6: *Crises in the World-System* (1983)
        Albert Bergesen, *Editor*

Volume 7: *Labor in the Capitalist World-Economy* (1984)
        Charles Bergquist, *Editor*

Volume 8: *States Versus Markets in the World-System* (1985)
        Peter Evans, Dietrich Rueschemeyer, and
        Evelyne Huber Stephens, *Editors*

Volume 9: *Crises in the Caribbean Basin* (1987)
        Richard Tardanico, *Editor*

Crises in the Caribbean Basin

Edited by
Richard Tardanico

Volume 9, **Political Economy of the World-System Annuals**
Series Editor: Immanuel Wallerstein

SAGE PUBLICATIONS
The Publishers of Professional Social Science
Newbury Park   Beverly Hills   London   New Delhi

For information address:

SAGE Publications, Inc.
2111 West Hillcrest Drive
Newbury Park, California 91320

SAGE Publications Inc.   SAGE Publications Ltd.
275 South Beverly Drive   28 Banner Street
Beverly Hills   London EC1Y 8QE
California 90212   England

SAGE PUBLICATIONS India Pvt. Ltd.
M-32 Market
Greater Kailash I
New Delhi 110 048 India

Printed in the United States of America

Library of Congress Cataloging-in-Publication Data

Crises in the Caribbean Basin.

   (Political economy of the world-system annuals ;
v. 9)
   "Based on papers presented at the ninth annual
Conference on the Political Economy of the World-System,
Tulane University, March 18-20, 1985"-—Pref.
   1. Caribbean Area—Economic conditions—
1945-   —Congresses. 2. Central America—Economic
conditions—1979-   —Congresses. 3. Caribbean
Area—Politics and government—1945-   —Congresses.
4. Central America—Politics and government—
1979-   —Congresses. I. Tardanico, Richard.
II. Political Economy of the World-System Conference
(9th : 1985 : Tulane University) III. Series.
HC151.C75 1986   330.9729   86-1852
ISBN 0-8039-2808-4

FIRST PRINTING

CONTENTS

Preface   7

Introduction: Issues in the Study of Caribbean Crises
    RICHARD TARDANICO   9

PART I: LABOR, ECONOMY, AND CRISIS

1. White Days, Black Days: The Working Day
   and the Crisis of Slavery in the French Carribean
       DALE W. TOMICH   31

2. Labor and Ethnicity: The Caribbean Conjuncture
       SIDNEY W. MINTZ   47

3. Economic Development and
   Dependency in Nineteenth-Century Guatemala
       RALPH LEE WOODWARD, Jr.   59

4. Industrialization, Labor Migration, and
   Employment Crises: A Comparison of
   Jamaica and the Dominican Republic
       DAVID BRAY   79

5. The Informal Sector Revisited: The Case of
   the Talleres Rurales Mini-Maquilas in Colombia
       CYNTHIA TRUELOVE   95

PART II: STATE, ECONOMY, AND CRISIS

6. State Responses to the Great Depression, 1929-1934:
   Toward a Comparative Analysis of "Revolutionary"
   Mexico and "Nonrevolutionary" Colombia
       RICHARD TARDANICO   113

7. Coffee and Politics in Central America
       JEFFERY M. PAIGE   141

8. Sandinista Relations with the West:
   The Limits of Nonalignment
       ROBERT P. MATTHEWS   191

9. Restratification After Revolution: The Cuban Experience
    SUSAN ECKSTEIN   217

10. The International Monetary Fund and Contemporary
    Crisis in the Dominican Republic
    MARTIN F. MURPHY   241

Notes on the Contributors   261

PREFACE

The contents of this volume are based on papers presented at the Ninth Annual Conference on the Political Economy of the World-System, Tulane University, March 28-30, 1985. The conference was sponsored jointly by the American Sociological Association Section on the Political Economy of the World-System and Tulane's Roger Thayer Stone Center for Latin American Studies. Special thanks to Richard E. Greenleaf, Director, for the Center's generous support; to Gene Yeager, Associate Director, for his valuable advice; and to David Bray, Assistant Director, for going far beyond the call of duty in helping with the conference's countless details. Marionita Williams and Jane Kuroda, Department of Sociology, took care of more than their share of details, including doing their very best to keep my head on straight. For quite a few months my phone was a virtual hotline to Martin Murphy, Helen I. Safa, and Evelyne Huber Stephens, whose long-distance help was appreciated almost as much as their participation in the conference. Besides all of these kind people and the contributors to the volume, a number of other participants greatly enriched the conference with commentary and with papers that will be appearing elsewhere. Additional thanks go to my colleagues at the Escuela de Historia y Geografía, Universidad de Costa Rica, and at the Facultad Latinoamericana de Ciencias Sociales (FLACSO), for making the first few months of my Fulbright year such stimulating, productive, and pleasant ones; and, most of all, to my wife Sally, whose warmth and challenges keep me afloat, especially when we manage to be in the same country.

Richard Tardanico
San Jośe, Costa Rica

INTRODUCTION
Issues in the Study of Caribbean Crises

Richard Tardanico
Florida International University

CARIBBEAN CHALLENGES
TO UNITED STATES HEGEMONY

Breakdown, struggle, transformation: The Caribbean region is indeed wracked by crises. At the heart of its crises lie two virtually inseparable issues. The first is the distribution of wealth and power ① throughout the zone. The second is the terms of its political and ② economic relations with the United States in particular and the global capitalist order as a whole.

The recent ascendance of Caribbean affairs to the headlines of world metropolises dates from 1978-1980 with a wave of challenges to the underpinnings of U.S. regional hegemony. Most prominent among these challenges were the Nicaraguan Revolution, the New Jewel regime of Grenada, electoral strife in Jamaica, and the intensification of conflicts in El Salvador and Guatemala. In the context of anti-American struggles elsewhere in the underdeveloped world, these and other political currents heightened strategic and scholarly interest in Cuba and focused attention on the revolutionary potential of what U.S. analysts have labeled the *Caribbean Basin* (see Dominguez, 1982; Erisman, 1984; Greene and Scowcroft, 1984; Insulza, 1985; Levine, 1983). Integral to the unfolding of crises in the Caribbean Basin was the emergence during the 1970s of Venezuela and Mexico as zonal powers. Riding the crest of the international petroleum boom to enhanced geopolitical autonomy and influence, their diplomatic and economic support for the area's popular-nationalist forces further eroded the traditional foundations of Washington's regional dominance (Bagley, 1984; Matthews, 1984; Payne, 1984). During a global capitalist downturn, the potential for circum-Caribbean movements and governments to exercise initiative against the United States and its oligarchic partners

9

received additional boosts from the loosening of U.S.-Western European relations, the strengthened economies of oil-producing countries in other areas of the Third World, and post-Vietnam political divisions within the United States (see Edelman, 1985; FLACSO et al., 1985; Matthews, this volume; Wallerstein, 1984a, 1984b).

Such potential, however, should not be overestimated; the United States' invasion of Grenada and stepped-up political, economic, and military intervention in Central America have delivered this sobering message. At issue is the capacity of popular-nationalist forces to gain bargaining leverage against U.S. dominance by building centralized, mass-inclusionary states, by diversifying their dependence among foreign powers, and by aligning with reformist and revolutionary elements throughout the underdeveloped world. To be sure, the smallness and extreme dependency of most circum-Caribbean nations militate against these strategies; Mexico and Cuba have been the most successful practitioners, the most obvious limitation being Cuba's deep reliance on Soviet aid. Although present international conditions do allow significant room for political-economic maneuvering against Washington, the latter's resources remain considerable. Washington's confrontation with revolutionary Nicaragua is a crucial example.

Western European aid and trade have proved essential to the Sandinista government's campaign to simultaneously offset U.S. opposition and minimize dependence on the Soviet Union[1] (Armstrong, 1985; Conway, 1985; Edelman, 1985; Matthews, this volume). Yet Western European states acknowledge the legitimacy of American interests in the Caribbean Basin and their own geostrategic priorities lie elsewhere. Broader U.S.-Western European considerations, which translate into American financial and diplomatic leverage, additionally limit the extent of active Western support for Nicaragua (FLACSO et al., 1985; Matthews, this volume). Meanwhile, Sandinista relations with the Eastern bloc were slow in developing and remain fraught with tensions, the most important reason being the low priority of Caribbean affairs in Soviet foreign policy (Edelman, 1985; Valenta, 1982). Nevertheless, Washington's political, economic, and military reprisals push Nicaragua into heightened dependence on the Eastern bloc. In so doing, the Reagan administration undercuts Sandinista leanings toward nonalignment and renders the new regime increasingly vulnerable to charges of Soviet complicity. At the same time its opposition diverts Nicaragua's minimal resources to intensified military buildup, thereby damaging programs of socioeconomic reconstruction and reinforcing domestic tendencies toward restricted civil liberties (Conway, 1985; Edelman,

1985; Kinzer, 1985; LaFeber, 1983; LeoGrande, 1986; Woodward, 1984).

Cuban foreign policy, of course, is tightly intertwined with that of the Soviet Union. Castro, nonetheless, is no Soviet puppet and his regime's independent stake in the Caribbean Basin is obviously considerable (LeoGrande, 1983; Pastor, 1983; Valenta, 1982). Until late 1978 Cuban backing of the Sandinistas was much more diplomatic than material, as Castro sought to reduce the chances of U.S. reprisal and to preserve a decade's progress in Cuban-Latin American diplomacy. When Cuba did begin supplying arms to the Sandinistas by no means did it act alone among Caribbean states; it followed the lead of Costa Rica and its shipments were probably worth less than those of Venezuela and Panama (Edelman, 1985: 35-36; LeoGrande, 1983: 46-47). In the international setting delineated above, Cuban military and nonmilitary support has grown substantially. But data indicate that the Sandinista military is far from being the regional threat portrayed by Washington (Edelman, 1985: 49-53; Kinzer, 1985). Further, Castro has urged a cautious Sandinista stance toward domestic business classes and the United States, and Nicaragua's loans and credits have flowed mainly from non-Communist nations and multilateral institutions (Conway, 1985; Edelman, 1985; LeoGrande, 1983; Matthews, this volume). Still, the Reagan presidency has persisted in highlighting Cuban involvement as a means of legitimizing its anti-Sandinista measures, including the actions of its Central American collaborators (Edelman, 1985; Kenworthy, 1985; LeoGrande, 1983, 1986).

A key dimension of Washington's interventionist strategy has been its ability to maneuver Costa Rica, El Salvador, and Honduras into objecting against Contadora provisions that would restrict U.S. presence in Central America[2] (Kenworthy, 1985; see also Anderson, 1985; Bagley, 1984; Baloyra, 1985; La Nación, 1985; LeoGrande, 1986; Lincoln, 1985; Morales, 1985). In view of today's internal unrest, regional instability, deteriorating trade conditions, and financial crises, such small, client states are especially amenable to U.S. diplomatic-military initiatives. Venezuela and Mexico, as Caribbean powers, possess much greater bargaining potential, yet their own willingness and capacities to counterbalance U.S. influence have been declining. Since 1979 Venezuelan foreign policy has shifted rightward, in spite of its Contadora participation. This shift has been rooted in national party forces, diplomatic tensions with Cuba, and, given a world oil glut, economic difficulties, and increased dependence on U.S. trade and aid (Ewell,1986; Matthews, 1984). The consistency of Mexico's commitment to popular-nationalist causes stems from its own heritage of revolution and confrontation with U.S. expansionism, as well as from its petroleum resources and large, diversified economy. Crises of its economy and one-party structure jeopardize both the institutional foundations of Mexican political stability and its state's independent foreign policy (Bagley, 1984; Levy and Székely, 1986). Mexico's postrevolutionary state structure and national development have done much to shield U.S. society from spillovers of the political violence and uncertainity that Central Americans know all too well. Should Mexico's crises deepen, and should Washington's regional posture remain inflexible, this shield will continue to erode. If it someday collapses, First World citizens will then find themselves face to face with Third World political realities.

It is clear, in sum, that the Reagan administration has not lacked for responses to Caribbean challenges. Economic and debt crises have been a source of leverage over Caribbean states, while militarization and the Caribbean Basin Initiative are the linchpins of its campaign to keep friendly forces afloat in the American Mediterranean (Baloyra, 1985; Kenworthy, 1985; LeoGrande, 1986; Lowenthal, 1984; Newfarmer, 1985; Payne, 1984). With this campaign, though, the administration exacerbates the zone's socioeconomic inequalities, fans its flames of political unrest, and escalates diplomatic tensions on a wider international scale. As part of a more basic political-economic realignment, this myopic foreign policy has profound implications for the daily lives of U.S. citizens, too. These have included the economic and social costs of militarization, the flight of American manufacturing jobs to low-wage sites in the Caribbean Basin and other Third World zones, and the influx of thousands of migrants fleeing the poverty, oppression, and violence of their homelands (see FLACSO et al., 1985; Portes and Walton, 1981; and the chapters by Bray, Murphy, and Truelove, this volume). We can only speculate about the probable consequences of intensified and expanded regional warfare for U.S. domestic civil liberties. By no means, then, are the ramifications of Caribbean crises restricted to that area of the globe; in spilling beyond its boundaries, they wash onto the shores of and permeate the soil of American society and the world at large.

ANALYZING PAST AND PRESENT CARIBBEAN CRISES

Identifying crises is one thing; analyzing their origins, development, and consequences is quite another. It is the analysis of past and present

Caribbean crises that commands this volume's attention. How to go about this task is itself a challenging issue, as evidenced by the history, depth, and intensity of controversy over the study of crises in general. Since Greek antiquity, crises have been approached from myriad perspectives and variously portrayed as morbid and threatening, vital and liberating; as cyclical and static, unpredictable and dynamic (Starn, 1971). Not that controversy has been restricted to the grandest of issues, as the study of crises has focused debate too on details regarding their causes, scale, duration, and outcomes. Such disagreement continues, not just between but within the many schools of thought. Both levels of disagreement flourish within the rapidly expanding literature on crises in the Caribbean Basin (see, for example, Ambursely and Cohen, 1983; Dixon and Jonas, 1983; Erisman, 1984; FLACSO et al., 1985; Greene and Scowcroft, 1984; Levine, 1983; National Bipartisan Commission on Central America, 1984a, 1984b; Payne, 1984).

The essays in this volume address various dimensions of past and present crises in the circum-Caribbean, and the contributors share no single theoretical and ideological viewpoint. What they do share is a common orientation—one that underscores the interplay of Caribbean crises with the world-historical development of capitalism. The contributors focus on various facets of Caribbean life—from work routines and ethnic identities to investment flows and state policies—as they have intersected with the global dynamics of capital accumulation and diplomatic-military relations. Even so, the contributors make little mention of capitalism as a "world-system" (Wallerstein, 1979). Theirs is generally a looser conception of world capitalism. Its point of departure, to be sure, is the history of colonial and neocolonial intrusion into the circum-Caribbean. Nonetheless, this conception does not regard the region's history as a mere by-product of North Atlantic economic and geopolitical expansion; on the contrary, it recognizes ample room for local initiative to grapple with and alter the terms of European and U.S. domination. The chapters tell us that such initiative has taken a variety of forms—social, cultural, economic, and political; and they suggest that we take local initiative seriously not only as it has mediated the forms of metropolitan penetration, but also as it has compelled metropolitan governments and enterprises to reconsider their strategies of operation both within the Caribbean Basin and worldwide.

The implications of this approach transcend the study of the Caribbean per se. They channel our attention to local processes and structures throughout the Third World as we attempt to make sense of historical and contemporary transformations of production, exchange, and politics at the global level. Thus the chapters build upon the growing literature that faults theory and research on the capitalist world-system for underestimating or ignoring the importance of social relations of production (Bergquist, 1984; Portes and Walton, 1981; Wolf, 1982), state organizations (Evans et al., 1985; Kraus and Vanneman, 1985; Skocpol, 1979), and the peoples of underdeveloped lands (Mintz, 1977; Portes and Walton, 1981; Wolf, 1982). Neither individually nor collectively do the chapters venture to account for capitalism's world-scale ups and downs. Instead they pose two challenges to scholars so inclined. The first is to recognize the multidimensionality of dominated societies— the depth and interplay of their elements of class, ethnicity, state building, geopolitics, and so on. The second is to incorporate into analyses of international capitalism the active role of dominated societies in the making of the modern world.

Regarding the volume, the two challenges raise a fundamental question: How do we define *Caribbean*? That this question sparks lively debate is no surprise; the lack of consensus itself attests to the tremendous diversity within the zone—however defined—as well as to the complexity of its linkages with the global order. Probably the most common definition takes as the Caribbean's essence its history of colonialism, plantations, slavery, and African influence. From this standpoint the area consists of the Caribbean archipelago and mainland Belize, Guyana, Suriname, and French Guiana. This definition does not deny the myriad divergencies that have characterized the region's societies during and since the colonial era. It nevertheless underlines the common sociocultural traits associated with the Caribbean's history as Western Europe's oldest bloc of overseas colonies (see Knight, 1978; Payne, 1984). An increasingly popular alternative takes as its point of departure political-military networks within the Caribbean and in the zone's relations with the wider world. Essential to this approach is the assertion of U.S. hegemony over the Caribbean from the late nineteenth century onward, and the way such hegemony has conditioned the area's intra- and extra-regional affairs. This definition focuses on the "circum-Caribbean," or "Caribbean Basin," which it views as embracing not simply the archipelago and the mainland territories mentioned above, but additionally the remaining countries of South America's northern coast, the entire isthmus of Central America, and Mexico (see Erisman, 1984; Greene and Scowcroft, 1984; Insulza, 1985).

Both definitions are inherently politicized. Barry Levine (1983: 4) acknowledges this fact and underscores their complementarity in capturing different yet overlapping realities of the Caribbean zone, saying that "nations will frequently invoke ethnic identifications in attempts to achieve geopolitical goals, or geopolitical concerns may reinforce sociocultural linkages." These tactics point us in the direction of comparative-historical research on the processes by which regions of the Americas, Asia, and Africa have been incorporated into the metropolitan orbit and the relationship of such processes to regional patterns of resistance and accommodation to metropolitan intrusion. In both respects, diplomatic-military rivalry, capitalist penetration, and the construction of ethnocultural groupings have played powerful, intersecting roles in Caribbean history. The Caribbean's past and present suggest that what constitutes a "region" of the world political economy by one or two of these criteria, or by some subset of their myriad dimensions, may not do so by the remainder; and that, like other political-economic phenomena, such regions are constantly being defined and redefined by class formation, statist actions, transnational production and trade and the like (see Giddens, 1981; Wolf, 1982).

The impact of such pressures on interstate relations within and between Third World areas merits special attention insofar as it receives little or none from most writings on imperialism and underdevelopment. This topic encompasses such issues as how Third World states, not merely in conjunction with North Atlantic powers but likewise on their own, undertake wars and peace-keeping measures as well as establish regional and extraregional blocs (e.g., OPEC, the Non-Aligned Movement, the Contadora Group). A related issue is how the developmental gains of underdeveloped countries may come at the direct or indirect expense of less fortunate counterparts within and outside their particular zones of the Americas, Asia, and Africa (see Tardanico, 1984; Wallerstein, 1979). For instance, what local and world conditions determine whether metropolitan investors choose the Caribbean Basin or the "Pacific Rim" for export-assembly manufacturing? What conditions determine which countries within the two zones, and which locales within the countries, capture such investments? What are the consequences of success or failure in attracting export-assembly for inter-and intraregional patterns of economic change, social struggle, and state building? What are the ramifications of such patterns for metropolitan economies and politics? Similar questions can be directed at earlier periods of Caribbean history and at the histories of other underdeveloped areas.

Thus we see that the intra- and interregional dynamics of the underdeveloped world deserve serious consideration as we examine the ever-changing fabric of global production, exchange, and politics. The Caribbean—as the first colonial site of European overseas expansion, as a vibrant amalgam of world cultures, as a generator of challenges to metropolitan domination—has been a vital contributor to capitalism's intenational transformations. It is from this standpoint that the volume addresses crises in the Caribbean Basin, past and present.

THE CONTRIBUTIONS

Labor, Economy, and Crisis

Labor, ethnicity, and struggle form the core of Dale W. Tomich's "White Days, Black Days: The Working Day and the Crisis of Slavery in the French Caribbean." Tomich explores the changing organization of the working day under slavery. He thereby traces slavery's changing social relations of production and evaluates their significance for the French Caribbean's transition to post-emancipation society. The material-technical demands of sugar production dictated a complex, highly regimented division of labor, which submitted slaves to the physical and cultural burdens of work as a cold, calculated, coerced routine. The organization and rhythm of Caribbean sugar production, then, stood in violent contrast to the traditional African subordination of work to kinship and community.

Yet sugar production did not monopolize the daily lives of slaves. Aside from the harvest season, the unit of labor time was the day—from sunrise to sunset. Tomich explains that this limitation guaranteed slaves a considerable degree of social autonomy. Adding a measure of economic autonomy was the masters' cost-reducing practice of allowing slaves marginal land and a free day to produce for their own subsistence. Though initially opposed by colonial authorities, such production expanded to become an essential, and legally recognized, part of the wider food supply. What is more, it signified the division of labor time between a portion claimed by the master and a portion claimed by the slaves. Hence the consolidation and extension of the slaves' "free time" became not only the focal point of their quotidian struggles, but also a driving force in the continual evolution of master/slave relations.

Tomich's chapter portrays the complexities of everyday accommodation and resistance to slavery. In doing so, it underlines the active role of the slaves' consciousness and initiative both in transforming the plantation regime from within and in establishing the social structure of the post-emancipation Caribbean. More generally, it highlights the interconnections of work, culture, and community in the underdeveloped world; the social and political pressures that emerge from these interconnections; and the impact of such pressures not just on local class relations but on global patterns of production.

To what extent did the labor process change with the demise of slavery? Sidney W. Mintz's chapter, "Labor and Ethnicity: The Caribbean Conjuncture," begins where Tomich's leaves off by examining the interplay of class, ethnicity, and the global labor market during the transition to post-emancipation society. Mintz's point of departure is the nineteenth century's massive and divided transoceanic flow of labor. Its division sent whites along the temperate belt from "Old Europe" to "New Europe" and nonwhites along the subtropical belt from Africa and Asia to the Caribbean. Mintz's concern lies with the receiving end of the underside of this flow: the movement of nonwhites to the Caribbean and the naked exploitation they encountered there. This movement and exploitation, he observes, was inextricably bound up with the epoch's evolving international market, specifically the rising demand in the temperate belt's industrializing economies for tropical foods. The tropical food in question here, of course, was sugar—the most basic of the "drug foods" that, by cheaply sustaining the growing metropolitan proletariat, subsidized the booming profits of metropolitan capitalists (Mintz, 1985).

Like Tomich, Mintz indicates that capitalists topped the class structure of the Caribbean, too; the machinery of Caribbean capitalists consisted mainly of slaves who, in Haiti, asserted their humanity in revolutionary fashion. The consequent collapse of Haiti's sugar industry meant expanded market opportunities for planters elsewhere in the Caribbean. There was new competition, though, from European beet sugar. There was also mounting metropolitan presure for the abolition of slavery and persistent fear among planters of another situation like Haiti. Herein lay what, from the planters' perspective, was crisis: How could they ensure the large, thoroughly exploitable work force necessary to undercut European competition and fill the Haitian vacuum? African slavery underwrote nineteenth-century Cuba's large-scale sugar expansion. Of increasing importance, however, throughout the Caribbean was a new supply of workers—East Indian and Chinese "contract" labor. Nevertheless, "free" labor it was not. Herein lay what, from the masses' perspective, was crisis: the persistence of brutal conditions of work and life. It was in this context—the enhancement of labor market segmentation for economic exploitation and political control in rigid, plantation societies—that Caribbean ethnicity unfolded. Mintz situates the political economy of ethnicity in concrete sociohistorical settings. His analysis raises fundamental issues about the linkages among class formation, ethnicity, and the world-historical development of capitalism. And it tells us that intertwined with ethnicity and the "American Dream" in the industrializing United States was ethnicity and nightmare in the post-emancipation Caribbean.

Ralph Lee Woodward, Jr.'s "Economic Development and Dependency in Nineteenth-Century Guatemala" extends the discussion of socioeconomic structure and the international division of labor to the western rim of the circum-Caribbean. In contrast with the Caribbean islands, Central America barely touched the emerging international division of labor until well into the nineteenth century. Guatemala's earliest involvement with the incipient global capitalist economy, and with commodity traffic across the Caribbean, was through its exports of cacao and indigo. During the nineteenth century, as metropolitan demand picked up, new agricultural exports—most significantly coffee, whose cultivation had traversed the Caribbean—energized Guatemala's liberal elite and nascent entrepreneurial classes. The sociopolitical structure that the liberals consolidated has been among the world's most oppressive (Paige, 1983; this volume; Torres-Rivas, 1981; Woodward, 1985).

Woodward informs us that the foundations of Guatemala's contemporary crisis were partially laid by seventeenth-century class relations and eighteenth-century political conflicts. The latter, which took the form of liberalism versus conservatism, intensified with the nineteenth century's quickened pulse of Guatemalan external commerce. Such exports as cochineal and cotton promoted the modernization of the country's economic infrastructure, even as conservatives ruled; but it was coffee expansion after mid-century that propelled the liberals to power for good in 1871. Their policies broke up the traditional barriers to commercialization, above all oligarchic paternalism toward the indigenous masses and aversion to metropolitan influence. Surging exports of coffee and, later, bananas meant prosperity for Guatemala's upper class and its foreign partners, cheaper metropolitan food costs, and some growth of the domestic middle class. It likewise meant crisis for the indigenous masses: shrinking landholdings, declining subsistence production, disrupted communal networks, and harsh work conditions. Eventually, too, it meant crisis for the middle classes, which began pressing—without success—for effective voice in government. Political polarization and repression became persistent features of Guatemalan life (Woodward, 1985).

Woodward's chapter complements Mintz's in that the two examine responses of commercial landowners in the periphery to expanding world market opportunities. The coffee and sugar estate owners they study were, as a class, successful in dominating land and labor. The Guatemalan planters did so by exploiting indigenous labor, whereas the Caribbean planters exploited immigrant labor. Thus arises a series of questions: Were their counterparts elsewhere as successful in responding to world market opportunities? If not, why? What were the ramifications of differing tactics of labor control, as well as differing degrees of success in implementing them, for comparative economic development, social relations, and state making in the periphery?

These comparative-historical questions bring us to chapters by David Bray and Cynthia Truelove on labor and transnational capitalism since World War II. Bray addresses "Industrialization, Labor Migration, and Employment Crises: A Comparison of Jamaica and the Dominican Republic." He begins by noting that in the face of severe unemployment and underemployment the governments of Jamaica and the Dominican Republic wrestle with contradictory pressures by the local populace for job-creating expenditures and by the International Monetary Fund for budgetary cutbacks (see Murphy, this volume). The Jamaican and Dominican employment crises, to be sure, are related intimately to the Caribbean history of colonialism and neocolonialism. Bray argues that within this setting they reflect the severe limitations of post-World War II strategies of economic development through industrialization, emigration, and tourism. He focuses on the first two strategies as they pertain to Jamaican and Dominican trends in employment structure and labor migration.

Neither Jamaica nor the Dominican Republic were viable candidates for import-substitution industrialization, which promises extensive participation by domestic capital but requires a substantial preexisting base of infrastructural and market development. Bray reports that the two countries did experience restricted amounts of import-substitution growth. Nonetheless, its job-creating capacity peaked early, a result of both the sector's capital-intensive nature and the structural limitations of agrarian-based economies. Not surprisingly, it is export manufacturing that has gathered steam-especially in the Dominican Republic, with the emergence of the "new" international division of labor and the introduction of the Caribbean Basin Initiative. Export manufacturing, however, is almost solely the domain of foreign capital; and though its job-creating capacity is significant, the sector's employment is overwhelmingly low-skill, low-pay, and geared to young, single females. Hence export manufacturing reinforces external dependence, aggravates class inequality, and "feminizes" the industrial work force (see Newfarmer, 1985; Portes and Walton, 1981). Bray concludes that it thereby combines with stagnation in import-substitution industry to promote the emigration of skilled labor and professionals to the United States. Their outmigration stands in sharp contrast to projections by post-World War II economic planners, who sought to channel workers into food production and manufacturing for the local urban market while exporting surplus rural workers to foreign agricultural zones of the Caribbean.

Truelove, in "The Informal Sector Revisited: The Case of the Talleres Rurales Mini-Maquilas in Colombia," stresses the role of the periphery's contemporary labor arrangements in generating what many theorists characterize as "unequal exchange" within the world economy (see Portes and Walton, 1981; Wallerstein, 1979). She writes that initial thinking pointed to rural subsistence production as underlying the transfer of surplus value from, first, countryside to city in the periphery, and second, periphery to core in the international division of labor. A basic question, though, is how the international transfer of surplus value is maintained in the face of declining rural subsistence production throughout the underdeveloped world. Recent thinking has pointed not to rural/urban mechanisms but to segmentation of the urban labor market of the periphery—specifically, the linkages between its "formal" and "informal" sectors—increasingly as the basis of unequal exchange at the global scale. Truelove claims that, without denying the importance of the urban labor market, this recent approach too quickly dismisses the rural sphere. Her own perspective synthesizes the initial and recent approaches. It highlights the dynamics by which the formal sector's enterprises, many of which are connected with metropolitan firms, offset today's crisis of capitalist accumulation by penetrating the rural sphere in the form of subcontracting arrangements, thus taking advantage of the cheap, informal labor made available by crises of agrarian society and economy. We therefore see the extension into the countryside of linkages between the formal and informal sectors. Simultaneously we see that this process interacts with another, more fundamental, set of linkages—the sexual division of labor—as rural women come to constitute the informal, underpaid industrial work force that undergirds the changing organization of unequal exchange.

The chapters by Bray and Truelove suggest several questions. Earlier we noted one of them: What regional, national, and local circumstances attract export-manufacturing investment? In addition, how does such investment affect linkages between the formal and informal sectors, as well as between men and women? How do these linkages foster sociopolitical unity or disunity among the rural and urban masses (see Murphy, this volume)? In what ways do women gain or lose socially, economically, and politically? How do evolving class and gender relations influence flows of labor migration? How do the socioeconomic networks and gender relations of the masses differ in capitalist and socialist countries of the periphery (see Eckstein, this volume)? With respect to Colombia, does export-manufacturing investment represent closer integration with the Caribbean Basin? If so, what are the implications for the political economies of both the Caribbean and Andean regions? The last two questions are theoretically pertinent to the volume's consideration of the forms and extent of historical and contemporary integration among the Caribbean islands, the northern rim of South America, Central America, and Mexico (see Levine, 1983; and the chapters by Woodward, Tardanico, Paige, and Matthews, this volume).

State, Economy, and Crisis

Richard Tardanico's topic is "State Responses to the Great Depression, 1929-1934: Toward a Comparative Analysis of 'Revolutionary' Mexico and 'Nonrevolutionary' Colombia." He begins by posing two questions: How does state making differ in revolutionary and nonrevolutionary settings? What are the consequences of its differences, not just for domestic sociopolitical and economic structures but for their relations with worldwide patterns of capital accumulation and geopolitics? With respect to Mexico and Colombia during the Great Depression, these questions direct research to the historical roots of contemporary tendencies of class struggle, state building, and economic development in the Caribbean Basin.

Tardanico points out that, in responding to the onset of world crisis, Mexican and Colombian policies were similar: Neither state's leadership took advantage of the weakened condition of the domestic upper classes and U.S. capital by attempting to stimulate national development by redistributing wealth at home and redefining linkages with metropolitan interests. A basic difference, though, was that Mexico's revolutionary experience had mobilized popular-nationalist forces toward the political defeat of the traditional oligarchy and the creation of a centralized state apparatus. Despite a conservative shift among many new regime elites, such forces imposed formidable constraints upon state making options. In Colombia, by contrast, the traditional oligarchy retained a powerful role in the formulation of government policy and the state apparatus was notably decentralized. Consequently, the Mexican state's conservative response to the onset of world crisis provoked a resurgence of populistic nationalism that further centralized the new regime state, definitively undermined the old regime oligarchy, altered the terms of metropolitan investment, and promoted large-scale capitalist accumulation. Colombia experienced a milder form of populistic nationalism that culminated not in statist and capitalist transformation but in oligarchic reaction, political chaos, and a relatively traditional dependence on foreign capital. The impact of revolution in Mexico and its absence in Colombia has continued to be evident in the comparative unfolding of their domestic sociopolitical crises and in their comparative relations with crises in the wider Caribbean Basin.

Like the contributions to Part I, Jeffery M. Paige's "Coffee and Politics in Central America" focuses attention on transnational commodity flows and local socioeconomic structures. He takes us a step further, however, by using this interrelationship to shed light on political diversity in twentieth-century Central America. Paige remarks that, at first glance, the marked diversity of Central American regimes is a puzzling phenomenon; after all, the countries have been hewn from a common bedrock of isthmian location, Spanish colonial heritage, postcolonial entaglements with foreign powers, and reliance on one or two agricultural exports, above all coffee. Yet the region lacks neither socioeconomic nor political diversity. Although the embryonic regional differences of the colonial era had reached adolescence by the era of independence, it was coffee that nourished them to adulthood in the nineteenth and twentieth centuries. Paige cautions us against reducing the political complexities of contemporary Central America to the class structure of coffee, but he underscores the extent to which their roots are intertwined.

Paige exposes these roots by delving into the socioeconomic arrangements by which Central America's oligarachies have extracted wealth from coffee, and then linking these arrangements to the region's differences in elite political responses to challenges from below. He concentrates on the socioeconomic side of this equation through a detailed, comparative discussion of the elite's involvement in coffee cultivation, processing, and export during the mid-twentieth century. Thus he brings us to the onset of the post-World War II economic growth and diversification that, mediated by Central America's class and state forms and geostrategic position, led to present-day crises (see LaFeber, 1983; Torres-Rivas, 1981; Woodward, 1985). Regarding reformist and radical challenges to the upper class, how has the comparative organization of coffee cultivation, processing, and exporting shaped the political interests and capacities of the sector's small holders and proletariat throughout Central America (see Paige, 1975, 1983)? How has this comparative organization intersected with that of other rural and urban commodities to influence wider intra- and interclass patterns? How have such patterns combined with pressures emanating from the bureaucracies of Central American and foreign governments to mold the region's state-class and state-state relations?

Robert P. Matthews's theme is "Sandinista Relations with the West: The Limits of Nonalignment." He writes that, in view of Nicaragua's history of extensive U.S. military and political intervention, nonalignment has been a fundamental point of both Sandinista foreign policy and U.S. opposition. Matthews observes that Nicaragua's smallness, poverty, and location have precluded the severing of relations with Washington as a feasible option. Hence the Sandinistas have undertaken to improve their ability to bargain with Washington by spreading Nicaragua's economic and military dependence among foreign states. This pragmatic stance parallels the foreign policy of nonsocialist revolutionary Mexico (Bagley, 1984; Meyer, 1972; Tardanico, this volume) more than that of socialist revolutionary Cuba, whose leadership more directly confronted U.S. interests (Dominguez, 1979; Pastor, 1983; Valenta, 1982).

Matthews's essay informs our earlier discussion of Sandinista-Washington relations. The significance of his contribution lies not just in its relevance to present-day crises in the Caribbean Basin, but also in its emphasis on the initiative taken by peripheral regimes to counteract the dominance of metropolitan states and capital. The degree to which such initiative can be successful depends in part on the availability of foreign allies that possess negotiating leverage against metropolitan powers. Relevant to the chapters by Matthews, Eckstein, and Tardanico is this question: How have global distributions of economic and diplomatic-military power fostered or impeded policies of revolutionary nationalism in Mexico (1917-1940), Cuba (1959-present), and Nicaragua (1979-present)? Favorable external circumstances, though, by no means guarantee that a revolutionary regime can take advantage of them. Whether or not a regime does so hinges on such domestic considerations as its state-class structure and its economy's size and development (see Skocpol, 1979). Revolutionary Mexico's distinct advantage of size makes for risky comparison with revolutionary Cuba and Nicaragua. Concerning the latter two, however, what similarities and differences characterized their economies and state-class structures during the early stages of their revolutions? How did such similarities and differences influence their capacities both to take advantage of favorable external circumstances and to withstand external pressures?

The volume's discussion of state policy in revolutionary and nonrevolutionary settings continues with chapters by Susan Eckstein and Martin F. Murphy. Eckstein examines "Restratification After Revolution: The Cuban Experience." Her point of departure is the contemporary crisis of worsening socioeconomic inequalities associated with the world recession and budgetary cutbacks by governments of the Caribbean Basin. Has Cuba—with its far-reaching socialist transformation—managed to escape the regional tendency toward class polarization? Eckstein demonstrates that, not only during the initial stages of the Revolution but more recently as well, Cuban policies have indeed cushioned the nation's masses against the dislocating effects of extreme dependency on agricultural exports. Her data tell us that postrevolutionary Cuba enjoys the least amount of inequality—in rural and urban property holdings, employment opportunities, gender relations, and income distribution—of all Latin American countries. Eckstein nonetheless indicates that state intervention on behalf of the Cuban masses has not been invariant; its history, rather, is one of shifting policies and distributional consequences.

Eckstein explores these policy and distributional shifts. They have occurred in the context of the old regime's demise and persistent U.S. opposition, the commitment of revolutionary leadership to socialist principles, and the nation's inability to reduce its dependence on agricultural exports. Under these circumstances the Castro regime has grappled with contradictory demands: on the one hand, the task of solidifying the political allegiance of strategic domestic groups; on the other hand, the task of stimulating economic and fiscal growth. Central to Eckstein's chapter is the fundamental tension between Cuban revolutionary ideology and the exigencies of consolidating the new regime state and economy. How has Cuban leadership attempted to resolve this tension? What do its attempts have to say about the possibilities and limitations of socialist revolution in a capitalist world-economy? (For comparative perspective see Chase-Dunn, 1982; Eckstein, 1985; Kraus and Vanneman, 1985; Skocpol, 1979; and the chapters by Tardanico and Matthews, this volume).

Murphy's "The International Monetary Fund and Contemporary Crisis in the Dominican Republic" addresses state policy in a nonrevolutionary situation. He comments that, according to IMF guidelines, the organization's measures should not inflict damage on the social and political fabric of borrowing countries. Yet such damage is inevitable, for the agency's policies support the interests of metropolitan states and capital at the expense of the living standards and political participation of the masses in underdeveloped countries. This contradiction is evident in the IMF's present-day relations with the Dominican Republic.

Murphy's study of government concessions to the IMF complements the chapters by Bray and Truelove on policies to attract export-manufacturing investment in the Dominican Republic, Jamaica, and Colombia. His firsthand account connects international and national economic policies to everyday life in Santo Domingo's lower-class neighborhoods and its broader "grass roots" political context. Also complementing the chapters by Bray and Truelove is Murphy's discussion of ties between the formal and informal sectors. An important issue is how such ties affect the political consciousness and actions of the lower classes. What social networks emerge from the formal and income-producing activities of the urban poor and their rural counterparts? What cooperative and conflicting interests arise from such networks, and what resources can be mobilized on behalf of the various interests? How do such networks, interests, and resources interact with the organization and control of production, as well as the structure and policies of government, to encourage or limit work-based and communally based political action? How do the forms, or absence, of such action influence local relations with the global capitalist order?

NOTES

1. Sequiera (1984), Armstrong (1985), and Edelman (1985) write that differences have always characterized Sandinista leadership regarding the desired role of the Soviet Union in Nicaraguan affairs. Sequiera (1984: 103, 105-107) notes that the faction of President

Daniel Ortega has been most inclined to a policy of nonalignment. All of these analysts acknowledge that it is Cuba—that, despite extreme dependence on the Soviets, has encouraged Sandinista pragmatism—to whom the new regime has looked for external guidance and support (see also LeoGrande, 1983; Matthews, this volume).

2. The Contadora Group consists of Mexico, Panama, Colombia, and Venezuela. A "support group" consists of Peru, Brazil, Uruguay, and Argentina.

REFERENCES

AMBURSELY, F. and R. COHEN [eds.] (1983) Crisis in the Caribbean. New York: Monthly Review.
ANDERSON, T. P. (1985) "Honduras in transition." Current History 84: 114-117, 132.
ARMSTRONG, R. (1985) "Nicaragua: sovereignty and non-alignment." NACLA Report on the Americas 19: 15-21.
BAGLEY, B. M. (1984) "The Politics of asymmetrical interdependence: U.S.-Mexican relations in the 1980s," pp. 141-159 in H. M. Erisman (ed.) The Caribbean Challenge: U.S. Policy in a Volatile Region. Boulder, CO: Westview.
BALOYRA, E. A. (1985) "Central America on the Reagan watch." Journal of Inter-American Studies and World Affairs 27: 63-90.
BERGQUIST, C. [ed.] (1984) Labor in the Capitalist World-Economy. Political Economy of the World-System Annuals, Vol. 7. Beverly Hills, CA: Sage.
CHASE-DUNN, C. [ed.] (1982) Socialist States in the World-System. Beverly Hills, CA: Sage.
CONWAY, M. E. (1985) "External dependence, external assistance, and economic aggression against Nicaragua." Latin American Perspectives 12: 39-67.
DIXON, M. and S. JONAS [eds.] (1983) Revolution and Intervention in Central America. San Francisco: Synthesis.
DOMINGUEZ, J. I. (1978) Cuba: Order and Revolution. Cambridge: Belknap Press.
———(1982) U.S. Interests and Policies in the Caribbean and Central America. Washington, DC: American Enterprise Institute for Public Policy Research.
ECKSTEIN, S. (1986) "The Cuban revolution in comparative perspective." Comparative Studies in Society and History 28: 502-534.
EDELMAN, M. (1985) "Lifelines: Nicaragua and the socialist countries." NACLA Report on the Americas 19: 33-53.
ERISMAN, H. M. [ed.] (1984) The Caribbean Challenge: U.S. Policy in a Volatile Region. Boulder, CO: Westview.
EVANS, P., D. RUESCHEMEYER, and E. H. STEPHENS [eds.] (1985) States Versus Markets in the World Capitalist System. Political Economy of the World-System Annuals, vol. 8. Beverly Hills, CA: Sage.
EWELL, J. (1986) "Venezuela: interim report on a social pact." Current History 85: 25-28, 39-40.
FLACSO et al. (1985) "Nuevas Formas de Cooperación Europa-Centroamericana. San José: FLACSO.
GIDDENS, A. (1981) A Contemporary Critique of Historical Materialism. London: Macmillan.
GREENE, J. R. and B. SCOWCROFT [eds.] (1984) Western Interests and U.S. Policy Options in the Caribbean Basin. Boston: Oelgeschlager, Gunn and Hain.

INSULZA, J. M. (1985) "Geopolítica e intereses estratégicos en Centroamérica y el Caribe." Polémica 16: 24-40.

KENWORTHY, E. (1985) "United States policy in Central America: a choice denied." Current History 84: 97-100, 137-138.

KINZER, S. (1985) "Nicaragua's edge in the arms race." New York Times (October 27): 2E.

KNIGHT, F. W. (1978) The Caribbean: The Genesis of a Fragmented Nationalism. New York: Oxford University Press.

KRAUS, R. and R. VANNEMAN (1985) "Bureaucrats versus the state in capitalist and socialist regimes." Comparative Studies in Society and History 27: 111-122.

La Nación (1985) "Contadora en la encrucijada." San José, Costa Rica, (September 12): 14A.

LaFEBER, W. (1983) Inevitable Revolutions. New York: Norton.

LeoGRANDE, W. M. (1983) "Cuba and Nicaragua: from the Somozas to the Sandinistas," pp. 43-58 in B. B. Levine (ed.) The New Cuban Presence in the Caribbean. Boulder, CO: Westview.

———(1986) "The United States and Latin America." Current History 85: 1-4, 40-42.

LEVINE, B. B. [ed.] (1983) "Geopolitical and cultural competition in the Caribbean—an introduction: Cuba versus the United States," pp. 1-18 in The New Cuban Presence in the Caribbean. Boulder, CO: Westview.

LEVY, D. C. and G. SZÉKELY (1986) "Mexico: challenger and responses." Current History 85: 16-20, 37.

LINCOLN, J. K. (1985) "Neutrality Costa Rican style." Current History 84: 118-122, 136.

LOWENTHAL, A. F. (1984) "The insular Caribbean as a crucial test for U.S. policy," pp. 183-198 in H. M. Erisman (ed.) The Caribbean Challenge: U.S. Policy in a Volatile Region. Boulder. CO: Westview.

MATTHEWS, R. (1984) "Oil on troubled waters: Venezuelan policy in the Caribbean." NACLA Report on the Americas 18: 23-43.

MEYER, L. (1972) México y los Estados Unidos en el Conflicto Petrolero, 1917-1942. Mexico, D. F.: El Colegio de México.

MINTZ, S. W. (1977) "The so-called world system: local initiative and local response." Dialectical Anthropology 2: 253-270.

———(1985) Sweetness and Power. New York: Viking.

MORALES, A. (1985) "El clima bélico y la alteración de la paz." Aportes 25: 4-6.

National Bipartisan Commission on Central America (1984a) Report of the National Bipartisan Commission on Central America. Washington, DC: Government Printing Office.

———(1984b) Appendix to the Report of the National Bipartisan Commission on Central America. Washington, DC: Government Printing Office.

NEWFARMER, R. S. (1985) "Economic policy toward the Caribbean Basin: the balance sheet." Journal of Interamerican Studies and World Affairs 27: 63-90.

PAIGE, J. M. (1975) Agrarian Revolution. New York: Free Press.

———(1983) "Social theory and peasant revolution in Vietnam and Guatemala." Theory and Society 12: 699-737.

PASTOR, R. A. (1983) "Cuba and the Soviet Union: does Cuba act alone?" pp. 191-210 in B. B. Levin (ed.) The New Cuban Presence in the Caribbean. Boulder, CO: Westview.

PAYNE, A. (1984) The International Crisis in the Caribbean. Baltimore, MD: Johns Hopkins University Press.

PORTES, A. and J. WALTON (1981) Labor, Class, and the International System. New York: Academic Press.

SEQUIERA, A. C. (1984) "The origins of Sandinista foreign policy," pp. 95-109 in R. S. Leiken (ed.) Central America: Anatomy of Conflict. New York: Pergamon.
SKOCPOL, T. (1979) States and Social Revolutions. London: Cambridge University Press.
STARN, R. (1971) "Historians and crisis." Past and Present 52: 3-22.
TARDANICO, R. (1984) "Revolutionary Mexico and the world economy: the 1920s in theoretical perspective." Theory and Society 13: 757-772.
TORRES-RIVAS, E. (1971) Interpretación del Desarrollo Social Centroamericano. San José: Editorial Universitaria Centroamericana.
———(1981) Crisis del Poder en Centroamérica. San José: Editorial Universitaria Centroamericana.
VALENTA, J. (1982) "Soviet foreign policy and the crisis in the Caribbean," pp. 47-82 in H. M. Erisman (ed.) Colossus Challenged: The Struggle for Caribbean Influence. Boulder, CO: Westview.
WALLERSTEIN, I. (1979) The Capitalist World-Economy. London: Cambridge University Press.
———(1984a) "The USA in the World Today," pp. 69-79 in The Politics of the World-Economy. London: Cambridge University Press.
———[ed.] (1984b) "Revolutionary movements in the era of U.S. hegemony and after," pp. 132-46 in The Politics of the World-Economy. London: Cambridge University Press.
WOLF, E. R. (1982) Europe and the People Without History. Berkeley: University of California Press.
WOODWARD, R. L., Jr. (1984) "The rise and decline of liberalism in Central America: historical perspectives on the contemporary crises." Journal of Interamerican Studies and World Affairs 26: 291-312.
———(1985) Central America: A Nation Divided (2nd ed.). New York: Oxford University Press.

PART I

LABOR, ECONOMY, AND CRISIS

WHITE DAYS, BLACK DAYS:
The Working Day and the Crisis
of Slavery in the French Caribbean

Dale W. Tomich
State University of New York, Binghamton

This chapter draws its title from two expressions, far apart in time and space, and without any apparent connection between them. In the French Antilles the practice—common throughout the sugar colonies of the Caribbean—of giving slaves a bit of land on which to grow their own food and a free day, usually Saturday, to cultivate it was called *samedi nègre*. On the other hand, in Brazil today the phrase *dia de branco* is used to refer to working days and particularly to Mondays. Although this expression evokes an image of the slave past, its origins remain unclear. It appears to be unfamiliar to many middle-class Brazilians, and it is described as an expression used by "poor people" (*gente pobre*) or, more provocatively, by "old-timers" (*gente antiga*). There is no evidence that the two terms share a common historical origin nor is the use of the analogous phrase apparent in either the Caribbean or Brazil. Yet the juxtaposition of the two expressions remains striking. The first is a term of contempt bestowed by aristocrats of the skin who measured their wealth, power, and prestige in sugar and slaves whereas the second registers the resignation and unsubmissiveness of those whose fate it is to have their time and labor appropriated by others. Together they divide the week into two distinct and contrasting parts distinguished by different types of economic activity and characterized by antithetical racial identifications and evaluations. The strength of these oppositions suggests both the complexity and the contradictoriness of the social construction, perception, and evaluation of time within the social relations of slavery. They thus provide the occasion for a reexamination of the evolution of the working day and its significance for the historical development of slavery. This task will be undertaken here with reference to the French Caribbean.

The sugar plantation engaged the slaves in a year-round cycle of work that followed the rhythm of the crop. Despite differences of law, religion, and culture, similar yearly and daily routines derived from the material-technical conditions of sugar production evolved in all the slave colonies of the Caribbean, whether French, British, or Spanish. The transformation of sugar from cane to crystals requires a series of agricultural, mechanical, and physical-chemical operations. Each step— planting, cultivating, harvesting, grinding, defecation, evaporation, and crystallization—is necessary in the proper sequence, and none can be omitted if a final product is to be obtained. The spatial concentration of these different aspects of sugar production and their integration within a continuous process are required by the physical properties of sugar. The interdependence of these phases is most apparent during the harvest season. Although the harvest might last from six months to a year because of the amount of cane planted, each individual stalk had to be converted into sugar within hours after it was cut or the juice would ferment and spoil, causing the yield to diminish and the quality of the product to decline. Thus, speed, continuity, and coordination were of vital importance throughout the entire manufacturing process (Ortiz, 1970: 21-36).

Large-scale commercial production required that the distinct technical operations entailed in sugar manufacture form a complex division of labor. All the sequential phases of the manufacturing process had to be carried out simultaneously, continuously, and as quickly as possible. To achieve this, each of these various constituent tasks was permanently assigned to different groups of workers who specialized in them. This division of labor not only established the qualitative differentiation of tasks, but also created a quantitative relation between these different sectors of production. The process of sugar production formed an organic whole whose constituent parts were related to one another in definite proportions. It was of crucial importance to coordinate the various separate yet interdependent operations throughout the crop cycle from planting to harvest. The capacity of the fields, transport system, mill, refinery, and curing house had to be assessed and synchronized with one another (Marx, 1977: 461-470; Ortiz, 1970: 33, 41).

The integration of the labor process could only be achieved on the assumption that a given amount of product could be obtained during a given period of time. The allocation of labor and resources was thus governed by a fixed mathematical ratio that set the parameters of the duration of labor time and the conditions for the possible transformation of the labor process. Regularity in the performance of each partial task was necessary to maintain the continuity of production. The specialized labor of each group of workers provided the raw material for the next phase of the process. Direct material dependence compelled each worker or group of workers to spend no more time than was necessary on the performance of their particular task. This regulation of the amount of time necessary to perform a particular task was imposed on the workers as a technical condition of the labor process itself and determined the number of workers in each sector and the intensity and duration of their efforts. (Marx, 1977: 461-470).

The imperatives of the market and the demand for surplus labor were imposed upon these material-technical conditions of sugar production and exerted pressure for the optimal utilization of available labor time. Within the limits established by the technically determined proportional relations between the various sectors, the need to maximize output and "efficiency" integrated the division of labor on each plantation ever more closely and filled in the "empty spaces" in the potentially available labor time. Historically, these conditions of commercial sugar production were developed via the use of African slaves. Slavery provided the means by which the combination of laborers into the collective social force necessary for large-scale production was organized and molded to the technical and economic requirements of the labor process. The superiority of slavery as a form of social labor lies in its capacity to forcibly concentrate large masses of workers and compel their cooperation. It secured a labor force that was abundant, cheap, and subject to strict work discipline and social control. Through coercion the level of slave subsistence was reduced to a minimum while the time spent in commodity production was extended. Slave labor was technically and socially disciplined to the requirements of commercial sugar production, and slaves were compelled to perform repetitive tasks for long hours over the course of the crop cycle for the duration of their working lives. Thus, the relations of slavery organized sugar production as the production of commodities and gave labor time its specific social form. Planting and harvesting dominated the agricultural year and defined its division. However, the agrarian rhythm formed by their alternation was not simply natural but rather was manipulated to make full use of the productive capacity of the slave gang over the entire course of the planting and harvest seasons. An agricultural routine was adopted that minimized the effects of the natural seasonal break while the crop matured and kept the slaves continuously engaged in sugar production throughout the greater part of the year. The rotation of the fields was carefully planned so that over the 15- to 18-month maturation period of the sugar cane the planting of one crop could be constantly alternated with the harvesting of a previous crop. Planting and harvesting the crop each took place over the course of a period of several months, and one followed upon the other as quickly as possible. In this way, the planter was able to extend his utilization of the productive potential of the slave labor force and to obtain an annual crop while increasing the yield within the natural limits of the planting and harvest seasons (Goveia, 1965: 127-129).

The demand for labor was most intensive during the harvest season, but even in the so-called "dead season" between harvests the slaves were kept continually busy with a variety of tasks essential to the operation of the plantation. These included not only planting and caring for the cane, but also auxiliary tasks such as clearing new fields; planting provisions; carrying manure to the fields; ditching; building and maintaining roads, buildings, and animal pens; cleaning canals; building and repairing carts; and other types of repairs and maintenance. If these jobs were not enough to keep the slaves occupied, new work was created for them. Such a routine encouraged the generalization rather than the specialization of slave labor. Individual slaves were constantly shifted from one task to another and thus acquired a broad range of general skills, but at the same time the development of the division of labor on the plantation and therefore the collective level of skill and the productive capacity of the slave gang as a group was retarded. Furthermore, although the dead season was in principle less demanding than the harvest season, this regime harnessed the slaves to a pattern of year-round drudgery that dulled their incentive and efficiency and exposed them to the burdens of prolonged fatigue and overwork. This situation was aggravated when heavy rains or prolonged drought impeded work during the off season. There then followed a push to make up for lost time and complete these tasks before the harvest season renewed its claim on the full energy of the labor force.

Superimposed on the agricultural calendar was the religious calendar. The Edict of 1685 (the *Code Noir*) and the Royal Ordinance of 1786 exempted slaves from labor on Sundays and holidays, and, according to all available accounts, these provisions were generally observed. In pre-revolutionary Saint Domingue, Dutrône (1791: 335-336) calculated that 52 Sundays, 16 feast days, and about 17 rainy days left the planter with 280 work days a year. After the French Revolution divine virtues gave way to secular ones, and the number of religious holidays was reduced to four: Christmas, Ascension Day, Assumption, and All Saint's Day. These provisions were suspended during the harvest season when the demands of production were continuous. The days remaining after the deduction of these exemptions were available for the labor of the estate (Ministère de la Marine et des Colonies, 1844: 301-302).

The unit of labor time in the Caribbean sugar colonies was the day. This was a variable natural unit of measurement lasting from sunrise to sunset. Marking the length of the parts of the working day depended upon the judgment of the overseer. Beyond the technical problems of measurement, this could lead to conflict between the overseer, who was under pressure to produce as much sugar as possible, and the master, who—particularly after the abolition of the slave trade—was desirous of protecting the well-being of his slaves. Collins (1811/1971: 162-163) in Jamaica admonished:

> In turning out in the morning, it is usual to prepare your negroes by the plantation bell, which, by the carelessness of the watchman, or by the difficulty of distinguishing between the light of the moon, and the first approach of morning, is rung an hour or two earlier than it ought to be. This you should prevent, by directing it not to be rung until twilight is very well ascertained.

Mechanical timekeeping was conspicuous by its absence, particularly in the French Antilles. Indeed, even bells were scarce there, and the elaborate system utilizing the clerical hours of the church bells to mark the working day in Cuba as described by Moreno Fraginals (1978) appears to have been unknown in Martinique and Guadeloupe. The divisions in the day there were more commonly signaled by the crack of the overseer's whip or the blowing of a whistle or conch shell (Lavollée, 1841: 122-123; Le Goff, 1980: 44-49).

In the French colonies, work in the fields before sunrise and after sunset was forbidden by law, and although it was sometimes attempted during the harvest season, fieldwork done in the dark was both dangerous and difficult to supervise. In order to take maximum advantage of the daylight hours, the slaves were awakened before dawn. After assembly for communal prayers, roll call, and the assignment of the day's tasks, they went off to the fields accompanied by the overseer and the drivers. The slaves' workday began between five and six a.m. with the rising of the sun. At eight or nine o'clock they stopped work for between 30 and 45 minutes while breakfast was brought to them in the fields. Work in the fields was avoided during the hottest part of the day, and the slaves had the period from noon until two o'clock to themselves in order to eat and rest. Many slaves devoted this time to the cultivation of their private garden plots or provision grounds if these were located near enough to the fields. At two o'clock they were summoned back for the afternoon work session, which lasted until five o'clock in the summer and sunset in the winter. At the end of the workday, and sometimes during the mid-day break as well, each slave was required to pick a bundle of Guinea grass for fodder for the animals and carry it back to the animal pens. There was a final assembly and an evening prayer, though this was not as regular nor as rigorous as the morning assembly. The remaining time belonged to the slaves. Each household prepared its own evening meal. The slaves were relatively free, and all that was required was that general order and tranquility be maintained (Lavollée, 1974: 122-123; Debien, 1974: 147-152).

Thus, the effective working day spent in the fields normally lasted between nine and ten hours depending on the amount of daylight. To this must be added the time spent going to and from the work site and gathering and carrying fodder. (Many planters thought that this latter task merely added to the fatigue of the slaves after a long day's work and ought to be given over to a special gang.) The need for continuity in sugar production established a regularity of activity during this period that was uncommon in pre-industrial work rhythms. The division of the canefields into carefully measured and geometric pieces as well as the organization of collective gang labor and its supervision by drivers and overseers represented attempts to guarantee the regular and constant application of labor throughout the day and to achieve a standardized and calculable daily output that could permit the integration of the production process over the course of the entire crop cycle. Explicit in the organization of the working day was a concern for the maximization of yield, technical efficiency, and quantification and measurement, the outcome of which is the increasing standardization of process and product (Lavollée, 1974: 123-124; Debien, 1974: 153-154).

Both pro- and anti-slavery writers agreed that this regime did not make excessive demands on the strength and health of the slaves even in the tropical climate. In the words of French abolitionist Victor Schoelcher: "The slaves do what they must, and today the masters do not demand more of them than they can do." The technical division of labor left gaps in the working day, and Schoelcher reported that there was much more give and take in the time discipline of the sugar plantations in Martinique than in a European factory. Not infrequently he witnessed the afternoon work periods begin at 2:15 or 2:20 rather than at 2:00 p.m. Further, many planters, especially after the abolition of the slave trade, were very attentive to rest periods and meals and thought them to be essential for the efficiency and well-being of their *ateliers* (Schoelcher, 1842/1976: 22).

The natural agrarian rhythm of the daily plantation routine was interrupted during the harvest season when the industrial character of sugar manufacture emerged and revealed its dominion over the organization of the entire crop cycle. During this period, the legal restrictions on the working day were suspended. Night work, regarded as what is described by Le Goff as as "urban heresy" in the agrarian societies of late medieval Europe, proliferated in the sugar mills of the colonial countryside, and the slaves were harnessed to the continuous mechanical movement of the mill and the flow of the boiling house where work went on ceaselessly around the clock. In order to maintain this effort, the *atelier* was divided into three groups called *quarts* that were successively rotated from the fields to the mill and refinery where they worked in 7½-hour shifts. According to Sainte Croix, (1822), 150 slaves were necessary to organize a complete system of shifts, and planters with fewer slaves had to restrict themselves to manufacturing sugar only during the day. However, other sources suggest that round-the-clock shifts were carried on with smaller complements of slaves, although night work appears to have been an exception on small- and medium-sized plantations. This schedule placed an enormous physical burden on the slaves. After a full day's work in the fields during the most demanding period of the year, they had to do a shift in the mill or refinery at night as well. During the harvest season, 18-20 hours of intensive effort without a break was common. The exhausting *veillées*, as the night shifts were known, led to fatigue and often to horrible accidents, as tired and overworked slaves got a hand or arm caught in the cylinders of the mill or fell into cauldrons of boiling cane juice (Debien, 1974: 149-153; Dûtrone, 1791: 149-153; Lavollée, 1841: 73, 122-123; Sainte Croix, 1822: 135).

The slaves' working activity was not confined only to the production of export commodities. A considerable amount of their time was also devoted to producing for their own subsistence. Commonly, slaves were given plots of marginal land and "free" time in order to produce at least a portion of their own consumption. This practice directly benefited the master. Imported consumption goods were always expensive and their supply was often irregular whereas both the land and the time for provision cultivation emerged almost naturally from the conditions of sugar production itself. Allowing the slaves to produce for their own subsistence from resources already at hand instead of purchasing the necessary items on the market represented a saving to the master and a reduction of the cash expenses of the estate. This arrangement shifted the burden of the reproduction costs to the slaves themselves and kept them usefully employed even during periods when there was not work to be done on the sugar crop. In addition, many planters hoped that it would give the slaves a stake in the plantation and instill in them regular habits and the virtues of work and property. Thus, instead of separating the direct producers from the means of subsistence, slavery provided them with the means of producing a livelihood. Although the slaves acquired access to the use of property and the possibility of improving the material conditions of life, for them the price of subsistence was work beyond that required for sugar production. With these developments, the time devoted to the slaves' reproduction became separate from commodity production and a de facto division between necessary and surplus labor time was created.

The practice of giving the slaves gardens and a free day per week to grow their own food was brought by Dutch refugees from Pernambuco who introduced the cultivation of sugar cane into the French Antilles during the first half of the seventeenth century. Thus, the diffusion of sugar cane entailed not merely the movement of a commodity, but the spread of a whole way of life. From the beginning of slavery in the French colonies, the slaves were given small gardens to supplement their rations, but with the introduction of sugar, planters tended to neglect subsistence crops for their slaves in favor of planting sugar cane. With the adoption of the "Brazilian custom," masters no longer distributed rations to their slaves. Instead, the latter were expected to provide their own food, shelter, and clothing from the labor of their "free" day. But this practice had negative consequences. Food production was anarchic, and the slaves were often poorly nourished. Indeed, frequent food shortages prevented the masters from dispensing with the distribution of rations altogether. Provisions for these rations were produced as an estate crop by compulsory gang labor under the supervision of drivers and overseers. Critics of the custom of free Saturdays claimed that it gave the slaves too much freedom and encouraged theft and disorder. Too many slaves neglected their gardens and preferred to hire themselves out rather than grow food during their free time. They squandered their earnings and robbed their masters and neighboring plantations for food (Debien, 1974: 178-186).

The colonial authorities were in agreement with the critics and both sought to stop what they perceived to be the excesses resulting from the free Saturday and to ensure adequate treatment for the slave population. The Royal Edict of 1685 (*Code Noir*), the Royal Ordinance of October 15, 1786, the Colonial Penal Code of 1828, and innumerable local ordinances sought to make the master totally responsible for the maintenance of his slaves and to prescribe standards for food, shelter, and clothing to be provided to the slaves. Masters were expressly forbidden to give their slaves the free Saturday in place of the legal ration or to permit them to furnish their own food. However, such regulations were not easy to enforce in a society dominated by slaveholders, and local authorities made little attempt to carry them out (Debien, 1974: 178-186, 205-207).

Despite the shortcomings and abuses of the practice of free Saturdays and slave provision grounds and the repeated attempts to suppress them, the scale of these activities increased steadily and they became more and more central to the functioning of the colonial economy. By the 1830s the masters, with few exceptions, encouraged their slaves to grow their own foodstuffs, and the substitution of free Saturdays for rations had become widespread in the colonies. The slaves were given as much land as they could cultivate. They produced and marketed their crops without supervision, and their produce was an integral part of the colonial food supply. Colonial authorities no longer regarded these practices as threats to order, but rather felt that they contributed to social harmony. The reports of local officials particularly stressed the social benefits of independent cultivation by slaves. One of them expressed the opinion that the free Saturday was an "effective means of giving [the slave] the taste for property and well-being, and consequently, to make them useful craftsmen and agriculturalists desirous of family ties." For another, writing in 1842, it meant nothing less than bringing the slaves up to the standards of the civilized world:

But the slaves, for whom the custom of free Saturdays is established, prefer it to the ration because they work on their own account and find some profit from that state of affairs. It is clear evidence that man, even though a slave, has an interest in money and likes to enjoy the fruits of his labors while freely disposing of that which belongs to him. The black is forced to enter into types of social transactions that can only serve as a means of civilizing him.

This latter aspect was seen to be especially important because of the imminent prospect of emancipation. The report continued: "In this regard, the custom of the free Saturday must be preferred to the legally sanctioned ration because, beyond everything else, it is a road toward free labor." In 1846, these practices received the sanction of law. The authorities saw in them not the source of disorder, but the means to regulate slavery and provide a transition to free labor (Ministère de la Marine et des Colonies, 1844: 183-184, 290).

The evolution of the working day in the French Caribbean needs to be understood not simply as the product of the political economic structure of the slave plantation, but also as a historical process in which the cultural definitions of work and its relation to the larger matrix of plantation life were contested. For the African bondsman, slave labor in the New World required a radical restructuring of the work process under brutal conditions. In the Antilles, the goals and organization of work were very different from what they had been in Africa. The purposes and organization of work were no longer defined by mutual obligation, kinship ties, or social duty. Instead, a complex system of political and legal sanctions established the domination of the master over the person of the slave, and imposed work upon the slaves as an alien activity. Work was separated from all other human activities and subordinated to the claims of production embodied in the master, while all other aspects of slave life were subordinated to work. Systematic production for the abstract market, not direct or indirect consumption, required that the slaves adapt to new purposes of production, appropriation, and distribution. The slaves were forced to adopt new work habits, adjust to new work discipline, and learn new values and incentives to work. They had to learn to accept the authority of the master and his supervisors, to become proficient at new skills, and to work together in large gangs continuously and regularly at repetitive tasks for a period of fixed duration, day after day. The burden of this transition was heavy on the minds and bodies of the enslaved, and it required a painful cultural adaptation on a vast scale.

This process of "creolization" can be seen in the historical evolution of the practice of the free Saturday. Although the free Saturday never ceased to be functional from the point of view of the interests of the master, it formed a nodal point within the social relations of slavery that allowed slave practices, values, and interests to emerge and develop and to assume autonomous forms of organization and expression. As they became socialized into the routine of plantation labor, the slaves were able to lay claim to the free Saturday and use it for their own ends. By the nineteenth century, the slaves by and large preferred to have an extra day to themselves and raise their own provisions rather than receive an allowance of food from the master. As one government official observed,

> This practice . . . is completely to the advantage of the slave who wants to work. A day spent by him cultivating his garden, or in some other manner, will bring him more than the value of the nourishment that the law prescribes for him. I will add that there is no *atelier* which does not prefer this arrangement to the execution of the edict [*Code Noir*]. Once it has been set, it would be dangerous for the master to renounce it.

Another document emphasizes:

> "There would be discontent if the proprietors took away the free Saturday to give the provisions prescribed by the edict. . . . The Negroes prefer this method which assures them of an extra day each week. Everywhere that it has not been adopted the blacks desire it and beg for it. To try to abolish it where it has once been established would be to provoke disorder and revolt." [Ministère de la Marine et des Colonies, 1844: 180, 290].

Labor time became divided, in practice, between time belonging to the master and time belonging to the slaves. For their part, the slaves felt that they had a right to such "free" time and resisted any encroachment upon it. According to one official:

> It would be almost impossible for a planter to take even a little bit of time belonging to his slave, even if the authorities ignored the situation. There is a spirit of resistance among the slaves that prevents anyone from threatening what they consider to be their rights.

Through this process of the appropriation of a portion of the available labor time, the slaves were able to elaborate what Sidney Mintz (1974) has described as a "proto-peasant" style of life. They displayed remarkable energy and skill and used the opportunities presented to them to secure at least relative control over their subsistence and a degree of independence from the master. Their initiative led to the development of new economic and social patterns and the mobilization of productive forces that otherwise would have remained dormant. The slaves who wanted to plant gardens were given as much land as they could cultivate. The plots were frequently extensive, and the slaves had complete responsibility for them. Access to this property meant that the slaves' consumption was no longer entirely dependent on the economic condition of the master. Rather, they could use their free time and the produce of their gardens to improve their standard of living. Beyond supplying the personal consumption needs of the slaves, the provision grounds produced a marketable surplus of food. The slaves sold this produce in the towns and cities and developed a network of markets that were an important feature of the economic and social life of the colonies. In this process, the slaves were able to improve and add variety to the material conditions of their lives as well as to acquire skills, knowledge, and social contacts that increased their independence and allowed them to assert their individuality (Ministère de la Marine et des Colonies, 1844: 303-305).

The consolidation of this position in subsistence production provided a base for the assertion of the slaves' purposes, needs, and cultural forms in other aspects of plantation life, including the organization of work and the composition of the working day. Time became a kind of currency, and a complex system of time accounting emerged. If the master found that he needed the slaves at a time when they were exempted from labor, such work was voluntary, and it was rare that the slaves were not compensated for their services. Often, the master indemnified the slaves with an equivalent amount of time rather than money. In Martinique, it was reported that the slaves on one plantation were made to work on Sunday during the harvest but were given the following Monday off. On the infrequent occasions when the master of another plantation needed the labor of his slaves on a free Saturday or a Sunday for some pressing work that could not be postponed, they were given an equivalent amount of time on a weekday. A government official reported that this latter planter kept a precise account of the extra time that the slaves put in and indemnified them scrupulously (Ministère de la Marine et des Colonies, 1844: 303-305).

Thus, the time belonging to the slaves became not only distinguished from the time belonging to the masters but opposed to it as well. At the extreme, the former encroached upon the latter. In the 1840s, for example, there were persistent attempts by the slaves in Martinique and Guadeloupe to refuse to do nightwork during the harvest season. More dramatically, in August 1791, at the beginning of the Haitian Revolution, the slaves of Saint Domingue demanded the system of *trois jours*, three days for the master and three days for their own gardens. For the slaves, the time separate from work became a sphere of autonomous activity—"free" time in which they could dispose of their energies as they saw fit and within which they created a community organized around their beliefs, values, and collective action. (According to Monk Lewis, a planter in Jamaica, the slaves on his plantation referred to their free Saturday as "playday.") The slaves' use of their free time became subversive of plantation discipline, as one observer in Martinique indicates:

> During the week, when work is finished, the slaves leave the plantation and run to those where they have women.... The liberty of the night, that is, the right to use their nights as they wish, is a veritable plague. With this type of liberty, the Negroes have every means to indulge in their debauchery, to commit thefts, to smuggle, to repair to their secret meetings, and to prepare and take their revenge. And what good work can be expected during the day from people who stay out and revel the whole night? When the masters are asked why the slaves are allowed such a fatal liberty, they reply that they cannot take it away from them.

For the slaves, their free time represented a social space to be protected and, if possible, expanded; the master, however, had to contain the slaves' demands within the limits of economic efficiency and social order (Debien, 1974: 209; Lavollée, 1841: 124; Lewis, 1929: 81).

The evolution of the practice of the free Saturday thus suggests the historical trajectory and limits of slave production and the master-slave relationship. The relation between master and slave was not static but underwent a process of continual evolution. Europeans and Africans encountered one another through the unequal relations of slavery and engaged in a day-to-day struggle—sometimes implicit, sometimes overt—over the organization of work and the norms and values that it entailed. The master sought to discipline the slaves to the technical and social conditions of plantation production and to inculcate in them appropriate skills, attitudes, and values. But if the enslaved successfully adapted to the exigencies of the new labor regime, their behavior and values were not imitative of those of their masters. Nor were their motives, meanings, and goals identical with those of the masters. For their part, the slaves, in a complex mixture of accommodation and resistance, struggled both within and against the framework dictated to them and, in the course of their struggle, developed other values, ideas, and cultural forms. These, in turn, enabled them to assert their own purposes, needs, and rhythms in work and social life and to resist the definitions imposed by their masters. Thus, the very ability of the masters to compel the participation of the slaves in the new conditions of life and labor altered the slave relation itself. New forms, meanings, and goals of social action emerged alongside older ones and became the focal points of a new constellation of conditions, needs, and capacities on both sides, which moved the struggle between them to a new terrain.

This process of the appropriation of the free Saturday by the slaves had far-reaching consequences for the development of slavery in the French West Indies and was itself an aspect of the crisis of the slave system. It represents not an attempt to reject or escape the system, but an initiative by a population that over the course of its historical experience had learned to adapt to the slave plantation's labor routine, discipline, and organization of time, and confronted slavery *within* its own relations and processes. The result was simultaneously to strengthen and weaken the slave system. On the one hand, the slaves became more effectively integrated into slavery and responsive to its rewards and punishments. The operating expenses of the plantation were reduced, and a greater surplus was available to the planter. On the other hand, the amount of labor time at the disposition of the planter was congealed, and the slaves acquired a means of resisting the intensification of work at the very moment that the transformation of the world sugar market demanded higher levels of productivity and greater exploitation of labor from French West Indian planters. In this process, the bonds of slavery began slowly to dissolve, and the activities of the slaves gradually transformed the foundations of slave society itself. Custom, consent, and accommodation assumed a greater weight in the conduct of daily life where coercion had prevailed. The acquisition of skills and property and the establishment of economic and social networks enabled slaves to realize important material and psychological gains. The slaves thus began to fashion an alternative way of life that played an important role not only in eroding the slave regime but also in forming a transition to a new society. In it can be seen nuclei of the post-emancipation social structure and the means for resisting the new encroachments of plantation agriculture.

REFERENCES

Anonymous [Dr. Collins] (1811) Practical Rules for the Management and Medical Treatment of Negro Slaves in the Sugar Colonies by a Professional Planter. London: Vernor, Hood, and Sharp, Hatchard.

DEBIEN, G. (1974) Les esclaves aux Antilles françaises (XVIIᵉ-XVIIIᵉ siécles). Basse-Terre: Société d'histoire de la Guadeloupe. Fort-de-France: Société d'histoire de la Martinique.

DUTRÔNE de la COUTURE, J. F. (1791) Précis sur la canne et sur les moyens d'en extraire le sel essential, suivi de plusieurs mémoires sur le sucre, sur le vin de canne, sur l'indigo, sur les habitations et sur l'état actuel de Saint-Domingue. Paris: Debure, DeSeine.

GOVEIA, E. V. (1965) Slave Society in the British Leeward Islands at the End of the Eighteenth Century. New Haven, CT: Yale University Press.

LAVOLLÉE, P. (1841) Notes sur les cultures et la production de la Martinique et de la Guadeloupe. Paris: Imprimerie Royale.

Le GOFF, J. (1980) Time, Work and Culture in the Middle Ages. Chicago: University of Chicago Press.

LEWIS, M. G. (1929) Journal of a West India Proprietor. Boston: Houghton Mifflin.

MARX, K. (1977) Capital (vol. 1). New York: Vintage Books.

Ministère de la Marine et des Colonies (1844) Exposé général des résultats du patronage des esclaves dans les colonies françaises. Paris: Imprimerie Royale.

MINTZ, S. W. (1974) Caribbean Transformations. Chicago: Aldine.

MORENO FRAGINALS, M. (1978) El ingenio: Complejo económico social cubano del azúcar (vols. 1-3). Havana: Editorial de Ciencias Sociales.

ORTIZ, F. (1970) Cuban Counterpoint: Tobacco and Sugar. New York: Vintage Books.

SAINTE CROIX, F. RENOUARD, MARQUIS DE (1982) Statistique de la Martinique. Paris: Chaumerot, Librairie Palais Royale.

SCHOELCHER, V. (1976) Des Colonies françaises. Abolition immédiate de l'esclavage. Basse-Terre: Société d'histoire de la Guadeloupe. Fort-de-France: Société d'histoire de la Martinique.

Chapter 2

LABOR AND ETHNICITY:
The Caribbean Conjuncture

Sidney W. Mintz
Johns Hopkins University

The nineteenth century witnessed an amazing international movement, both in scale and in variety, of persons seeking work. But much of it was concealed by an unsurprising distinction, within the world press, between what might be called "newsworthy" and "unimportant" events. W. Arthur Lewis (1978) tells us that perhaps as many as 100 million persons changed countries by international migration in that century; but the movement of most of them was of little genuine interest to anyone other than their own relatives.

The transoceanic movement of nearly 50 million Europeans—the circumstances of whose migration, though bad enough, were probably less sordid, on balance, than those of the 50 million non-European migrants—eventually did win international press attention. These people were mostly moving from one European country (such as Italy or Germany) to another (such as Canada or Australia); their migration was in this sense entirely "Western." Yet these movements were paralleled by others of equal scale, even if considered far less newsworthy. Involved were the migrants who left no European country and, in most cases, could be said to have entered none. There were, to be sure, certain exceptions to this assertion, but their numerical importance was slight. Thus, we confront a phenomenon of world importance that received only half as much attention in the international press.

The acknowledged historical impact of this divided migration has been similarly divided. Every community migrant to the United States, for instance, has commemorated itself in literature—the literate children of Italians, Jews, Hungarians, Germans, Swedes, Armenians, and all the rest of the migrants have told us what it was like to be poor, foreign, and powerless. But the children of those others who left no European country and arrived in none—except for the aesthetic product of an occasional Naipaul—have bequeathed to us and to their descendants no such stories.

To some extent this dual and divergent movement reflected two rather different developments in the world-economy. On the one hand, the rapid economic growth of countries such as the United States, Australia, South Africa, and Argentina created labor needs that their then-available populations apparently could not satisfy. On the other hand, accompanying the growth of these countries was their rising importation of various sorts of foods, a trend that stimulated agricultural production in other, even less developed portions of the world-economy.

To illustrate this latter trend, passing reference will be made here to sugar, the history of which as a Western food of mass consumption is in large measure a nineteenth-century phenomenon. Even allowing for the vast nineteenth-century increases in production that marked the beet sugar industry—the first time in food history that a subtropical commodity (cane sugar) would be supplanted in important degree by competitive production in the temperate zone (beet sugar)—the loci of sugar production increases otherwise were subtropical, though the loci of their consumption were mainly temperate.

The migration of nearly 100 million persons, almost equally divided into two sectors of about 50 million each, involved movement toward two different climatic termini, one mostly temperate and the other mostly subtropical or tropical. Not surprisingly, perhaps, the "subtropical migrant stream" went mostly from tropic to tropic, the "temperate migrant stream" mostly from one part of the temperate zone to another. Finally—though it need hardly be said—"the temperate migrant stream" was white, the "tropical and subtropical migrant stream" nonwhite. Whereas Europeans moved from more to less developed (or frontierlike) European states, the non-Europeans moved mainly from one set of tropical colonies to another set. To this picture can be added several other sociological features deserving of mention.

In the neatest formulation of this contrast, Lewis has developed a persuasive argument for the differential flow: the widely varying agricultural productivity of the migrant-supplying countries. Stated oversimply, Lewis's argument is that Africans and Asians were prepared to migrate to engage in wage labor at rates that could not successfully attract Europeans, who came from countries with relatively more efficient agriculture. But the direction of the two migrant streams was not, of course, a function only of differential agricultural productivity, for the nonwhite migrants were in most cases barred from entry into those selfsame countries that were admitting European migrants. Thus, if Lewis's retrodiction is correct, the distribution of these 100 million newcomers over the course of the nineteenth century was the precipitate not only of differential agricultural productivity at home, but also of racism abroad.

There were, of course, other ways in which these migrations differed. With only a few exceptions, the movement of nonwhite migrants in the nineteenth century carried them to colonial (which is to say, economically and politically dependent) countries. In most cases, the majority of inhabitants already in place in the receiving colonies had absolutely no political voice or influence with regard to the issue of additional migration, even though they sometimes ended up financing it (Mintz, 1979). In the Caribbean region, this often meant in practice an unwilling but forced subsidization of the planter class by the ex-slaves—in effect, a lowering of the prevailing wage rates through increases in the labor force by migration, with a resultant intensified competition among wage laborers. When one contrasts the picture in Trinidad or erstwhile British Guiana—both of which received large numbers of Indian contract laborers in the nineteenth century—with the movement of European migrants to the United States or to Argentina, for example, it is clear that the power of local populations to affect decisions on such matters as migration was strikingly different from case to case.

The specific economic conditions under which such migrants came to grips with the terms of their employment were also radically different, but will not be dealt with here. Several other aspects of the migrations to sugarcane-producing areas—which gave a distinctive character to the nature and intensity of ethnic identity—do merit attention. But first some idea of the scale of migration to the Caribbean region during the nineteenth century is called for, to suggest the major sources of origin, note the statuses of the migrants, and suggest the reasons—at the receiving end—why such movements did in fact occur.

In 1804, the first Caribbean island nation, and the second in the New World, was to declare its independence from France. Haiti had won its freedom in a terrible and costly war, and began its career as a free nation having committed a cardinal sin—that of having freed its people (*all* of its people, including the slaves) by revolution, at a time when slavery was still an acceptable custom for the Europeans. The sugar industry in Haiti was, to all intents and purposes, dead as a consequence of its revolution. But the rest of the Caribbean remained colonial, its economies slave based. Sugar and slavery would flourish even more, for the Haitian Revolution had destroyed Europe's biggest, most lucrative colony and largest sugar producer.

Yet with that event two specters had arisen to haunt the Caribbean planters. One resulted from a politicotechnical achievement: the creation of a beet sugar industry in Europe, largely under Napoleon's stimulus. The other was sociopolitical: the haunting vision of another, perhaps even fiercer, Haiti of the future. As other producers struggled to fill the vacuum in tropical production that Haiti's revolution had created, the political pressure for abolition in the rest of the Caribbean colonies also increased. Usually taking the form first of an initiative to abolish the slave trade (ostensibly to improve the treatment of the slaves by masters, the worth of whose chattel property would presumably appreciate upon the end of the trade), this only preceded demands for outright emancipation, with or without compensation. (It need only be noted in passing that demands for compensation were always intended to compensate the masters for their investment, and never the slaves for their labor.)

The first abolition came in the British possessions (1834-1838); the second, third, and fourth in the French, Danish, and Dutch possessions (1848, 1859, 1863); and the last in the Spanish possessions, Puerto Rico (1873-1876) and Cuba (1880-1886). Each such event brought in its wake what the promises of abolition had foretokened: a determined attempt by the planters to secure the same sort of adequate and dependable labor force that slavery had previously guaranteed. But the terms "adequate" and "dependable" deserve a cultural definition. The planters everywhere wanted assurances that the *particular* character of their everyday relationships to legally defenseless people—people whose civil rights were formerly nonexistent—would be zealously protected *after* emancipation; and when one thinks about it in the light of the history of planter power, this is not so absurd as it may seem. Why, after all, should laws passed in a distant metropolis, by people who had not the slightest idea either of the ostensibly limited capacities of the slaves or of the difficulties of plantation management, be permitted to interfere with the serious business of business? Freedom was bad enough; that it might seriously be allowed to affect the character of the sugar industry would be intolerable.

The problem of labor was addressed by the planters and by their colonial governments (which were in most cases and at least to some extent the same thing) in a number of different ways. Migration was one obvious answer—though these economies could not have been said to be "developing" in the manner in which that term might be applied to Australia, say, or the United States, which were also receiving migrants. This does not mean that the Caribbean "labor problem" was not perceived as real, or even that in all cases it was unreal. Thus, to take one instance, Adamson points out that emancipation in British Guiana, by reducing the legal workday for field laborers from nine to seven and one-half hours, increased the local need for plantation labor by 13,000 persons (1972: 31). But why did not the then-available free laborers supply this extra effort? A good question and—given what the planters were prepared to pay, accustomed as they were to slavery as a basis for setting wages—one with a good answer. As Adamson has shown, the planters could maintain profitable sugar production in the face of both labor "shortages" and available land for the freedmen by

> several deliberate acts of policy. These included (1) the inhibition of the Negro village economy as a viable way of life; (2) the radical reconstruction of the plantation labor force through indentured immigration; and (3) the massive injection of public capital into the sugar sector, a kind of reverse transfer payment through which the Guyanese peasant and indentured immigrant paid an annual subvention to the planter [Adamson, 1972: 32-33].

It is by a consideration of steps such as these, designed by the planter class in each colony to frustrate the aspirations for economic autonomy of the freed people, that one approach to the subject of ethnicity or ethnic persistence may be developed. But what of the numbers of the migrants and of their origins?

Inasmuch as slavery ended at different points in different Caribbean colonies, it is not surprising that the probable major source of imported labor, even in the nineteenth century, should have been Africa. Moreover, the move to import other, nonslave labor began in some cases even before emancipation was secured—as in Cuba. Although we are by no means entirely sure of the number of enslaved Africans who reached the Caribbean region in the nineteenth century (i.e., 1800-1886, up to when the last slave in Cuba was freed), some very reliable estimates have been prepared. (As for the nonslave migrants during that century, our figures are not noticeably more reliable, but again, there are careful estimates.) Curtin's (1969) calculations for the nineteenth century for the Caribbean come to 606,000 for the Hispanic colonies (Cuba and Puerto Rico) and 96,000 for the French colonies (Martinique, Guadeloupe, and French Guiana). The biggest Caribbean buyer for the nineteenth century would be Cuba, where slavery flourished after the Haitian Revolution, and in spite of some international pressure—chiefly British—against the trade. The demographic, cultural, and political impact of the newly arrived Africans upon Cuban society constitutes far too large and complex a subject to be considered here. But there is no doubt that the distinctive vivacity and intensity of Afro-Cuban culture is owing in substantial measure to the recency, scale, and politicocultural controversiality of this vast movement. Curtin's figures (which still may be revised upward on the basis of more recent work; see Lovejoy, 1982) indicate the following *yearly* averages of importation to Cuba during particular nineteenth-century decennia: 1811-1820: 7,990; 1821-1830: 11,250; 1831-1840: 12,610 (Curtin 1969: 234). The consequences for cultural change and cultural persistence in a slavery situation where new slaves were arriving at the rate of perhaps 1,000 per month surely must have been remarkable.

But other migrations besides those of enslaved Africans also merit attention here. For the nineteenth century, the next largest movements to the islands were of Indians (sometimes labeled "East Indians," ostensibly to distinguish them from Amerindians) and Chinese. Both groups arrived as contracted laborers. Both were thought of by people in Europe as being very different in every way from the enslaved Africans who preceded them; and as being much the same (though a somewhat different color) by everyone in the colonies. The term *contract,* used to describe a written document stating the legal conditions under which such persons were reciprocally bound, had almost no meaning at all in the case of these migrants.

Nonetheless, they did know who and what they were; and their story is only now beginning to be told. If one looks, for instance, at an 1876 report on Chinese emigration to Cuba (Cuba Commission, 1876), the words of the Chinese laborers in Cuba interviewed by the commissioners at that time indict stunningly the system that entrapped them and reveal the naked criminality concealed behind the term "contract." The Commission's report indicates that, of 114,081 landed Chinese laborers during a 20-year period, there remained alive at its conclusion 58,400 (Cuba Commission, 1876: 69). Some of the details collected by the Commission members hardly bear repeating, though each informant quite literally took his life in his hands by volunteering information to its members. For instance:

> Chou Jun-ch'ing deposes that the unbaptised are not admitted to a cemetery. Hsu Li-sheng and 98 others depose that Chinese receive neither coffin nor grave, and that their bodies are cast out anywhere. Ch'en Te-lin and 2 others depose that when buried they are not placed in coffins, and that their clothing is removed. Kuo A-mei and 1 other depose that they made coffins (used on the plantation where they served) and that these were provided for Negroes but not Chinese. Huang Chieh and one other depose that their employers use one coffin, which was brought back after the bodies had been carried to the hills and buried . . . Lo A-chi deposes that the bodies are placed in a shallow hole, that in the course of time the bones are turned up by the spade, and piled up in little heaps, dissolve under the sun and rain; he also remarks that as the charred bones of oxen are required for the refining of sugar, the mixture of those men would produce an even purer whiteness.

> Again the petition of Jen Shih-chen and 2 others contains the following statement: "We have been here 17 and 18 years, and are so environed by the devices of the Commission of Colonization and others interested that egress is hopeless. We are old and weak and it is only uncertain whether we shall die in a depot or in a fresh place of service, or be cast out as useless by the roadside; but it is certain that for us there will be neither coffin nor grave, and that our bones will be tossed into a pit, to be burnt with those of horses and oxen and to be afterwards used to refine sugar, that neither our sons nor our sons' sons will ever know what we have endured [Cuba Commission, 1876: 79-80].

The picture is not significantly different for other migrant groups, ostensibly protected by their contracts. Donald Wood, describing the immigration to Trinidad in the post-Emancipation years, and remarking on the good reception given Indian contract laborers in the 1840s, adds:

> There was in fact a darker side to the picture. If many coolies had settled down, yet others were misfits who found their only escape in vagrancy. In a decade when destitute immigrants were a common sight, the Indian beggars were in a worse plight than indigent Europeans who aroused some pity, at least in other white breasts. They were far more isolated in

their misery than vagrant Africans who found companionship and shelter in the slums of Port of Spain or among the squatters of their own race. The Indians, on the other hand, lay unattended and sick on the roads and pavements. As an emergency measure, Lord Harris set up two temporary hospitals in June 1847 to relieve the overcrowding in the Colonial Hospital in Port of Spain. But a year later the Colonial Hospital was still caring for over 200 instead of its usual ninety in-patients. The only token that others had ever existed were their skeletons, stumbled across in the canefields and the woods [Wood, 1968: 114-115].

In addition to Africans (many of them freed people, somewhat deviously rerouted to work in the Antilles, rather than repatriated), Chinese, and Indians, the migrants included other Asians and some Europeans, particularly from the south of Europe. Neither their total numbers, nor a full list of their origins, need be provided here. The point, for present purposes, is the consequence of the particular settings—political, social, economic—for the character and content of ethnicity in this region. In all, the British Caribbean colonies received about 430,000 Indians between 1838 and 1917; Martinique and Guadeloupe received about 70,000, and the Dutch colony of Suriname (Dutch Guiana) about 35,000. The total number of Chinese who went to the Caribbean islands in the nineteenth century probably reached about 150,000. Between 1890 and 1931, about 33,000 Japanese reached Suriname (perhaps one quarter of whom were later repatriated). As many as 500 persons from old French Indo-China probably reached the French islands and French Guiana, while at least some political radicals from Indo-China were deported to Cayenne (Mintz, 1969).

Not all such movement was of nonwhite persons. Spain and Portugal supplied many migrants to the islands; in the period 1835-1882 some 40,000 Portuguese reached the British Caribbean. Spaniards emigrated to Cuba and to Puerto Rico; between 1882 and 1895 about 80,000 Spaniards landed in Cuba. Smaller numbers of Germans, English, Irish, and so on also reached the islands. But their movement was dwarfed by that of what might be referred to today as Third World people. What can we say of these migrations from tropic to tropic, beyond what has been said already? To begin with, these were unfamiliar migrations, unlike those of Europeans to the big European frontier states. They were, moreover, "unfamilial" migrations, in the sense that it was much more difficult for these migrants quickly to recreate their ethnic hearths in these new settings, in the absence of their wives or women of the same culture. It is not without reason that the woman is seen as the maker of the family in European migrant settings; in these settings, too, the obstacles to the recreation of the family—including the absence of culturally familiar partners of the opposite sex—gave to any motive for the perpetuation of ethnicity a particular and distinctive pathos. These Caribbean post-slavery adjustment situations are marked by other features. First of all, a severely restricted upward mobility is noted, defined generally by the economic conditions of plantation colonies. Second, there is the competition for work, often phrased in ethnic terms, pitting an earlier arriving ethnic group against a more tardily arriving group. A third factor, somewhat difficult to describe exactly, has to do with the presence or absence of a "national culture" in the host colony. In Cuba, for instance, a creole culture—an authentic Cuban culture, detached in certain important ideological features from the metropolis— did exist from quite early in colonial history; there are good grounds for the contention that such a culture was absent in a colony such as Jamaica. But in both cases, the ability of the new migrant group to acculturate to some national (creole) model was somewhat restricted by the lack of social and economic mobility, and of political representation. Ethnicity in these Caribbean cases, then, is not a matter simply of cultural content, but also of the relations among different groups whose stakes are defined in good measure by external, imperial, and remote power. How different from the situations in independent countries, such as Australia or the United States, where immigration policy was in much larger measure a domestic political consequence, where the newly arrived soon took their place in the body politic, and where "becoming" included becoming a *citizen*.

Hence it can be argued that "ethnicity" was a different phenomenon in societies such as the United States, for example, from what it was in a plantation colony such as Jamaica, because the conditions under which group identity would take on its characteristic form and intensity differed so greatly. If it is useful to think of ethnicity as being "ethnicity *for*" something, then it matters greatly *what* for—and under what specific circumstances. Said another way, being Indian in (former) British Guiana must have been radically different from being Italian or Jewish in the United States—not simply because the intrinsic cultural features of Indian ethnicity are so different (though, of course, they are), but because what one can do with one's ethnicity can come to depend so much on what other groups can do with *their* ethnicity. In the Caribbean region, the children of the nineteenth-century immigrants could look forward principally to cutting sugarcane as their fathers had done before them; what is more, the grandchildren of such immigrants could do the same. To such inescapable continuity of fate, ethnicity holds up a special mirror.

Ethnicity as an aspect of these developing Caribbean societies, then, was linked inseparably to the "crisis" attributable to dislocations in the labor supply created by revolution and emancipation. So far as the migrants themselves were concerned, it was a crisis produced not so much by change as by the *absence* of change. The ethnic identities of these populations were in this connection a coefficient of the political and economic rigidities characteristic of plantation economies. Hence to speak of such identities in terms of cultural content—cuisine, costume, coiffure, custom—though extremely illuminating in some regards, may also miss the point in others. Part of being what one *is,* is being unable to suppose that one could ever be anything else. The Caribbean conjuncture of labor and ethnicity is a product of particular forces at a particular time, and of necessity it raises serious questions about the linkages between class and culture. To understand Caribbean ethnicity we need to understand the social fields within which it took on and maintained its characteristic shape.

Too little has been said here, of course, of the major economic activity of these various migrant peoples, the sugar industry and its nineteenth-century development. But it may be worth noting in conclusion that the divided migration referred to earlier resulted—among its other consequences—in a sharp division in consumption: while one category of these migrants planted, cultivated, cut, and ground the cane to make sugar, the other such category produced finished products in the temperate-zone Western nations, and learned to eat ever-larger quantities of the sugar. The growth of the world division of labor continued unabated, while the world percentage of calories derived from this odd product—now both a temperate- and tropical-zone commodity—continued to rise (Mintz, 1985). Although it would be misleading to claim that the particular character of Caribbean ethnicity is linked in some invariant fashion to nearly five centuries of production of a single commodity, it is also the case that without that linkage there would not be such ethnicity in the Caribbean region. There is no intent embodied in this assertion to argue against any cross-culturally valid definitions of ethnicity, or against a theory of ethnicity that transcends—as good theory must—particular cases. Yet without a serious specification of the particular social conditions—in this case the conditions of the labor process—under which ethnicity is to be studied and understood, it may be difficult to construct a theoretically effective model of the relationship between content and structure in the definition of ethnicity itself.

REFERENCES

ADAMSON, A. H. (1972) Sugar Without Slaves. New Haven: Yale University Press.
CUBA Commission (1876/1970) Chinese Emigration. Taipei: Ch'eng Wen Publishing.
CURTIN, P. D. (1969) The Atlantic Slave Trade: A Census. Madison: University of Wisconsin Press.
LEWIS, W. A. (1978) The Evolution of the International Economic Order. Princeton, NJ: Princeton University Press.
LOVEJOY, P. E. (1982) "The volume of the Atlantic slave trade: a synthesis." Journal of African History 23: 473-501.
MINTZ, S. W. (1969) "A brief visit to the Third World: Guyana and Vietnam." Yale Review 59, 1: 51-60.
———(1979) "Slavery and the rise of peasantry." Historical Reflections 6, 1: 215-42.
———(1985) Sweetness and Power. New York: Viking.
WOOD, D. (1968) Trinidad in Transition. London: Oxford University Press.

Chapter 3

ECONOMIC DEVELOPMENT AND DEPENDENCY IN NINETEENTH-CENTURY GUATEMALA

Ralph Lee Woodward, Jr.
Tulane University

The economic history of nineteenth-century Guatemala has only begun to be studied in detail or as a chronological unit. Periodization of the century in political terms, however, has been well defined in four distinct segments. The first two decades of the century (1800-1821) were the closing years of three centuries of Spanish rule. Although spared the bloody wars of independence that scarred much of the rest of Latin America, Guatemala was nonetheless passing through a turbulent time politically, as New Guatemala City, founded only in 1776 after the destruction of the old capital, was struggling to maintain its hegemony over the Kingdom of Guatemala, stretching from Chiapas to Costa Rica (Woodward, 1985b). The next two decades were a chaotic period in which Liberals generally held office, with Guatemala as a state in the ill-fated United Provinces of Central America (1823-1840), dominated by the figure of Francisco Morazán. Then followed the emergence of the Republic of Guatemala, with only a few brief exceptions dominated by Conservative governments, in which the popular figure of Rafael Carrera stands out. Finally, the Liberal Revolution of 1871 initiated a long period of Liberal rule (1871-1944), characterized by the military dictatorships of Justo Rufino Barrios (1873-1885), Manuel Estrada Cabrera (1898-1920), and Jorge Ubico (1931-1944) (Woodward, 1984, 1985).

   The only general economic history of Guatemala (Solórzano Fernández, 1947) is a creditable overview. It can be supplemented by a
number of monographs dealing with the nineteenth century, as well as
with the outline economic history of Central America by Cardoso and
Pérez (Castellanos, 1978, 1984; McCreery, 1983a; Woodward, 1966).
This chapter draws upon these and other secondary works and my own
recent research in Guatemala, to present a synopsis of nineteenth-
century Guatemalan economic development, with particular attention
to the Conservative years between 1840 and 1871.
   The three centuries of Hispanic development of Guatemala (1524-
1821) represent a long transition from feudalism to capitalism. Although
the sixteenth-century Spanish Habsburgs had encouraged mining and
agro-exports, the conquistador generation and their descendants were
culturally more acquainted with feudal than capitalist traditions and
institutions. In the seventeenth century, declining Spanish commercial
and military strength contributed to retrenchment among the creole
landholding elite into feudal patterns that emphasized self-sufficient
estates and forms of labor control resembling medieval serfdom.
Master-serf relationships evolved that have characterized Guatemalan
rural life ever since (Romano 1984: 124-134). There existed throughout
the colonial period, however, a small capitalist element, and an
important segment of the economy dedicated itself to agro-exports, first
of cacao and later of indigo (MacLeod, 1973). Yet it is probable that the
majority of the declining population were engaged in economic activity
more akin to feudalism than capitalism (Martínez Peláez, 1970:
618-627.)
   The eighteenth-century Bourbons, however, put great emphasis on
capitalist development and particularly on agro-exports and mining in
underdeveloped areas of the empire such as Central America. This
resulted in the rise of the Salvadoran indigo industry and in greater trade
and economic interdependence among the Central American states.
Although this augmented productivity and exports, it threatened the
security that many creoles had developed in their feudal traditions. As
elsewhere in Latin America, the Bourbon effort to make the colonies
profitable put pressures on the creole landholding elite that divided
them into Liberal and Conservative factions, the former supporting the
development of agro-exports and the latter clinging to feudal traditions.
These factions formed the basis for the emergence of the two political
parties of nineteenth-century Guatemala (Woodward, 1965). The Liberal
economic philosophy became especially evident in the Cortes of Cádiz

(1810-1814), which influenced enormously the early independent Guatemalan leaders (Rodríguez, 1978). The Constitution of 1812 ignited an enthusiasm among young liberals in Central America, which translated into a fiery commitment to political and economic reform in the nation that emerged after independence from Mexico in 1823.

Export of indigo, mostly produced in El Salvador, dominated the late colonial economy. The wealthy merchants of Guatemala City controlled this trade and protected their monopoly through the merchant guild, or *Consulado*—one of eight such institutions erected in Spanish America by the government of Carlos IV between 1792 and 1795 to encourage more economic development by breaking the monopoly of the merchant guilds of Cádiz, Mexico, and Lima. The new Consulados not only gained their own tribunal to adjudicate commercial litigation in a court friendly to mercantile interests, but also received a strong charge to develop roads, ports, and agro-exports. Separate from the tribunal, the Consulado's royal charter established a governing board (*Junta de Gobierno*) whose principal purpose was

> the protection and development of commerce . . . to be fulfilled by procuring by every possible means the advancement of agriculture, improvement in the cultivation and yield of production, the introduction of the most advantageous machines and tools, facilitation of interior transportation, and , in sum, everything that appears conducive to the greatest increase of all aspects of cultivation and commerce [Carlos IV, 1793: Art. XXII].

Moreover, the charter ordered the Junta

> to undertake immediate consideration of the necessity to construct good roads and to establish settlements in unpopulated regions for the convenience of transportation, so that commerce might flourish, and . . . also note the benefit that would result from making some of the rivers near the capital navigable, thereby avoiding the dangers which presently burden shipping of imports and exports [Carlos IV, 1793: Art. XXIII].

Subsequent articles emphasized port development and assigned a half of one percent *avería* tax on commerce to the Consulado to fund these projects (Carlos IV, 1793: Arts. XXIV, XXXI, and XXXII).[1] Although the Consulado never exercised these functions to any great extent in the other states, within Guatemala it became the principal agency for economic development until its suppression in 1871. This privileged position granted to the merchants of the capital met with resentment from less favored economic interests, such as planters and merchants outside the capital, and was a considerable element in the rivalry that led to the separation of El Salvador from Guatemala. Moreover, the decline of the indigo trade—resulting from insect plagues, shipping losses during the Napoleonic Wars, and the disadvantageous Pacific coast location of Central American indigo production in competition for European markets with Atlantic producers like Venezuela and South Carolina—further contributed to the resentment against the Consulado by the close of the colonial era. Embued with notions of free trade and laissez faire, Liberals regarded the monopoly afforded the Guatemala City merchants as a barrier to the unrestrained economic growth they envisioned.

Shortly after independence, the Consulado made a detailed study of the economy, calling for expanded production and diversification to offset the declining indigo exports. It urged that machinery be imported and that cotton cultivation be expanded to boost textile production, an important cottage industry in Guatemala since pre-Columbian times. It warned against the importation of cheap English cotton goods, which it said had paralyzed the Guatemalan industry. It called for high protective tariffs to protect native industry and reflected a xenophobic fear of foreign—especially British—mercantile competition with the merchant elite of the capital (Batres Jáuregui, 1883: 56; Consulado de Guatemala, 1822; Dunn, 1829: 211-212). These were views inconsistent with the Liberal philosophy of José Francisco Barrundia and the other *exaltados* who dominated the Guatemalan government after secession from Mexico, and the Consulado found itself abolished altogether in 1826, although it continued to function in a limited form during the bloody civil war, after Conservatives regained control of the Guatemalan state government. But the Liberal victory in 1829 and ascendancy of Francisco Morazán ended the Consulado existence for a decade (Woodward, 1966: xv-xvi).

Liberal policy under the United Provinces favored promotion of private sector economic development and expansion of exports, but expectations far outstripped achievements (Woodward, 1985: 92-119). Inexperienced in government, faced with civil war in every state, and deprived of revenues because of their abolition of most taxes and the decline of commerce, the Liberal plans to develop a broad network of roads and ports progressed little further than the drawing boards. Yet confident that their policies of free trade and encouragement of expanded agro-export production would bring rapid economic growth, they turned to a loan of 5 million pounds from the London firm of Barclay, Herring & Richardson. Few of the bonds were sold, and the Central American government never received more than a few hundred thousand pounds spent on diplomatic expenses in Europe. Yet the indebtedness remained for years and provided important leverage for the British to garner trade and other economic concessions from the Central American states (Smith, 1963).

When the Liberals in Guatemala, under the government of Dr. Mariano Gálvez, sought to develop a transportation infrastructure using forced labor and a head tax on the rural peasants, they revolted behind the leadership of Rafael Carrera, resulting in the fall not only of the Guatemalan Liberal government in 1838, but ultimately of the entire federation by 1840 (Woodward, 1972).

Notwithstanding the political turmoil and the general failure of the Liberal economic program during the federation period, there was a notable increase in agro-exports from Guatemala and a clear beginning of the trend toward dependency on foreign markets that would characterize the more recent economic history of the country. Implementing Bourbon developmentalist policy, Captain General José de Bustamante in 1811 had introduced cochineal dye into Guatemala from Oaxaca, where it had been a major export for some time. Bustamante correctly envisioned the crimson dye as a possible replacement for the declining indigo trade. Cultivation of the nopal cactus, upon which the cochineal insect that produced the crimson dye thrived, spread quickly in the Antigua and Amatitlán regions, encouraged by both the government and the *Sociedad Económica* (Batres Jáuregui, 1916, 1929: 467-468; 1949; Dunlop, 1847: 95, 123ff.; Dunn, 1829: 16ff.; Gazeta de Guatemala, 1811: 209-210; El Amigo de la Patria, 1821: 137-138; Periódico de la Sociedad Económica de Guatemala, July 15-November 1, 1815: 93-96, 108-112, 141-144, 172-176, 187-191, 204-208, and April 15, 1816: 378-382; Squier, 1858: 507, 519-525; Stephens, 1841: 277ff., vol. 1). In 1818 the Consulado published a 34-page pamphlet promoting cochineal culture (López, 1818) and cooperated with the government's effort to develop the crop. By 1822 Guatemalan merchants were exporting significant amounts to Spain and England (Baily, 1850: 164). Beginning in 1823 the Liberal trade laws allowed the commerce to expand even more. The merchants financed the crops, advancing money to the growers with the expected crop as security, and charging interest at the rate of 2%-3% per month. Investors enjoyed large profits from this industry in the 1820s, as much as 100% every year but the first, providing the weather was normal (Obert, 1840: 135-137; Thompson, 1829: 281). The Guatemalan merchants thus gained control of all phases of the production and export of the raw dye. This arrangement placed the merchant class in a far more advantageous position than it had enjoyed during the Spanish period when the production of indigo was largely in the hands of a separate group of Salvadoran farmers with their own Growers' Society to finance the crops and bargain with the merchants for higher prices (Floyd, 1961, 1965; Indigo Growers Society, 1950; Rubio Sánchez, 1976; Smith, 1959). By 1825 cochineal, mostly produced in Guatemala, had become Central America's most valuable export (Solórzano Fernández, 1947: 244-245).

By 1835 cochineal exports had brought considerable prosperity to both planters and merchants in central Guatemala and were contributing to a rapprochement between elite Liberals and Conservatives before the Carrera revolt plunged the country into a bitter civil war once more (1837-1840). Conservative alliance with Carrera and his peasants brought a new government to power, but there continued to be strong support of the cochineal industry, which expanded notably in the 1840s and reached its peak of production and exports in the 1850s. The greatest harvest of Guatemalan history came in 1854 when 2,587,000 pounds of the dye produced a return of 1,757,300 pesos. Cochineal amounted to roughly 79% of the total value of Guatemalan exports between 1851 and 1855, with indigo accounting for another 15% (Solórzano Fernández, 1947: 528).

The discovery of mauve aniline dye by Sir William Henry Perkin in 1856 eventually resulted in the destruction of the natural dye industry in Central America (Meldola et al., 1906: 66). By 1860 this had begun to cause considerable alarm in Guatemala. The Consulado, which had been restored along with other Hispanic institutions in 1839, made a study of the new dyes and warned of the danger of falling prices. It recommended that cochineal workers be excused from military service to neutralize this effect, and that other crops be encouraged. The government complied with the recommendation (Gaceta de Guatemala, September 21, 1860: 2, and October 14, 1860: 1-2), but although the Consulado and the government tried to calm the fears of the producers, near panic resulted as prices steadily fell and the number of cochineal plantations for sale increased. The financial difficulty for the merchants and planters was reflected in litigation in the Consulado tribunal. By

1865 both prices and imports by the principal buyers in London were declining regularly (Gaceta de Guatemala, October 17, 1860: 1, March 23, 1861: 3, April 8, 1865: 26; Machado, 1862: 3-4; Salazar, 1957: 9-10). Nevertheless, in 1867 a French traveler wrote: "It is cochineal, still, . . . on which is founded the prosperity of Guatemala and which constitutes today, in the favorable years, her richest resource of exploitation" Belly, 1867: 144-145, vol. 1). Cochineal remained the single most important export for two more years, but other crops, chiefly coffee, began to challenge the dye's position in the economy. The decline of cochineal in Guatemalan exports following the discovery of the new chemical dyes is reflected in Table 3.1 (Boletín Oficial, August 11, 1871, and March 15, 1872: 4-5; Gaceta de Guatemala, October 13, 1869: 4, and May 24, 1870: 4-6; La Semana, December 3, 1865: 1; Rubio Sánchez, n.d.).

Coffee cultivation, although often associated with the Liberal return to power in Central America, had already become an important export under Conservative rule. Noting its importance in Costa Rica, both the Consulado and the Sociedad Económica encouraged its cultivation from the 1840s forward. In 1845 the Consulado appropriated funds to guarantee a fixed minimum price for the commodity (Consulado de Guatemala, 1845: 6-7), and published a pamphlet on coffee raising in Costa Rica, where the crop was already widely cultivated (Aguilar, 1845). These institutions also distributed seed and plants throughout the highlands and encouraged both Indian communities and private landowners to plant the crop (Batres Jáuregui, 1916, 1929, 1949: 233; Belly, 1868: 131, vol. 1; Shafer, 1958: 352). The government encouraged production by exempting coffee from export taxes and by offering premiums to producers (Gaceta de Guatemala, May 13, 1853: 1). These efforts began to bear fruit as coffee exports rose from a value of 690 pesos in 1852 to 4680 pesos in 1859 (Solórzano Fernández, 1947: 264). In the 1860s coffee exports rose rapidly and overtook the declining cochineal in value (see Table 3.2) (Boletín Oficial, August 11, 1871, and March 15, 1872: 4-5; Cardoso, 1975; Gaceta de Guatemala, October 13, 1869: 4, and May 24, 1870: 4-6; Mosk, 1955; Rubio Sánchez, 1953-1954: 185).

A more serious downturn in total exports in the transition from cochineal to coffee was avoided in Guatemala by circumstances quite beyond local control, but of which Guatemalan planners were able to take advantage. Secession and civil war in the United States (1861-1865) drove up the price of cotton in the world market, prompting the

TABLE 3.1
Value of Guatemalan Exports in Pesos

Year	Cochineal	Total Exports	Percentage
1855	977,460	1,104,923	88
1856	1,381,240	1,496,980	92
1857	1,017,270	1,309,203	78
1858	1,407,410	1,796,313	78
1859	1,222,680	1,533,320	80
1860	1,274,240	1,632,735	78
1861	788,650	1,106,583	71
1862	837,986	1,368,150	61
1863	855,838	1,490,811	57
1864	688,080	1,551,716	44
1865	975,933	1,833,325	53
1866	975,132	1,680,341	57
1867	1,068,047	1,919,650	57
1868	891,514	2,188,197	41
1869	1,266,614	2,497,127	51
1870	865,414	2,562,391	34
1871	876,025	2,657,715	33

TABLE 3.2
Value of Guatemalan Coffee Exports in Pesos,
1859-1871

Year	Coffee Exports (pesos)	Percentage of Total Exports
1859	4,680	0.3
1860	15,350	1
1861	53,110	5
1862	119,076	9
1863	199,076	13
1864	192,762	12
1865	265,404	17
1866	384,936	23
1867	415,878	22
1868	788,035	36
1869	790,228	32
1870	1,132,298	44
1871	1,312,129	50

Consulado in 1861 to initiate a campaign to increase Guatemalan cotton production. The government subsidized export shipments of more than 1000 quintals[2] and exempted the commodity from the export tax. The

Sociedad Económica joined the campaign and propagandized cotton cultivation, distributed free seed, and imported ginning and bailing machinery that it sold at cost. Cotton production had already been given a boost in Guatemala with the free distribution by the British Consul, on behalf of the Manchester Association for the Propagation of Cotton Cultivation, of a large amount of seed in 1858. The establishment of a national cotton-spinning mill in Quezaltenango with the support of the Consulado further stimulated production in 1860. Cotton was not exported in any significant quantity before 1862, but it expanded fairly rapidly thereafter and by 1864 Central American cotton commanded a high price on the London market. Unfortunately, although much land was put into cotton in these years, various types of insects appeared to have ruined many crops, causing those who planted cotton to lose large sums (Woodward, 1964).

Table 3.3 shows the place of cotton in Guatemalan exports in 1862-1868 (Gaceta de Guatemala, October 13, 1869: 4). Other products—silk, sugar, indigo, tobacco, and a variety of minor exports—were also encouraged, but none achieved much importance as exports except for sugar, which enjoyed modest success in the California market in the 1860s (Woodward, 1966: 51-54).

During the Conservative years then, and under the aegis of the merchant guild, Guatemalan foreign trade increased significantly. Figures for the 1840s are fragmentary, but the annual value of exports does not appear to have greatly exceeded $1 million in any year prior to 1850. Exports grew steadily thereafter and amounted to 1.8 million in 1865 and 2.7 million by 1871. From 1854 through the end of the period the state enjoyed a favorable balance of trade. In addition to a policy of protective tariffs, the maintenance of this balance after 1860 must be attributed to the successful development of coffee production and the development of a primitive but serviceable infrastructure of roads, bridges, and port improvements by the merchant guild. A major boost to Guatemala's overseas trade was the opening of the Panama Railway in 1855, allowing Guatemala dramatically to shift her trade from Caribbean to more accessible Pacific ports (Woodward, 1966: 51-104).[3] This development was a devastating blow to the British settlement at Belize, which had been the principal entrepôt for Guatemalan trade in the first half of the nineteenth century. It now languished into poverty from which it has not yet recovered (Clegern, 1967). The British continued to dominate Guatemalan trade, even after the decline of Belize. Import valuations in the Guatemalan customs houses reveal that

TABLE 3.3
Value of Guatemalan Cotton Exports in Pesos

Year	Cotton Exports (pesos)	Percentage of Total Exports
1862	1,230	0.1
1863	16,240	1.1
1864	240,600	15.4
1865	351,425	19.2
1866	77,875	4.6
1867	114,943	6.0
1868	20,485	0.9

between 1850 and 1870 61% of Guatemalan imports (in pesos) came from Great Britain, with another 6% from Belize; 17% came from France, 5% from Germany, 4% from Spain and Cuba, 3% from the United States, and 2% from Belgium (Gaceta de Guatemala, 1851-1871.

Conservative economic policy thus laid the foundation for the subsequent rapid conversion to agro-exporting in Guatemala, especially of coffee. Conservative economic growth was slow, however, when compared to the later period, and although it contributed to the prosperity of a small elite, the economy remained for the most part a subsistence-oriented agricultural society. The government of Rafael Carrera was ever mindful to the attitudes of the Indian peasant masses, and repeatedly blocked efforts by the elite to seize their communal lands and to convert them to plantation workers. The memory of the peasant revolt of 1837 served to keep the Conservative elite cautious in any major change in Guatemalan land and labor patterns throughout the mid-nineteenth century (Miceli, 1974; Woodward, 1979). In 1848 Carrera reminded the legislature that "the restoration to the masses of their customs, traditions and peculiar way of life" had been among his major obligations (Carrea, 1848).

The increase in foreign trade provided the principal revenues for the Guatemalan government. The expenses of this highly decentralized government were not great and it did not share the ambitious public works and development goals of either its Liberal predecessors or successors. The Consulado, the church, and other private or quasi-private agencies carried on most of the public works construction, as well as education, public health, and other expenditures that government would later assume. Even the construction of the Teatro Carrera (later renamed the Teatro Colón), the most impressive architectural monument of the regime, was largely paid for with private subscriptions. The government bureaucracy was very small and the government prided itself on keeping expenditures low and maintaining solvency. Indeed, this had to be considered one of the major achievements of the Conservative administration. The principal expenditures were on the military, both for foreign defense and internal security.

The government inherited a substantial debt from the Federation and the civil war of 1837-1839, to which was added considerable military expenditure in the 1840s. With most taxes abolished the government was forced to depend upon trade duties, the liquor and tobacco monopolies, and minor taxes, with loans from the Consulado, the church, and private individuals, including a number of forced loans on the property holders. Never popular, these forced loans were nevertheless tolerated by the elite, and in the long run turned out to be good investments. Initially the government paid interest at the standard rate of 3%, but resistance forced the government to offer more attractive rates of up to 12%. On other loans that the government contracted with private individuals and firms in the 1840s, both domestic and British, the government had to pay as much as 50% annual interest.[4]

During the fiscal year 1839-1840, the first year following the overthrow of the Liberal government, total government revenues, including loans, were $588,665.38. Of that sum, $274,412.03 (47%) went toward payment of the debt whereas $255,898.41 (43%) went to military expenses, leaving only $58,354.94 (10%) for civil administration (El Tiempo, August 26, 1840: 493). The debt inherited from the previous government totaled nearly 400,000 pesos (El Tiempo, January 7, 1841: 607). A proposed operating budget for 1841-1842 projected expenditures of $263,428, with $140,000 (53%) dedicated to the armed forces (Gaceta Oficial, November 5, 1841: 135).[5]

Military expenditures prevented the Conservative government from coming closer to balancing the budget and eliminating the debt altogether. Loans were guaranteed by the import export revenues. By the end of the decade, the size of the budget had grown considerably, but debt and military expenditures still were the principal payments. Of a total budget of $701,750.37 for 1848-1849, not including police, the military accounted for $297,688.82 (42%), and debt service for $261,342.62 (37%) (Gaceta de Guatemala, June 18, 1849: 274). The following year, however, with Carrera back in control of the military after a brief exile, the budget amounted to only $443,526.03, but with the military consuming 69% of that amount and debt service only 10%

(Gaceta de Guatemala, June 7, 1850: 393).[6] Peace and the increase of
cochineal exports allowed the government to reduce the total debt from
more than $500,000 in 1851 to less than $300,000 by the end of 1852
(Gaceta de Guatemala, November 12, 1852: 3, and December 17, 1852:
4), but war with Honduras forced it back up again in 1853 (Carrera,
1853: 8; Gaceta de Guatemala, February 24, 1854). A new British loan of
100,000 pounds in 1856 contracted at 5% per annum with 50% of
customs receipts pledged to guarantee the loan reflected the improved
credit of the regime (Corporation of Foreign Bondholders, 1936: 282ff.;
Gaceta de Guatemala, 31, 1856: 1-2). The war against William Walker
(1856-1857) and war with El Salvador in 1863 were further major
military expenditures. By the end of the Carrera period annual expenditures exceeded a million pesos, of which more than 40% was annually
pledged toward debt retirement, with the military consuming about
a third (Gaceta de Guatemala, 1865-1871). The actual amount of
indebtedness did not decrease very much during the Conservative years,
but it was managed effectively and Guatemala enjoyed good public
credit by the close of the Conservative period (Gaceta de Guatemala,
1845-1871).

The death of Carrera in April 1865 and the continuation of
Conservative rule under his deathbed selection, Vicente Cerna, began a
period of transition to the Liberal Reforma of 1871. Cerana was a
competent military and administrative leader, but lacked either Carrera's charisma or his sympathy for the Indian masses. The Guatemalan
archives reflect a rapid increase in Indian complaints of encroachment
on their lands during the Cerna years, accompanied by the rapid
increase in coffee production already mentioned (Castellanos Cambranes, 1978, 1984; Clegern, 1979: 98-110).

Guatemalan economic growth under the Conservatives, although
impressive when compared to the first decades after independence, was
slow compared to the general pace of economic growth in the Western
world in the mid-nineteenth century. Moreover, the economy was
developed exclusively for the benefit of a small class of merchants and
planters concentrated in the capital and central part of the country, with
a paternalistic and protective attitude toward the masses. As coffee
began to extend into the western highlands, Pacific slopes, and the
Verapaz, planters in those areas believed that the Conservative regime
failed to serve and protect their interests and thus they were attracted to
the Liberal Revolution, which promised greater government development of infrastructure, support of land and labor acquisition for the

expansion of coffee cultivation, and a favorable taxation policy.

The new Liberal government that took power in 1871, and was dominated by Justo Rufino Barrios until his death in 1885, promoted a rapid expansion of coffee cultivation and began a massive program of road, railroad, and port construction to facilitate its export. The Consulado essentially was nationalized, and became a national Ministerio de Fomento (Development Ministry). Exports of coffee increased nearly fivefold between 1871 and 1885, leading Guatemala into dependency on foreign markets. Table 3.4 reflects the growth of coffee exports during the last third of the nineteenth century (McCreery, 1983b: 737).

The government actively encouraged and supported the process of acquisition of land and cheap labor by a planter class (McCreery, 1983a, 1983b). Both natives and foreigners received such support, and Germans became especially important in the Guatemalan coffee industry (Castellanos Cambranes, 1975, 1977).

The Liberal revolution occasioned a substantial restructuring of the Guatemalan economy and changed the development philosophy of the government.[7] Although agro-export development had been encouraged under Conservative rule, there was a conscious effort by the government to protect Indian lands and to limit exploitation of their labor. Xenophobia on the part of Carrera and many of the Conservative elite limited the influence of foreigners in the economy. Although British merchants were important, the government generally opposed the granting of the country's land and resources to foreign owners. After 1871, foreigners were openly welcomed and came to have a major influence in the development of both coffee and, subsequently even more of bananas. The new Liberal ideology was markedly affected by positivism and, as David McCreery (1976: 438) has aptly phrased it:

> consisted of an amalgam variously compounded in the light of local circumstances of popularized Comtean dogmas, racist interpretations of Social Darwinism and postulates of Free Trade. National Progress, the Liberals proposed, demanded not simply political constitutionalism but the transformation of material life to admit as rapidly as possible such visible characteristic of North Atlantic civilization as railroads, export industries and a "modern" working class.

Expansion of agro-exports took land formerly producing the local food supply and ultimately drove food prices up. The prices of basic

TABLE 3.4
Guatemalan Coffee Exports, 1871-1899:
Five-Year Averages

Year	Quintales
1871-1874	141,113
1875-1879	206,399
1880-1884	324,312
1885-1889	484,662
1890-1894	543,223
1895-1899	760,200

staples fluctuated considerably, owing to weather and other variables, but the Conservative governments had made sincere efforts to maintain a plentiful supply of food, and average prices increased only slightly during the period (Woodward, 1983: 12-13). It appears certain that the Liberal Reforma resulted in lower standards of living for many, if not most, Guatemalans. Although data are fragmentary for both wages and prices, available data suggest a decline in real wages in terms of current corn prices. This trend became more obvious in the twentieth century than in the nineteenth (Table 3.5) (Woodward, 1983; McCreery, 1983b: 748-50).

Emphasis on agro-exports at the expense of subsistence allowed Guatemala to modernize its capital city, develop its transportation infrastructure, develop a middle class and enrich a small elite, which preserved its position through control of the government and an expanded military force. It also made Guatemala dependent on the north Atlantic market for coffee, bananas, and other agro-exports. This culminated a century-long struggle, as David McCreery (1976: 438) has suggested, "between Enlightenment ideals and Hispano-traditionalism" as gradually there emerged "a general agreement among all segments of the elite—producers of new bulk export crops, their adjunct commercial sectors, and reformist caudillos—on the desirability of national development."

Nineteenth-century Guatemalan economic development, then, is a clear example of what Bradford Burns (1980: 132) has called the "poverty of progress," as "Westernization triumphed over folk culture." Progress meant agro-export production, international trade, and an increase in the volume of economic activity. It meant the eventual emergence of a middle class who would demand more political participation than the elite would be willing to grant. It meant the

TABLE 3.5
Daily Wages Expressed in Terms of Corn at Current Price

Year	Pounds
1853-1866	7-12
1870-1889	7.5
1890-1899	10
1900-1917	2.5-4.5
1917-1921	5.5
1920-1939	4-4.5

exploitation of the majority of the rural population and the destruction of their traditional way of life, replaced by conditions for most that were not only materially less satisfying, but culturally abominable. The native culture and economy gave way to one dependent upon foreign capital, technology, and markets. It promised prosperity and achievement of the high expectations of earlier Liberals. It produced wealth for the few and poverty for the masses in the twentieth century, making inevitable the conflicts that our own times have inherited.[8]

Although the economic growth during the Conservative years was less dramatic than that which occurred after 1871, it was less destructive of the country's social and cultural fabric. Now, a century later, we are beginning to understand that economic development measured solely in terms of exports and trade balances often overlooks the inherent condition of the population. The Guatemalan Conservative recognition of indigenous subsistence patterns and cultural indentity while at the same time supporting modest agro-export development with an emphasis on native ownership may have been doomed in the face of the assault of foreign capital from the nations that had already experienced the industrial revolution. But the nineteenth-century Conservative approach does suggest some alternatives for underdeveloped countries that wish to preserve traditional lifestyles within a framework of gradual modernization.

NOTES

1. The *Real cédula de erección,* along with other documents pertaining to the history of the Guatemalan merchant guild, have been reprinted in Woodward (1981: 231-252).

2. One *quintal* = 101.4 English pounds.

3. Trade figures, by ports, were published annually in the *Gaceta de Guatemala.* A comparison of imports for the period reflects the shift from Caribbean to Pacific ports.

Value of Imports (in U.S. dollars)

Years	Via Caribbean Ports	Via Pacific Ports
1853-1858	4,231,642	2,100,994
1859-1864	1,720,659	5,549,598

4. Detailed records of the forced loans of the 1840s are found in the Archivo General de Centro América, Guatemala, B, Legajos 2370 and 2371. The Belize-based firm of Hall, Klee and Skinner collected 50% interest on a loan of $30,000 to the Guatemalan government in 1844. The text of that loan contract was published in the *Gaceta Oficial* (July 1, 1844: 655-656). A comprehensive discussion of the Guatemalan debt management and forced loan procedures will be included in my forthcoming monograph on the Carrera period.

5. The breakdown by categories was as follows:

Asamblea.	$ 15,000
Su Secretaría.	1,744
Poder Ejécutivo.	8,680
Poder Judicial.	13,690
Jueces	5,040
Gobernación.	11,800
Policía	1,440
Hacienda:	
Contaduría Mayor.	1,860
Tesorería General	2,300
Crédito Público	500
Administración General	4,896
Correos.	996
Casa de Moneda.	2,150
Aduanas foráneas	6,100
Resguardo	10,700
Pensiones.	3,180
Instrucción Pública	7,192
Réditos de Capitales	5,000
Temporalidades	1,560
Gastos Generales	19,600
Fuerza Armada	140,000
TOTAL.	$263,428

6. Actual debt payments were higher than 10%, however, as creditors were able to use the *vales* issued them by the government to pay duties at the customs houses, and these amounts are not reflected in the annual treasury accounts cited here. A more thorough analysis of government accounts must be done before final conclusions can be drawn on this matter.

7. For a descriptive catalog of economic legislation of the Liberal Revolution, see Díaz Castillo (1973).

8. For a provocative discussion of these consequences, see Kautsky (1972).

REFERENCES

AGUILAR, M. (1845) Memoria sobre el cultivo del café, arreglado la prática que se observa en Costa Rica. Guatemala: Consulado de Comercio.

BAILY, J. (1850) Central America. London: T. Saunders.

BATRES JAUREGUI, A. (1883) Bosquejo de Guatemala, en la América Central. New York: Las Novedades.

———(1916) La América Central ante la historia (vol. 1). Guatemala: Marroquin Hermanos.

———(1920) La América Central ante la historia (vol. 2). Guatemala: Sanches & De Guise.

———(1949) La América Central ante la historia (vol. 3). Guatemala: Tipografia Nacional.

BELLY, F. (1867) A travers l' Amérique centrale (vols. 1 and 2). Paris: Librairie de la Suisse Romande.

Boletín Oficial (1871-1872) Guatemala.

BURNS, E. B. (1980) The Poverty of Progress: Latin America in the Nineteenth Century. Berkeley: University of California Press.

CARDOSO, C.F.S. (1975) "Historia económica del café en Centroamérica (siglo XIX): estudio comparativo." Estudios Sociales Centroamericanos 10: 9-55.

———and H. PEREZ BRIGNOLI (1977) Centro América y la economía occidental (1520-1930). San José: Editorial Universidad de Costa Rica.

CARLOS IV (1793) Real cédula de erección del Consulado de Guatemala Expedida en San Lorenzo a XI de diciembre de MDCCXCII. Madrid Spain.

CARRERA, J. R. (1848) Informe que dirijió el Presidente de la República de Guatemala al Cuerpo Representativo, en su instalación el día 15 de agosto de 1848. Guatemala: Imprenta de la Paz.

———(1853, November 25) Informe dirigido por el Exmo. Señor Presidente de la República de Guatemala, Capitán General Don Rafael Carrera, a la Cámara de Representantes en la apertura de sus segundas sesiones, Guatemala.

CASTELLANOS CAMBRANES, J. C. (1975) Aspectos del desarrollo económico y social de Guatemala a la luz de fuentes históricos alemanes, 1868-1885. Guatemala: Instituto de Investigaciones Económicas y Sociales de la Universidad de San Carlos de Guatemala.

———(1977) El imperialismo alemán en Guatemala. Guatemala: Instituto de Investigaciones Económicas y Sociales de la Universidad de San Carlos de Guatemala.

———(1978) Introducción a la historia agrícola de Guatemala. Guatemala: Facultad de Agronomía, Universidad de San Carlos de Guatemala.

———(1984) Coffee and Peasants in Guatemala: The Origins of the Modern Plantation Economy in Guatemala, 1853-1897. Stockholm: Institute of Latin American Studies.

CLEGERN, W. M. (1967) Colonial Dead End: British Honduras, 1859-1900. Baton Rouge: Louisiana State University Press.

———(1979) "Transition from conservativism to liberalism in Guatemala, 1865-1871," pp. 98-110 in W. S. Coker (ed.) Hispanic-American Essays in Honor of Max Leon Moorhead. Pensacola, FL: Perdido Bay Press.

Consulado de Guatemala (1822, August) "Informe del Consulado sobre el estado de suma decadencia á que se mira reducida nuestra industria fabril, sus causas, y remedios que deben aplicarse." Transmitted to Capitán General Vicente Filísola. Unpublished manuscript in Archivo General de Centro-América, B, legajo 67, expediente 1847, Guatemala.

Corporation of Foreign Bondholders (1936) Sixty-Second Annual Report of the Council. London: Corporation of Foregin Bondholders.

DÍAZ CASTILLO, R. (1973) Legislación económica de Guatemala durante la Reforma Liberal. Guatemala: Editorial Universitaria de Guatemala and Editorial Universitaria Centroamericana.

DUNLOP, R. G. (1847) Travels in Central America. London: Longman, Brown, Green, and Longmans.

DUNN, H. (1829) Guatemala, or, the Republic of Central America, in 1827-8. London: J. Nisbet.

ECHEVERRÍA, M. (1845) Memoria leída por el secretario del Consulado de Comercio del Estado de Guatemala al abrirse la sesión de 19 de mayo de 1845. Guatemala: Consulado de Comercio.

El Amigo de la Patria (1821) 1, 12 (January 20): pp. 137-138.

El Tiempo (1840-1841) Guatemala

FLOYD, T. (1961) "The Guatemalan merchants, the government and the *provincianos,* 1750-1800." Hispanic American Historical Review 41, 1: 90-110.

———(1965) "The indigo merchant: promoter of Central American economic development, 1750-1808." Business History Review 39, 4: 466-488.

Gaceta de Guatemala (1847-1870) Guatemala.

Gaceta Oficial (1841-1847) Guatemala.

Gazeta de Guatemala (1811) Vol. 15, (May 16): 209-210.

HERRICK, T. R. (1967) "Economic and political development of Guatemala during the Barrios period." Ph.D. dissertation, University of Chicago.

Indigo Growers' Society (1950) "Statutes of the Guatemalan Indigo Growers Society." Hispanic American Historical Review 30, 3: 336-345.

KAUTSKY, J. H. (1972) The Political Consequences of Modernization. New York: John Wiley.

La Semana (1865) Vol. 1, No. 48, (December 3). Guatemala.

LÓPEZ, A. (1818) Instrucción para cultivar los nopales y beneficiar la grana fina. Guatemala: Consulado de Comercio.

MACHADO, R. (1862). Memoria sobre los trabajos en que se ha ocupado el Consulado de Comercio de la República de Guatemala, durante el año corrido de 8 de mayo de 1861 a igual fecha de 1862. Guatemala: Consulado de Comercio.

MacLEOD, M. J. (1973). Spanish Central America, a Socioeconomic History, 1520-1720. Berkeley: University of California Press.

MARTÍNEZ PELÁEZ, S. (1970). La patria del criollo, ensayo de interpretación de la realidad colonial guatemalteca. Guatemala: Editorial Universitaria Guatemalteca.

McCREERY, D. J. (1976) "Coffee and class: the structure of development in Liberal Guatemala." Hispanic American Historical Review 56, 3: 438-460.

———(1983a) Development of the State in Reforma Guatemala, 1871-1885. Athens: Ohio University Center for International Studies, Latin American Program.

———(1983b) "Debt servitude in rural Guatemala, 1876-1936." Hispanic American Historical Review 63, 4: 735-759.

MELDOLA, R., A. C. GREEN, and J .C. CAIN [eds.] (1906) Jubilee of the Discovery of Mauve and of the Foundation of the Coal Tar Colour Industry by Sir W. H. Perkin. London: Perkin Memorial Committee.

MICELI, K. (1974). "Rafael Carrera: defender and promoter of peasant interests in Guatemala, 1837-1848." The Americas 31, 1: 72-95.

MOSK, S. (1955) "The coffee economy of Guatemala, 1850-1918: development and signs of instability." Inter-American Economic Affairs 9, 3: 6-20.

OBERT, L.H.C. (1840) Mémoire contenant un aperçu statistique de l'état de Guatemala, ainsi que des renseignements précis sur son commerce, son industrie, son sol, sa température, son climat, et tout ce qui est relatif a cet état. Brussels: Lesigne.

Periódico de la Sociedad Económica de Guatemala (1815, July-November; 1816, April) Guatemala.

PINTO SORIA, J. (1983) Raíces históricas del estado en Centroamérica (2nd ed.). Guatemala: Editorial Universitaria.

RODRIGUEZ, M. (1978) The Cádiz Experiment in Central America, 1808-1826. Berkeley: University of California Press.

ROMANO, R. (1984) "American feudalism." Hispanic Americans Historical Review 64, 1: 121-134.

RUBIO SÁNCHEZ, M. (1953-1954) "Breve historia del desarrollo del cultivo de café en Guatemala." Anales de la Sociedad de Geografía e Historia de Guatemala 27: 169-238.

———(1976) Historia del añil o xiquilite en Centro América (2 vols.). San Salvador, El Salvador: Ministerio de Educación.

———(n. d.) "Historia de la grana o cochinilla en Guatemala." Unpublished manuscript, Tulane University Latin American Library.

SALAZAR, R. (1957) Tiempo viejo, recuerdos de mi juventud (2nd ed.). Guatemala: Editorial del Ministerio de Educación Pública.

SHAFER, R. J. (1958) The Economic Societies in the Spanish World, 1763-1821. Syracuse, NY: Syracuse University Press.

SMITH, R. S. (1959) "Indigo production and trade in colonial Guatemala." Hispanic American Historical Review 39, 2: 181-211.

———(1963) "Financing the Central American Federation, 1821-1838." Hispanic American Historical Review 43, 4: 483-510.

SOLÓRZANO FERNANDEZ, V. (1947) Historia de la evolución económica de Guatemala. Guatemala: Seminario de Integración Social Guatemalteca.

SQUIER, E. G. (1858) The States of Central America. New York: Harper & Brothers.

STEPHENS, J. L. (1841) Incidents of Travel in Central America, Chiapas and Yucatan (2 vols.). New York: Harper & Brothers.

THOMPSON, G. A. (1829) Narrative of an Official Visit to Guatemala from Mexico. London: J. Murray.

WOODWARD, R. L., Jr. (1964) "Guatemalan cotton and the American Civil War." Inter-American Economic Affairs 18, 3: 87-94.

———(1965) "Economic and social origins of the Guatemalan political parties (1773-1823)." Hispanic American Historical Review 45, 4: 544-566.

———(1966) Class Privilege and Economic Development: The Consulado de Comercio of Guatemala, 1793-1871. Chapel Hill: University of North Carolina Press.

———(1972) "Social revolution in Guatemala: the Carrera revolt," pp. 45-70 in M.A.L. Harrison and R. Wauchope (eds.) Applied Enlightenment: 19th Century Liberalism. New Orleans: Tulane University, Middle American Research Institute Publication 23.

———(1979) Liberalism, conservatism and the response of the peasants of la montaña to the government of Guatemala, 1821-1850." Plantation Society in the Americas 1, 1: 109-129.

———(1981) Privilegio de clase y desarrollo económico, Guatemala: 1793-1871. San José de Costa Rica: Editorial Universitaria Centroamericana.

———(1983) "Population and development in Guatemala, 1840-1871." Journal of the Southeastern Council on Latin American Studies 14: 5-18.

———(1984) "The rise and decline of liberlism in Central America: historical perspectives on the contemporary crises." Journal of Inter-American Studies and World Affairs 26, 3: 291-312.

———(1985a) Central America, a Nation Divided (2nd ed.). New York: Oxford University Press.

———(1985b) "The economy of Central America at the close of the colonial period," pp. 117-134 in Duncan T. Kinkead (ed.) Estudios del Reino de Guatemala. Seville, Spain: Escuela de Estudios Hispano-Americanos, and Durham, NC: Duke University Press.

Chapter 4

INDUSTRIALIZATION, LABOR MIGRATION, AND EMPLOYMENT CRISES:
A Comparison of Jamaica and the Dominican Republic

David Bray

Inter-American Foundation

Two of the major capitalist economies of the insular Caribbean currently are immersed in seemingly insoluble economic crises. Jamaica, despite a determined effort to practice a Reaganesque policy of tropical trickle-down, has a reported unemployment rate of 26%, down only slightly from the highs of the late Manley period (1972-1980); the Dominican Republic's underemployment and unemployment have been estimated at 50% as recently as 1983. In both countries IMF-imposed austerity programs have led to outbreaks of violence as the political systems strain to cope with diametrically opposed demands from domestic labor for more state-generated jobs and international banks for a balanced budget (see Murphy, this volume).

The failure of these economies to generate a sufficient number of jobs is in striking contrast to the high hopes for economic development evidenced in the first decade after World War II. In that period, three

AUTHOR'S NOTE: An earlier version of this chapter was presented at the annual meeting of the Caribbean Studies Association, St. Kitts, W. I., May 29-June 1, 1984.

major strategies were put forward for the expansion of Caribbean economies: industrialization, emigration, and tourism. Their major goal was to address the problem of a vast supply of surplus labor in the rural areas that was just beginning its march to urban labor markets. The first and third strategies were designed to supply jobs; the second, to reduce the supply of labor. In this chapter, I review the accomplishments and failures of industrialization and emigration. The reasons for their successes and failures are many and ramify throughout the political economies of the two countries. Here, however, I concentrate on patterns of job creation and migration, as well as a few of the problems associated with these patterns. The first section discusses the theoretical and policy orientations that promoted industrialization and emigration. The second section reviews the two strategies in Jamaica and the Dominican Republic. The last section compares the two cases and attempts to evaluate what can be learned from thirty years of development history. The data from some periods are fragmentary, and what follows is exploratory with an eye toward generating research hypotheses.

INDUSTRIALIZATION AND EMIGRATION

The small countries of the Caribbean Basin began their industrialization programs during the decade after World War II from an almost completely agrarian and artisan economic base, with sugar plantations supplying the bulk of "industrial" employment. It was hoped that manufacturing would be the key both to freeing these latest of the "late industrializers" from their overwhelming dependence on monocrop export agriculture and to promoting modern, diversified economies. The paramount goal was the creation of manufacturing jobs to reduce high unemployment.

In order to reduce unemployment, two major industrialization strategies have been followed: import substitution industrialization (ISI) and export-oriented industrialization (Felix, 1977). ISI has fostered the manufacturing of light consumer goods and some consumer durables behind tariff walls for the internal market. It has tended to import relatively advanced manufacturing technology. Although ISI is usually characterized as foreign-dominated, there is substantial domestic participation. Export industrialization—frequently called "export-processing" as it involves the assemblage and reexport of products of components manufactured elsewhere—is an attempt to enter into global competition for the consumer markets of advanced capitalist countries. Although this sector is notable for its simple technology and labor-intensity, it is almost wholly dominated by foreign capital. This characteristic raises the issue of the degree of foreign capital penetration as one variable in evaluating industrialization and emigration programs.

W. Arthur Lewis (1951) played a leading role in conceptualizing the impact of both kinds of industrialization on Caribbean migration patterns. Lewis clearly had the smaller Caribbean economies in mind when he theorized that rural labor surpluses, foreign capital, and an export orientation were the keys to successful industrialization. His theory was built on the presence of large supplies of surplus labor in rural areas. He felt that the focus of development would shift from agriculture to industry through the reallocation of labor from stagnant subsistence sectors to dynamic industrial sectors. The large reservoir of cheap labor from the rural areas would create favorable conditions for industrial development. Besides supplying surplus manpower, the streamlined rural sector was expected to supply a "saving fund" in the form of a marketable agricultural surplus that could serve as a "wages fund," that is, cheap food for the new urban working classes (Fei and Ranis, 1964; Lewis, 1954). This approach saw migration as essential to economic modernization. Lewis's general model became the official development strategy in the region during the period (Mandle, 1982: development strategy in the region during the period (Mandle, 1982: 56).

But Lewis felt that industrialization, even rapid industrialization, would not be sufficient to solve the rural surplus labor problem. Thus, he also proposed emigration from the rural areas of Jamaica to British Honduras and British Guiana. Lewis (1951: 33) argued that if they could be drained at a reasonable cost the coastal areas of British Guiana between the Essequibo River and the Venzuelan border in particular could absorb a population of half a million. The chief benefit of emigration would be the simple removal of surplus rural laborers.

It has long been evident that neither internal nor international migration has occurred as Lewis predicted. Internally, urban surplus labor has become even more widespread than rural surplus labor (see Todaro, 1976: 23-24). The strategy of exporting farm labor internationally seems to have been partially effective when one observes that the international migratory flows examined in this chapter have, in certain periods, been dominated by the rural poor. But in other periods these flows have been dominated by the urban middle sector (Bray, 1984; Mills et al., 1950: Palmer, 1974). The latter fact is not easily explained by Lewis's vision of international migration as a displaced internal migration of the rural poor. It suggests that the structural changes wrought by industrialization have had unexpected consequences for Caribbean labor forces and the larger class structure.

In light of recent history, Lewis's theory on industrialization and emigration is clearly in need of reevaluation. An important step in this direction is the analysis of recent Caribbean experience from structuralist and international perspectives. By "structuralist" I mean a focus on how development strategies affect class structure, that is, how they change access to the means of production for large sectors of the population. By "international" I refer to the place of Caribbean industrialization within the international division of labor.

A structural and international perspective finds its most frequent vehicle of analysis today in the notion of the "new" international division of labor (Froebel et al., 1980; Nash and Fernandez-Kelly, 1983; Portes and Walton, 1981). What is "new" about this international division of labor is that certain segments of manufacturing production are being exported to Third World sites. The segmentation of production allows multinational corporations to take advantage of the cheap labor, tax incentives, and infrastructure offered by Third World countries, and has given them great flexibility and mobility in their investment decisions. As an example, one U.S. apparel company has established manufacturing plants in five different Caribbean Basin countries (Caribbean/Central American Action, 1985: 7). Increasing "capital flight" since World War II has been paralleled by a great influx of Latin American and Caribbean migrants into the United States. For some purposes different fractions of multinational investors have found it beneficial to employ Caribbean peoples directly in U.S. labor markets; for other purposes they have found it beneficial to employ such peoples on their home ground. The flexibility of capital in this regard has led to a situation where "labor circuits [are] overloaded with unused reserves while idle capitals scout for surer and quicker returns on investments" (Campos and Bonilla, 1982: 571; see also Sassen-Koob, 1983). A major consequence of this process is that transnational capital has been restructuring global labor forces at the expense of sovereign dependent capitalist states (McMichael, 1982; 126; Petras, 1980). Hence, Caribbean countries have lost the benefits produced by their labor forces through both international migration and direct employment of Caribbean labor by foreign subsidiaries.

This leads to one of the principal arguments of this chapter, that Caribbean industrialization has increasingly come under the sway of transnational capital and has dramatically failed to meet its original goals. ISI had some success in fostering the development of a domestic capitalist class, in expanding "stabilizing" middle sectors, and in reducing import dependence on some items. Nevertheless, the capital-intensive techniques of ISI have generated relatively few jobs. Export manufacturing, on the other hand, has employed far more labor-intensive techniques but has been completely dominated by multinational capital and makes little contribution to the development of middle sectors or to reduction of import dependence (see Felix, 1977: 79). Thus, one effect of export industrialization is reduced participation of Caribbean petty bourgeois sectors in economic opportunities generated by industrialization. Furthermore, Portes (1983: 83-84) uses the example of Asian export economies to argue that export manufacturing is likely to promote emigration. He does not, however, consider the variable impact of foreign investment on industrialization, a theme to be pursued here.

From 1945-1975 the Jamaican and Dominican economies have shared common experiences: U.S. political and/or economic hegemony, major industrialization programs, and major international migratory flows. They also present contrasts: differing legal relationships to their metropoles, differences in the timing and nature of industrialization, differences in the role of foreign investment, and differences in the class composition of their international migratory flows. These similarities and differences will be explored in the remainder of this chapter, with the concluding section comparing the cases and addressing the potential impact of the Reagan administration's Caribbean Basin Initiative (CBI) on the region's industrialization and emigration patterns (Feinberg and Newfarmer, 1982).

JAMAICA

After stiff opposition from both the colonial authorities and their British counselors, Jamaica began to grope toward an industrial policy in the late 1940s. Industrial legislation was enacted in 1949 and 1952, with further legislative boosts given to manufacturing in 1956 (Ayub, 1981: 16; Widdicombe, 1972: 71). Although the legislation of 1949 and 1952 had encouraged capital intensive manufacturing, that of 1956 promoted labor-intensive industry (Widdicombe, 1972: 215). Unlike the export model of Puerto Rico, the legislation provided different sets of incentives for ISI and export industrialization. The strategy consisted of encouraging local capitalists to invest in production for the local market while courting foreign capital to invest in export industries.

The Jamaican program generated substantial employment during the 1950s, when the number of Jamaicans employed in "large" (more than 15 employees) manufacturing plants more than doubled. Most of this expansion occurred in the import substitution sector with the fastest rate of growth achieved in cement and clay products, textiles, garments and footwear, metal products, and food processing (Jefferson, 1972: 132-135). By 1968 there were 179 firms operating under the three industrial incentive laws providing employment for 13,139 workers. This is an average of 73 workers per firm with an average investment per worker of J$4,425. Figures are not available to compare capital intensity in foreign versus domestic firms or export manufacturing versus import substitution. The capital investment per worker in all firms ranged from J$506 in textiles to J$18,831 in chemicals. Foreign capital investments during this period amounted to J$32.4 million through 1969—not an impressive sum for that period of time. Manufacturing employment, after the rapid rise in the 1950s, actually contracted slightly during the 1960s. In 1967 there were a reported 43,226 employees in all manufacturing, a slight drop from the 1960 figure (Government of Jamaica, 1968; Jefferson, 1972).

Manufacturing employment began to grow again at a very slow rate in the early 1970s before going into a decline during the Manley years (1972-1980). Prime Minister Michael Manley's democratic socialism and warm relationship with Cuba created unease among domestic and international capitalists and sharply reduced new investments in manufacturing (Stone, 1983: 58). From the 1950s to 1970s the trends in unemployment paralleled the fortunes of manufacturing employment. From an official rate of 18% in 1953, unemployment dropped to 14% by 1960. By 1972, however, unemployment had risen all the way to 23% (Government of Jamaica, 1972)

What about patterns of foreign ownership? Of the ISI companies started from 1956-1970, 51% were wholly owned by Jamaican interests, 19% were half or more owned by Jamaican interests, and only 6% were wholly by U.S. interests. On the export side, however, 77% of the firms started under these laws were wholly owned by U.S. interests (Widdicombe, 1972: 250). Of the ISI firms established in the early 1970s, about 33% were foreign-owned or controlled. The export-oriented firms, on the other hand, were 68% foreign owned or controlled. Contrary to many assumptions, foreign capital is investing in labor-intensive production techniques. The export firms invested a mere $613 per job created for the period 1968-1973 whereas the ISI firms averaged over $10,000 investment per job created in the same period (Ayub, 1981: 23-24).

Widdicombe (1972: 257) supports the finding that foreign investment in export manufacturing is more effective than ISI in creating working-class employment. It is clear, moreover, that Jamaican industrialization has reached a contradictory position. Labor-intensive manufacturing, promoted for decades as the most appropriate for Jamaican needs, is being carried out by foreign capital. This development would seem to provide some benefits for the Jamaican working class but few benefits to the society as a whole. Particularly damaging is the failure to use local raw materials and the denial of access for the Jamaican middle sectors to this important entreprenuerial activity.

Turning to emigration—Jamaica's second "development" strategy— it is obvious that this approach did not develop quite as Lewis had hoped. Jamaican farmers found the factories of Great Britain more attractive than the fertile coastlands of British Guiana and British Honduras, with 176,049 Jamaicans migrating to Great Britain from 1953-1962 (Petras, 1980: 184). Up to two-thirds of this migratory flow apparently originated in rural areas, some of the migrants having sold their land to the bauxite companies then just entering Jamaica (Koslofsky, 1981). A substantial number of skilled craftsmen and other "middle sector" occupations also left (Jefferson, 1972: 23-24). These findings suggest that the migratory flow was fairly representative of the population as a whole.

This flow underwent dramatic change after 1962, when Jamaica became independent. Great Britain passed restrictive immigration laws that favored highly skilled adults. But as the British closed one door for Jamaican migrants, the United States soon opened another. The 1965 U.S. Immigration Act, which became effective in 1967, gave Jamaicans new opportunities to migrate there. From 1967 to 1975, 108,843 Jamaicans legally migrated to the United States; the number of illegal immigrants has been estimated possibly to double that figure. The legal migratory movement to the United States, because of restrictions against the migration of the poor and unskilled, has taken on a strongly middle-sector composition (Foner, 1979; Palmer, 1974). A particularly high percentage works in health services. As Palmer (1974: 156) comments, "Jamaica is not only one of the world's leading exporters of bauxite but also one of the world's leading exporters of nurses." Hence, Jamaica's two development strategies have not had their desired effects. Industrialization, after a quick start, has absorbed very little labor over the long haul, whereas in recent years, those who are able to migrate are not the "redundant" but rather those who cannot be easily replaced.

DOMINICAN REPUBLIC

The Dominican Republic, under the dictator Rafael Trujillo (1930-1961), also launched its industrialization program during the same period as Jamaica's, although with little of the debate that accompanied it in Jamaica. Trujillo fostered the first phases of ISI in building materials, food processing, and apparel during the 1950s. After stagnating for decades, total manufacturing employment grew by 82% during this period. But much of this growth was in sugar. When sugar employment is subtracted, the labor force expanded at a lower but still substantial rate of 63%. Unlike the Jamaican case, this industrialization did not seem to be guided by any consciously articulated policy. It seems to have been primarily a response to Trujillo's sense of new investment opportunities provided by changing markets. In addition, the Dominican industrialization of the 1950s seems to have been almost exclusively import substitution, with little or no attention given to manufacturing for export. The assassination of Trujillo in 1961 unleashed nearly six years of both political turmoil (see Gleijeses, 1978) and economic uncertainty compounded by low commodity prices. As a result, the growth of manufacturing employment in the 1960s stopped dead in its tracks, remaining virtually unchanged from 1960 to 1968.

In 1968 the administration of Joaquin Balaguer passed the country's first major industrial incentive law—19 years after Jamaica passed its first such law, making the Dominican Republic one of the most laggard of the late industrializers. This law, the "Ley de Incentivo y Protección Industrial," provided the legislative impulse both to launch a new phase of ISI and to promote export-processing in free trade zones. The incentives had a considerable impact on employment in the first few years of operation. From 1968 to 1977 manufacturing employment more than doubled, almost 25% of it being in the export sector. The most dynamic sector of manufacturing from 1975 to 1980 was export, where the number of workers nearly tripled. But in recent years the onset of world recession appears to have stagnated new employment in manufacturing until the export sector began to grown again, albeit at a slow pace, in 1984.

There are no figures available on the percentage of foreign capital in ISI but it appears that there is major participation by Dominican capitalists in this sector. The industrial free trade zones, however, are almost completely foreign owned. There are three free trade zones in the country, one owned by U.S. interests, one owned by the Dominican government, and one owned by the Dominican private sector. In all three free trade zones the resident enterprises are almost entirely foreign and predominantly North American. The free trade zones have been quite profitable. In the period when employment was tripling (1975-1980) remitted profits were quintupling, from U.S.$7 million to U.S.$35 million (Duarte and Corten, n.d.: 7).

As in the Jamaican case, domestic investment is concentrated in ISI and shows a high degree of capital intensity. New ISI factories spent about $14,000 for each new job created. In export-processing zones the ratio of investment to jobs was $3,621:1 (Bell, 1981: 351-353) and other reports have placed the rate of per worker investment even lower. Like its Jamaican counterpart, the Dominican government is encouraging foreign investment in export manufacturing, including investment procurement missions to the United States headed by the President of the Republic.

Slow to industrialize, the Dominican Republic was also late in evidencing major international migratory flows. International migration from the Dominican Republic to the United States was insignificant in the 1950s, averaging less than 1000 a year (U.S. Immigration and Naturalization Service, 1961). This low level has been attributed to Trujillo's restrictive emigration polices. These policies were pursued both to ensure a supply of laborers for his own projects and to control the flow of information in and out of the republic. Those who did leave were mainly upper and middle class, including Dominicans who had ties to Trujillo and those who were militantly opposed to him (Georges, 1984: 13-14).

The numbers of migrants to the United States grew slowly in the first years after Trujillo's 1961 asassination. "Political push" factors clearly played a role, particularly in the early years, with peaks in 1963 (the year of the election and subsequent overthrow of Juan Bosch) and 1965 (the year of the "April Revolution" and invasion by U.S. marines). From 1968 to 1972 Dominican migration averaged about 10,800 a year but the numbers for the remainder of the decade were higher, averaging nearly 15,000 a year. Most current estimates place the total number of legal and illegal Dominicans in the United States and Puerto Rico at around 700,000.

Although a few early studies emphasized the rural origins of Dominican international migrants, the consensus of more recent studies is that the flow as it developed in the 1960s and 1970s has a predominantly urban, middle-sector composition (Bray, 1984; Georges, 1984; Grasmuck, 1983; Ugalde et al., 1979). The class composition of emigration is strongly influenced by its demand side, that is, the country's relationship to external powers. Unlike Jamaica, the Dominican Republic has not been a colony since the nineteenth century. Hence, entry of Dominican citizens into the United States has always been regulated by immigration laws specifically designed to exclude the poor and unskilled. Although many of the rural and urban poor would clearly migrate if they could, it is difficult and expensive to enter the United States illegally from an island (Bray, 1984). In brief, Dominican industrialization is beginning to recapitulate the Jamaican experience of declining industrial employment, although the Dominican Republic seems to be a stronger competitor in export manufacturing due to its cheaper labor. But like Jamaica, the patterns of industrialization have contributed to a "middle-class bottleneck" (Bray, 1984) that, in combination with demand-side restrictions, means that it is the relatively skilled and not the redundant who migrate.

COMPARISONS AND CONCLUSIONS

Jamaica's industrialization program of the 1950s and 1960s attempted to develop both ISI and export capabilities, but the former played the leading role. Both sectors stagnated in the 1970s, followed by a strong push toward exports in the early 1980s. The Dominican Republic began a program of import substitution in the 1950s but would not launch a combined strategy similar to Jamaica's until 1968. It has also seen a strong push towards export during the 1980s.

The two economies have followed similar policies in their handling of foreign capital investment. In Jamaica, there was some effort to channel domestic capital into ISI while reserving export manufacturing for foreign capital. It is commonly held that foreign capital moved into the most profitable and technologically advanced sectors of ISI as well, although evidence either way is sparse. What is evident is that domestic capitalists had major participation in ISI but virtually none in export; this is an important distinction because all Jamaican manufacturing is commonly categorized as "industrialization by invitation" (Beckford and Witter, 1980), with no attempt being made to distinguish degrees of foreign involvement in the various sectors. Another notable feature is that ISI has been capital intensive whereas export industrialization has been labor intensive. Dominican data suggest a pattern similar to that of Jamaica's. The Dominican export sector is principally foreign owned, with domestic capitalists having a substantial investment in the ISI sector. Once again, the evidence substantiates the ISI/capital intensive and export/labor intensive relationship.

The rates at which jobs were created by the two countries' industrialization programs are also similar, once the different historical periods in which they occurred are considered. The initial decade or so of industrialization was the period of greatest intensity in new job creation. Newly protected markets provided a great initial push and early investments tend to be relatively labor intensive. The ISI employment entered a period of stagnation and even decline from which the countries have not yet emerged. Export manufacturing, on the other hand, started slowly and then gathered more dynamism after the first five years or so. Currently, export manufacturing has received a major push from the CBI, but it remains unclear whether the new jobs created in this sector will offset the stagnation and decline in ISI employment.

As for international migration, in the late 1940s and 1950s Jamaica— but not the Dominican Republic—experienced major out-migration. Jamaican migration was dominatd by flows from rural areas but was basically representative of the island's population; those who did leave the Dominican Republic were mostly middle and upper class. Emigration from both countries became strongly middle-sector in its orientation during the 1960s and 1970s, reflecting their common vulnerability to the demand-side restrictions of the recipient country. In brief, industrialization only had a fluctuating and, in recent years, faltering impact on new employment. International migration now does more to remove the skilled middle sector than to drain off redundant rural labor. What are the theoretical and policy implications of these outcomes?

Individuals do gain or lose through industrialization and emigration development strategies (see Lucas, 1982; Todaro, 1976); yet they do so as aggregates with common relations to the means of production. The concept of the new international division of labor allows us to see industrialization and emigration not only as bundles of individual costs and benefits but as a new structural phase in the Caribbean economies— one that leads to an increasing loss of economic sovereignty. The structures that define the context of individual investment are created by political and economic actors in the setting of local and transnational patterns of struggle and accumulation. Development strategies are designed to change the structural context of individual decisions in order to induce individuals to act in a new way. The results of the two development strategies suggest that politicans have paid insufficient attention to the structural context of their decisions, leading to a progressive decrease in the access of Caribbean working and middle class to the means of manufacturing production.

It is curious that policies designed to ameliorate the political-economic crises of the 1980s seem to do no more than recapitulate policies designed for the political-economic crises of the 1940s. Lewis argued that industrialization should be export-oriented and rely on foreign capital, precisely the argument of CBI theorists who envision the "Taiwanization" of the Caribbean (Dam, 1984; for an opposing view, see Latortue, 1985). The proponents of foreign-controlled export sectors legitimately argue that they are now delivering what has long been the demand of economic nationalists: labor-intensive industrialization.

In arguing for alternative policies, it would indeed be unrealistic to suggest that Caribbean economies—like so many mini-Chinas—could be entirely self-sufficient. But dependence does not have to mean complete surrender of the economy to export-oriented foreign interests who have little concern for the long-term social consequences of their actions. And to argue that foreign-controlled export industrialization is the best response to today's employment crisis is to overlook both the advantages of a redesigned ISI strategy and the disadvantages of the current export strategy.

What appears most beneficial to the Caribbean economies is not the consignment to stagnation and decline of the ISI sector and the enthusiastic promotion of the export sector, but a balanced approach that tries to develop the positive features of each while diminishing their deleterious consequences. In brief, this would involve the labor intensification of ISI and the domesticization of capital investment in export. ISI sectors should be encouraged to develop productive techniques that rely less on imported technology and more on domestic labor. Encouraging the development of the artisan sector would be one way of accomplishing this. These shops may have lower wages than the more capital-intensive segments of ISI but they could provide both more employment and economic opportunities for capital-poor domestic entrepreneurs. In the export sector, what the multinationals bring is not capital—which is what in theory they are supposed to bring—but rather a segment of their global production processes and access to marketing networks. This suggests that domestic capitalists need to find ways to gain access to those markets that do not simply involve turning the country's cheap labor over to foreign investors. In terms of developing a more balanced class structure, the thrust should be toward increasing working-class employment opportunities in ISI and increasing opportunities for the entrepreneurial classes in export. The deleterious consequences of giving free rein to foreign capital is a strong argument for policies that restrict the access of foreign capital to Caribbean labor. Politically this is, of course, an extremely difficult proposition. But the partial success of some Third World countries in negotiating for a greater degree of economic sovereignty in pharmaceuticals and mining suggests that it is not impossible (see Gereffi, 1983; Girvan, 1976).

Unlike industrialization, international migration is no longer advanced as an explicit development strategy by the Caribbean nations. Nonetheless, if removing labor was the goal emigration has certainly been consistently successful. The reorientation of industrial policy suggested above is designed in part to increase opportunities for the middle sectors in industrialization. An expansion of opportunities for the working class would also presumably have multiplier effects through increased ability to purchase goods and services from the middle sector. Thus, such a reorientation could substantially increase employment opportunities for the middle sectors and decrease the need for middle-sector emigration. However, it is unlikely that such pressure will decrease in the short term, suggesting that remittance income from these emigrants will remain important for some time to come. Given this reality, Caribbean governments could devise means to capture these remittances for investments in industrialization projects (Swamy, 1981). After more than 30 years of industrialization and emigration the unemployment rates in the two economies are higher than they were in the early 1950s. Unless Caribbean governments are prepared to make a break from a simple recapitulation of previous policies, the employment crises of the 1990s are likely to be the most explosive of all.

REFERENCES

AYUB, M. A. (1981) Made in Jamaica. Baltimore: John Hopkins University Press.
BECKFORD, G. and M. WITTER, (1980) Small Garden . . . Bitter Weed: Struggle and Change in Jamaica. London: Zed Press.
BELL, I. (1981) The Dominican Republic. Boulder, CO: Westview.

BRAY, D. (1984) "Economic development: the middle class and international migration in the Dominican Republic." International Migration Review 17, 2: 217-236.
———(1987) "The Dominican exodus," in Barry B. Levine (ed.) The Caribbean Exodus. New York: Praeger.
Caribbean/Central American Action (1985) "Apparel industry thrives in Caribbean." Caribbean Action (Summer): 7.
CAMPOS, R. and F. BONILLA (1982) "Bootstraps and enterprise zones: the underside of late capitalism in Puerto Rico." Review 4: 556-590.
DAM, K. (1984) "The Caribbean Basin Initiative and Central America." Department of State Bulletin 84 (2802): 80-83.
Dirección General de Estadística (1950-1976) Estadistica Industrial de la República Dominicana. Santo Domingo.
DUARTE, I. and A. CORTEN (n.d.) "Processos de proletarización de mujeres: las trabajadores de industrias de ensemblaje en la República Dominicana." Unpublished manuscript, Universidad Autónoma de Santo Domingo, Departamento de Sociología.
FEI, J. C. and G. RANIS (1964) Development of the Labor Surplus Economy. Homewood, IL: Richard D. Irwin.
FEINBERG, R. E. and R. S. NEWFARMER (1982) "A bilateralist gamble." Foreign Policy 47: 133-138.
FELIX, D. (1977) "Latin American power: takeoff or plus c'est la même chose?" Studies in Comparative International Development 12, 1:59-85.
FONER, N. (1979) "West Indians in New York City and London: a comparative analysis." International Migration Review 13, 2: 284-297.
FROEBEL, F., J. HEINRICHS, and O. KREYE (1980) The New International Division of Labor. Cambridge: Cambridge University Press.
GEORGES, E. (1984) New Immigrants and the Political Process: Dominicans in New York. Occasional Paper 45, New York University Center for Latin American and Caribbean Studies.
GEREFFI, G. (1983) The Pharmaceutical Industry and Dependency in the Third World. Princeton, NJ: Princeton University Press.
GIRVAN, G. (1976) Corporate Imperialism: Conflict and Expropriation. New York: Monthly Review Press.
GLEIJESES, P. (1978) The Dominican Crisis: The 1965 Constitutionalist Revolt and American Intervention. Baltimore: Johns Hopkins University Press.
Government of Jamaica (1968, 1972, 1983) Economic and Social Survey. Kingston, Jamaica.
GRASMUCK, S. (1983) "The consequences of Dominican out-migration for national development: the case of Santiago." Presented at the Conference on The New International Division of Labor at the Center for Latin American Studies, University of Florida, Gainesville, April 7-8.
JEFFERSON, O. (1972) The Post-War Economic Development of Jamaica. University of the West Indies, Institute of Social and Economic Research.
KOSLOFSKY, J. (1981) "Going foreign—causes of Jamaican migration." NACLA Report on the Americas. 15, 1: 2-31.
LATORTUE, P. R. (1985) "The Taiwan model and economic development of Haiti," in A. Jorge et al. (eds.) External Debt and Development Strategy in Latin America. New York: Pergamon Press.

LUCAS, R.E.B. (1981) "International migration: economic causes, consequences and evaluation," pp. 84-109 in M. M. Kritz et al. (eds.) Global Trends in Migration. New York: Center for Migration Studies.

LEWIS, W. A. (1951) Industrial Development in the Caribbean. Port of Spain, Trinidad: Caribbean Commission, General Secretariat.

———(1954) "Economic development with unlimited supplies of labor." Manchester School of Social and Economic Studies 22: 139-191.

MANDLE, J. (1982) Patterns of Caribbean Development. New York: Gordon and Breach.

McMICHAEL, P. (1982) "Social structure of the new international division of labor," in E. Friedman (ed.), Ascent and Decline in the World System. Beverly Hills, CA: Sage.

MILLS, C. W., C. SENIOR, and R. K. GOLDSEN (1950) The Puerto Rican Journey: New York's Newest Migrants. New York: Harper and Brothers.

NASH, J. and M. P. FERNANDEZ-KELLY [eds.] (1983) Women, Men and the International Division of Labor. Albany: State University of New York: Press.

PALMER, R. W. (1974) "A decade of West Indian migration to the United States." Social and Economic Studies 23, 4: 571-587.

PESSAR, P. R. (1982) Kinship Relations of Production in the Migration Process: The Case of Dominican Emigration to the United States. Occasional Paper 32, New York University Center for Latin American and Caribbean Studies.

PETRAS, E. (1980) "The role of national boundaries in a cross-national labour market." International Journal of Urban and Regional Research 4, 2: 155-195.

PORTES, A. (1983) "International labor migration and national development," in M. Kritz (ed.) U.S. Immigration and Refugee Policy. Lexington, MA: D.C. Health.

PORTES, A. and J. WALTON (1981) Labor, Class, and the International System. New York: Academic.

SASSEN-KOOB, S. (1981) "Labor migration and the new industrial division of labor," pp. 175-204 in J. Nash and M. P. Fernandez Kelly (eds.) Women, Men and the International Division of Labor. Albany: State University of New York Press.

STONE, C. (1983) "Decolonization and the Caribbean state system: the case of Jamaica," pp. 37-62 in P. Henry and C. Stone (eds.) The Newer Caribbean. Philadelphia: Institute for Study of Human Issues.

SWAMY, G. (1981) International Migrant Worker's Remittances: Issues and Prospects. World Bank Staff Working Paper 48, Washington, DC.

TODARO, M. P. (1976) Internal Migration in Developing Countries. Geneva: International Labour Office.

UGALDE, A. D., F. BEAN, and G. CARDENAS "International Migration From the Dominican Republic: Findings from a National Survey." International Migration Review 13, 2: 235-254.

United States Immigration and Naturalization Service (1961) Annual Report. Washington, DC: Author.

WIDDICOMBE, S. H. (1972) The Performance of Industrial Development Corporations: The Case of Jamaica. New York: Praeger.

Chapter 5

THE INFORMAL SECTOR REVISITED:
The Case of the Talleres Rurales
Mini-Maquilas in Colombia

Cynthia Truelove
Johns Hopkins University

The last decade of research on the genesis of unequal exchange in the world-economy spans issues from a unique focus on the subsistence agricultural sector in the periphery to renewed attention to the urban-based informal sector in both the core and periphery. This shift reflects the efforts of many theorists to come to grips with the structural changes endemic to the recessionary world-economy since the 1970s. Thus, a marked shift has occurred in their explanation of the structural origins of unequal exchange between core and periphery. Earlier theories posited the critical role of the rural subsistence sector in the functioning of unequal exchange mechanisms in the world-system (e.g., Amin, 1976;

AUTHOR'S NOTE: I am grateful for the comments of Alejandro Portes, Helen Safa, and Richard Tardanico, and to Ruth Finkelstein for her encouragement and insights into the social construction of gender. I remain responsible for the material presented in this chapter. The field research upon which this chapter is based was conducted while I was a Summer Research Fellow of the Central American and Caribbean Program of The Johns Hopkins University School for Advanced International Studies.

de Janvry and Garramon, 1977). More recent theories, however, virtually eliminate the rural context from the analyses and point to the segmentation of the urban labor market in the periphery as the basis of unequal exchange in the world-system (e.g., Portes and Walton, 1981). The following discussion reconsiders these most recent hypotheses regarding the urban basis for the perpetuation of unequal exchange between and within the core and periphery. In so doing, it presents preliminary evidence supporting the existence of a segmented labor force in the periphery that incorporates rural informal proletarians—or disguised wage laborers—into formal sector national and multinational firms as well as strategic commercial agricultural production.[1] It is hoped that the case study of the Talleras Rurales del Valle Precooperative Program will inform our renewed efforts to build upon the theoretical insights of those who have eloquently meshed labor market segmentation and unequal exchange theories.

This chapter begins by reviewing approaches to the study of unequal exchange in the world-system and by introducing the context of labor market segmentation in the coffee-producing region of southwesten Colombia. It then focuses on the development of the Tallers Rurales del Valle Precooperative (TRV) *mini-maquilas*.[2] The discussion of the TRV mini-maquilas centers on four issues:

(1) the ramifications of the "pre-cooperative" status of the TRV enterprise under Colombian legal statutes and its internal organizational structure and operations;
(2) the nature of the TRV's subcontracting arrangements with national and international industry;
(3) TRV labor relations with those of other offshore assembly operations; and
(4) the role of rural female, disguised wage laborers in the reproduction of the seasonal agricultural labor force utilized by adjacent coffee plantations, and their role in assuring the small-scale cultivation and marketing of coffee by semiproletarians.

The chapter concludes by briefly considering the implications of this case for other areas in the periphery where strategic commercial agricultural interests are considering similar programs to attract multinational industry as a means of reducing the outmigration of the rural manual labor force.

UNEQUAL EXCHANGE THEORY: A REVIEW

One result of the critiques of early dependency theory is that a vast literature has emerged on the origins of unequal capitalist exchange between and within nations in the core and periphery. Critics of dependency theory allege that, taken alone, its metropolis/satellite hypothesis is too general to reveal the specific mechanisms responsible for unequal exchange at the level of the world capitalist system.[3] They propose to unveil the more specific processes through which peripheral social relations constitute the foundations for unequal exchange between the core and periphery.

An essential assumption of the original unequal exchange argument is that pre-capitalist, or semicapitalist, exchange relations in the rural areas of peripheral economies maintain low labor costs for urban capitalist enterprises (Amin, 1976; de Janvry and Garramon, 1977; Emmanuel, 1972). The argument contends that rural semiproletarians reproduce their own labor by maintaining subsistence production while working for marginal wages in commercial agriculture. This process is said to reduce the labor costs assumed by the commercial agricultural sector. In turn, it is claimed, the provision of inexpensive foodstuffs to the urban market allows for the reproduction of the urban labor force within the confines of extremely low wages. The difference between the capital produced by the urban labor force and the low wages it receives is presumably passed along in the form of surplus to the urban capitalist sector. As de Janvry and Garramon (1977: 211) succinctly state:

> The capitalist agriculture-subsistence sector binomial is the structural reflection of the rationality of peripheral accumulation. It constitutes a functional system that symptomises and embodies the contradictions of peripheral capitalism.

This model suggests that the structure of the capitalist world-economy is dangerously contradictory. For the continued loss of land by rural subsistence producers foretells not only the decline of the urban market's access to relatively inexpensive food, but also the inability of urban laborers to reproduce themselves at extremely low wages.

These assumptions recently have been challenged by social scientists studying the urban informal sector (see Portes, 1985; Portes and Walton, 1981). They maintain that because the absolute size of the subsistence sector is diminishing relative to the expanding capitalist sector, the argument presented above is an inadequate explanation of the structural factors promoting unequal exchange.

For these theorists, the primary mechanism that fosters unequal exchange within the periphery, as well as between core and periphery, is the use of urban-based, extramarket means of production by the formal sector. Such means, whose locus is the informal sector, ensure a "decrease in the costs of the reproduction of labor employed by the capitalist sector while decreasing the relative size" of the protected and organized labor force (Portes and Walton, 1981: 85). Portes (1984a) examined the segmented urban labor market in Latin America and found evidence of a substantial "informal proletariat" that provided the urban formal sector with the extramarket means of production. According to his hypothesis, the urban informal proletariat is readily identifiable as it (a) does not receive regular money wages; (b) does not receive the "indirect" wage of social security coverage; and (c) does not retain contractual relations with its employers. Prates (1983) similarly characterizes these semisalaried laborers as caught between two worlds because they neither receive the usual benefits of protected workers nor enjoy the independence and limited accumulation of fully self-employed artisans. She notes that urban women who work in subcontracting arrangements must assume all costs associated with "dead time" and their own reproduction, including food, clothing, housing, and transport. They likewise absorb the material and resource expenditures invested in production, such as machinery and electricity, and perform production activities that are not easily automated.

Although the latter informal sector/unequal exchange arguments surpass the former focus on subsistence agriculture, neither directly addresses the rural context of informal/formal sector exchange relations. Those who emphasize labor market segmentation in the periphery clearly enhance the explanatory power of unequal exchange theory relative to previous approaches. Yet specific studies of peripheral labor markets may call into question the purely urban basis of extramarket means of production that link peripheral and core capitalists. I am investigating regions and countries in the periphery, such as Colombia, that have extensive rural infrastructural development and that have the need for rural manual labor in the seasonal cultivation of strategic crops (e.g., coffee). The research tests the hypothesis that such regions and countries demonstrate a high incidence of formal sector firms subcontracting to rural disguised wage laborers, who themselves are responsible

e.g.
Taussig's work
(not eve cited!)

for the social reproduction of the seasonal agricultural labor force.

The above approach provides for the convergence of the subsistence sector and labor market segmentation theories of unequal exchange as we explore the structural role of female disguised wage laborers in the rural periphery. De Janvry and Garramon (1977) recognize that "woman's subordination originates in her role as a production agent of use-values to cheapen semiproleterian labour." They go on to say, however, that with the decline of small-scale landholdings and resources for the maintenance of the rural agricultural subsistence sector, the nature of the exploitation of the rural female semiproletarian labor force changes. In order to reproduce the cheapened semiproletarian male labor force in the rural periphery in the absence of the subsistence agricultural sector, female rural informal proletarians are exploited through "under-remuneration"; that is, characteristic of the segmented capitalist labor market discussed above, they receive less than minimum wage and no benefits. Under this model, surplus value is passed along through the low wages of informal proletarians to national and multinational industry, as well as through the relatively cheapened wage bill in commercial agricultural production. This process results in lower prices for these commodities on the world market.

Any macrotheory that seeks to explain a process as complex as unequal exchange in the world-system is subject to the host of variants arising out of unique cases. It is nonetheless hoped that the questions raised by Colombia's TRV mini-maquila case will provide insights into the nature of labor market segmentation and unequal exchange in the periphery.

COFFEE AND THE CONTEXT FOR
LABOR MARKET SEGMENTATION
IN SOUTHERN COLOMBIA

Since the mid-1880s coffee has constituted one of the key sources of foreign exchange for the Colombian national economy. Consequently, the particular interests of coffee growers and producers have been among the most articulate of private sector interests in Colombia. The Federación Nacional De Cafeteros Colombianos (FNCC)—The Colombian Federation of Coffee Growers—is by far the key private sector organization in Colombia in terms of the international, national, and regional resources it commands. Many interest groups merely articulate desired political and economic outcomes in the countries where they operate. The FNCC, however, is particularly powerful at the regional and local levels because its decisions regarding exports clearly affect coffee cultivation.

The FNCC is made up of local departmental, or state, committees through which all coffee in Colombia is officially required to pass prior to its internal sales or export. Each departmental committee contributes a tallied amount of coffee to the FNCC, and based upon a formula that gives preference to the departments in order of the amount of coffee they produce annually the FNCC apportions departmental contributions to the national exports. Based upon this system of differential contributions, departmental committees receive different budgets for their productive and political activities (Palacios, 1980).

Of particular interest to our discussion of the changing labor market in the Valle Department of Colombia is the decline in total coffee exports attributable to this particular department since the mid-1970s. During this period, the Valle Department has dropped from second place to fourth place among departments in terms of its contribution to coffee exports. In this context, the Valle Department's Committee of Coffee Growers has faced diminished output by small-scale coffee producers as well as increased rates of rural to urban migration by the manual laborers who work in the seasonal harvesting of coffee on large plantations in the Valle Department's highland communities. The Committee has responded by initiating a variety of social welfare programs to "improve the lives of small producers and those of the small towns and villages where they reside"(Central de Cooperativas Agrarias de Occidente, Ltda., 1978).

One of the first social assistance agencies organized by the Valle Committee, the Central de Cooperativas Asrarias de Occidente, Ltda. (CENCOA) has worked to promote rural cooperatives of small-scale coffee producers and their families throughout the Valle Department. Its stated goal is the improvement of coffee production through cooperativism. As a recognized nonprofit organization involved in social development programs, CENCOA has received grants from international development assistance agencies as well as from the multilateral regional development bank, the Inter-American Development Bank. CENCOA has become the direct channel through which the Valle Departmental Committee of Coffee Producers has sought to ameliorate the social conditions that threaten the level of coffee production in the Valle Department. From our perspective on the social and physical reproduction of the labor force, CENCOA and its related programs have served as a conduit for the investment of funds whose primary return has been the survival of a relatively healthy and nourished rural labor force for seasonal work in coffee harvesting.[4]

The Valle Departmental Committee of Coffee Growers became particularly concerned with "dead time" between the harvesting seasons, the decline in small plots held by individuals who cultivate subsistence crops during the off-season, and the potential out-migration of large numbers of persons in search of more steady and remunerative work. Thus, the committee's director began to search for programs that CENCOA might organize to bring additional sources of income to the families of small-scale coffee producers and of seasonal laborers in coffee. In 1973, after consultation with multinational and national industrial managers, the Valle Departmental Committee of Coffee Growers decided to assist CENCOA in the organization of the Programa Grupos Precooperativos Talleres Rurales del Valle, Ltda. (TRV), which shall now be discussed at length.

TALLERES RURALES DEL VALLE PRECOOPERATIVE MINI-MAQUILAS

The TRV Program was established jointly by the Valle Departmental Committee of Coffee Growers and CENCOA on September 15, 1974 with the following stated objectives:

> a) to lend dignity to the peasant woman; b) to diminish rural to urban migration; c) to diversify the income of rural families; d) to diversify the income of rural families; e) to provide educational experiences to rural women; f) to integrate women into the national economy; g) to unleash the productive processes which can come through the applied use of cooperative methods; and h) to establish a sound foundation for the development of a legally recognized cooperative at a later date [CENCOA, 1978b: 4].

The two initial "workshops" were located in the small rural towns of Venecia and San Antonio in the Valle Department. They were chiefly dedicated to the production of commercial clothing and to the stitching of the uppers for the cloth shoe industry. Because the level of production remained fairly low for the first two years of the workshops' operations firms, representatives of the Valle Department Committee of Coffee Growers pursued more formal ties with national and multinational industry. By late 1975, arrangements were completed with Croydon/UniRoyal of Colombia for the subcontracting of work from Croydon to the TRV Program.

According to the present Executive Director of the TRV Program, Croydon was eager to link its operations with the TRV Program as part of its larger campaign to dismantle its formal sector plant operations in nearby Cali. The reason was that the costs of social benefits for the factory workers had risen to the point of making Croydon's athletic shoes fare more expensive than similar shoes imported to Colombia or sold on the black market. Thus, having established sub-contracting agreements with the TRV Program, Croydon closed its formal operations in southern Columbia. The company gave part of the machinery to the TRV Program and provided the remaining portion to retired Croydon employees who themselves became labor contractors exploiting informal sector workers.

Throughout the 1970s, Croydon remained one of the TRV program's chief clients, with the number of the rural mini-maquilas growing in order to meet the contracts for the stitching of athletic shoes, jute sandals, and other products. By 1976, the two initial workshops legally annulled their individual status as separate nonprofit enterprises and were incorporated, along with the six newer "workshops," into the Talleres Rurales del Valle Precooperative, Limited.

The legal documents creating the TRV Program state that the Valle Departmental Committee of Coffee Growers and CENCOA were the legal advisors and responsible entities to whom the TRV Precooperative Program was subject for a term of 10 years. This arrangement, which is a standard clause in the Colombian statutes, supposedly favors newly constituted groups that may not possess the administrative training necessary for accepting the legal responsibilities associated with producer cooperatives. Although the latter is certainly the case for a number of newly organized agricultural producers' cooperatives, the consequences of the precooperative arrangement for the women who work in the TRV Program's rural mini-maquilas merit particular attention.

Under the precooperative arrangement with the Valle Departmental Committee of Coffee Growers, the Talleres Rurales Program and, particularly, the individual mini-maquilas cede their right to participate in the negotiation of contracts for the piece-rate wages for which they work. In addition, the program and its mini-maquilas retain less than half ownership of the program's assets and have limited representation in the direction of the enterprise. Management of the program rests in the hands of an executive director who is appointed by the committee and who must report directly to them in the daily management of the program.

As one publication about the TRV program states:

> The Coffee Growers' Committee is in charge of the planning and financing of the groups according to the proposals which are presented by the local municipalities regarding the installation of a new "taller" (workshop) based on socio-economic studies of each region. The Committee will select according to criteria related to coffee production and social conditions in its determination of the most viable locations for erecting workshops. As well, the Committee will be involved in the planning of production in the workshops, in the arranging of contracts pertaining to the sale of manual labor and in the diversification of lines of production [CENCOA, 1977: 8].

The precooperative arrangement is clearly beneficial to the interests of the committee as they are ultimately the negotiators with national and international industry. Industrial firms, in turn, are favored by this arrangement because they are able to turn contracts with rates favorable to their cost-saving interests without having to negotiate directly with labor.

The women who participate in the TRV program do have general membership assemblies and, upon proving their loyalty to the program, may be appointed to submanagerial positions at the level of the workshop; however, they have been unable to alter the policies that most affect their lives as piece-rate workers. It is important to note, though, that the legal statute permitting the precooperative arrangement was no longer valid as of December 1984, and unless some legal act provides for its extension, the women now have the legal right to increase their participation in the management of the program.

SUBCONTRACTING AND THE
COLOMBIAN MINI-MAQUILAS

During the 10 years of its operation, the TRV program has retained subcontracting arrangements with a variety of national and international firms. Under Colombian legislation entitled "the Plan Vallego," partially processed industrial goods, such as those assembled in the TRV mini-maquilas, are given duty-free entry into the country and are protected for reimportation into the United States under the well-known article 806.3. Under the provisions of article 806.3, U.S. firms pay duties based only on the value-added abroad (Nash and Fernandez-Kelly, 1983). Given the relative ease in organizing subcontracting arrangements with multinational firms, the TRV program has become one of Colombia's leading providers of informal proletarian labor to international capital.

According to estimates provided by an official of the Colombian Agency for Export Promotion (PROEXPO), the TRV program's contracts with U.S. industry rank among the top five Colombian firms in terms of foreign exchange generated through the offshore assembly arrangements with multinational industry.[5] Subcontracting agreements have included London Fog, Bobbie Brooks, College Town, and Levi-Strauss. During the summer of 1984, the executive director referred to a potential contract with Levi-Strauss that would necessitate the construction of a new mini-maquila workshop for 300 additional women, an increase of half the size of the entire program.

The mini-maquilas are also a key source of disguised wage labor for the ailing Colombian textile industry located in the Antioquia Department. Since the decline of the Colombian textile industry in both the national and international markets, Colombian textile producers strategically have pursued segmented production arrangements. Thus, simple garments are cut in the formal factories and sent to the mini-maquilas for stitching. Those firms with which the TRV program retains contracts include Fabricato, Linea Senorial, MultiHogar, Manizol, Lindo Hogar, and Everfit of Colombia. Ironically, though Antioquia is Colombia's leading coffee producing department, the Valle Departmental Committee of Coffee Growers has retained a monopoly on this income-generating scheme for rural women, and has managed to prevent the Antioquia Committee from establishing a similar program to bolster the household income of small-scale producers and seasonal laborers.

Any simple comparison of working conditions and labor relations in the TRV Program's mini-maquilas with those of other offshore assembly operations is difficult. The TRV program functions, at least legally, as a worker's precooperative. Hence, there is access to limited benefits including medical services, family educational loans, rotating loans for domestic crises, limited life insurance, and dormitory facilities for some workshops where women live too far away to commute. Nevertheless, these services are in no way "given" to the women, but are considered as overhead in the initial calculation of the piece-rate wage of which the women receive only 70% as base pay. They may earn more than the base pay through a production incentive system that, according to the executive director of the TRV program, represents the equilibrium point at which most of the program's costs are covered.[6] However, relevant to our discussion of the informal sector is the fact that the women themselves are responsible for generating the 30% margin necessary for the social services and other benefits; industry *does not* provide this indirect wage.

The TRV program claims to function as a cooperative education program for women in the countryside. Yet, like other maquila industries, it clearly discriminates in the terms by which women are allowed to enter. In the past, potential candidates had to fall within the ages of 15 to 40. Furthermore, they were expected to pass through a "test" period to ensure their "adaptation" to the work and to demonstrate their ability to work in the "spirit" of cooperativism. Researchers have identified the various mechanisms that maquila industries in other countries have employed to engender "dedication" to the work and to alleviate potential tension between the women that might arise from the competitive conditions associated with piece-rate work (Fernandez-Kelly, 1983). As an ideology, cooperativism promotes a sense of teamwork among TRV laborers and helps isolate those who question whether all of the workshops receive equal treatment as precooperatives.

Beginning in 1984, the TRV program began to administer manual dexterity tests to potential cooperative members in order to weed out those who might be less efficient and productive than desired by the management. Dexterity tests have been utilized regularly in maquila programs elsewhere. The women who were interviewed did not have any specific reaction to the test. Nonetheless, the chief social worker for the TRV program admitted that she had heard complaints from women whose daughters, sisters, and other relatives wanted entry into the program. The social workers responsible for receiving applications for entry into the program explained to this researcher that they are coached by management to judge the physical attributes of the women whom they interview. For example, they are told to "look for good hands" because management presumes that calloused and cracked hands are less adept at producing fine and intricate sewing patterns. The social workers check as well for eye strain, unusually thick glasses indicating vision problems, and general attitude. Again, comparable judgment techniques are employed in the Mexican, Central American, and Asian maquila programs to select women workers.

Labor relations in the TRV program have begun to show signs of worker/management tensions in the last few years. Perhaps the keenest example is the Venecia workshop's strategy two years ago, when management would not provide the Christmas vacation benefits the members felt they deserved. Summoning the executive director for consultation, the women called a workshop meeting at which point they surrounded the executive director and locked him in the workshop without the possibility of escaping for an entire day and part of the evening. Work stoppages have occurred in some workshops whose workers felt that they were being forced to work too many shifts and that the negotiated piece rate underestimated the time it took to produce a product. A prime example is the piece rate negotiated with Catalina for the production of bathing suits. According to the women involved, sewing bathing suits necessitates precise manipulation of miniscule stitches, tiny straps, and small pieces of elastic. According to the women in the workshop, this process requires that a single woman work for much more than the time estimated by the production engineers who calculate the piece rate based on time-production studies. The women have asked to be included in these studies as they have a realistic view of efficiency, timing, and the like. They have been told, however, that "production engineers have to go to college to learn to do these studies" and that such studies require skills that the women do not possess.

To the outside observer who spends time with the women in the various workshops, it is clear that labor/management relations in the TRV program more characteristic of profit-making industry than of production cooperatives. Several of the social workers interviewed predicted an increase in tension in the coming months and years as management attempts to expand the number of workshops while seemingly less productive ones remain without full-time work.[7]

THE INFORMAL PROLETARIAN/SEASONAL WORKER RELATION: INITIAL FINDINGS

To make empirical statements about the precise mechanisms through which the mini-maquilas undergird the reproduction of the seasonal agricultural labor force, we need indepth studies of the household income pooling units to which the TRV laborers contribute part or all of their earnings. Unfortunately, we lack such studies; my current research agenda addresses this gap. The fact remains that available data regarding the demographic and economic attributes of the women and their families support our hypothesis.

Surveys completed by the TRV program's social work staff indicate that over half of the women are between the ages of 15 and 22; that over half are unmarried and living with their parents; that 70% of the TRV labor force has been part of the program for less than four years; that at least 60% of their fathers own very small plots of land less than 6 plazas; that 60% to 70% of their fathers, husbands, and brothers work as day laborers; and that the portion of the family income contributed by the women is half to three-fourths, depending upon which workshop is surveyed (Central de Cooperativas Agrarias de Occidente, Ltda., 1983). It is evident that the work of the women in the mini-maquilas constitutes far more than supplementary income to the family unit: For most families, the women's wages may be the only steady source of income available to the household unit.

CONCLUSION

The Talleres Rurales del Valle Precooperative Program is certainly not the only example of the use of rural females as rural informal proletarian labor in Colombia or elsewhere in the periphery. Evidence indicates similar cases in other parts of Colombia as well as in Costa Rica, Taiwan, and Malaysia. And, at the time my field research in Colombia, plans were being made for the TRV program's staff to visit Uruguay, Ecuador, and Peru to discuss the potential for organizing similar programs in rural areas of those countries.

As the level of infrastructural development improves in the rural areas of the periphery, rural residents join the urban-based reserve army of labor that multinational industry pursues in order to lower production costs. When requirements of industrial production mesh with those of commercial agriculture, we can expect to find evidence of segmented labor markets along formal and informal lines, with a marked gender-specific division of the labor force.

Recent technological developments that have facilitated the component-by-component assembly of industrial goods create the possibility of more elaborate production hierarchies that incorporate the skills derived from women's socialization (Beneria, 1985). As rural regions of the periphery become more accessible by means of modern transport and possess a modicum of infrastructure such as adequate electrical and communication services, rural residents are likely to become the next source of inexpensive industrial labor. As in the case of the women discussed in this study, a major portion of these rural laborers who are newly incorporated into industrial production are likely to be women whose contributions to household income are either primary or substantial. The income that they contribute is critical to maintaining other members of the household such as males and other females who are employed in less remunerative agricultural work. Through this mechanism, the industrial employment of women in rural zones directly subsidizes commercial agriculture and permits the consistent payment of less than subsistence-level wages in that sector.

Only recently have scholars rigorously attempted to determine the functional relationship between unequal exchange and the status of women in peripheral economies. The expanded participation of female workers in the global assembly line since the 1950s has become the subject of research regarding the nature and extent of women's work in the periphery (Safa, 1981, 1984; Sassen-Koob, 1984; Nash and Fernandez-Kelly, 1983; Fernandez-Kelly, 1983) and has provided critical data on the working conditions associated with multinational subcontracting industries in the periphery. The latter research, as well as current theoretical debates treating the physical and social reproduction of the labor force (Beneria, 1978), are fundamental to developing an understanding of the various "modes of labor absorption" that are responsible for unequal exchange (Portes and Benton, 1984).

The world-economic crisis of the last decade has spurred the emergence and reemergence of a host of modes of labor absorption in the periphery. Countries in Central and South America and the Caribbean have already become the recipients of numerous off-shore assembly operations that employ primarily women in formal and informal sector firms. Recent state policies for regional economic development, such as the Caribbean Basin Initiative, have according to some analysts supported this form of employment generation in the periphery. Observers of past experiences with similar programs for economic development, such as Operation Bootstrap in Puerto Rico, continue to underscore the negative consequences that these policies have for women who often constitute the most exploited segment of the informal and formal production hierarchy (Safa, 1984).

NOTES

1. According to Portes's findings in the urban labor markets of Latin America, the urban informal sector is primarily distinguishable from the formal sector by the absence of

state intervention through the provision of social welfare benefits or the collection of taxes. For a more elaborate discussion of the informal sector, see Portes, 1985.

2. The term *maquila*, or assembly plant, originally referred to assembly-oriented operations in Mexico and has since been applied to industrial processing arrangements elsewhere (Fernandez-Kelly, 1983).

3. For an insightful discussion of the history of dependency theory, see Bornschier and Chase-Dunn, 1985. The work of Ward (1984) also contributes to this analysis of dependency theory by specifically analyzing dependency theory and the status of women in the world-economy.

4. The information related to the creation and current goals of CENCOA was obtained by the author through numerous personal interviews conducted at different times between 1978 and 1984 with former and current employees of the Valle Departmental Committee of Coffee Growers and of CENCOA.

5. PROEXPO's staff was still calculating the previous year's foreign exchange earnings from offshore assembly at the time of the interview. Hence, absolute dollar values for the portion of the portfolio belonging to the TRV program were not included here.

6. There is not space here to discuss the intricate details of how the piece-rate wage is derived and how the process bears on the reproduction of the informal proletarian labor force in the TRV workshops. Still, it is important to note that the majority of the costs for the program are covered by the subcontracting work itself or by international donor agencies. Not all of the workshops are in full operation 100% of the time as they depend on staggered contracts. Consequently, the operating costs are pooled in such a fashion as to distribute the excess over the entire program in order to protect the program from market fluctuations inherent in the offshore assembly business. Hence, the three or four workshops with large contracts are forced to cover the "dead time" of the smaller workshops that do not retain permanent contracts.

7. Substantial evidence exists for the internal segmentation of labor within the TRV program. It is highly possible that a "twin-plant syndrome" is developing in the TRV program whereby less skilled and more isolated mini-maquila workers perform one set of tasks and more established branches of the cooperatives perform relatively more elaborate tasks within the production hierarchy. For a discussion of the twin-plant syndrome in offshore assembly operations, see Safa (1984).

REFERENCES

AMIN, S. (1976) Unequal Development, An Essay on the Social Formation of Peripheral Capitalism. New York: Monthly Review Press.

BENERIA, L. (1979) "Reproduction, production and the sexual division of labour." Cambridge Journal of Economics 3: 203-225.

BENERIA, L. (1985, May) "Gender, skill and the dynamics of women's employment." Prepared for the Gender in the Work Place Conference, Brookings Institution, Washington, DC.

BORNSCHIER, V. and C. CHASE-DUNN (1985) Transnational Corporations and Underdevelopment. New York: Praeger.

BROMLEY, R. and C. GERRY (1979) Casual Work and Poverty in Third World Cities. New York: John Wiley.

Central de Cooperativas Agrarias de Occidente, Ltda. (1983) Informe sobre los talleres del punto de visto socio-económico de las socias. Cali, Columbia.

———(1978) Investigación socio-económica del Grupos Precooperativos. Cali, Colombia.

de JANVRY, A. and C. GARRAMON (1977) "The dynamic of rural poverty in Latin America." Journal of Peasant Studies 5: 206-216.

EMMANUEL, A. (1972) Unequal Exchange. London: New Left Books.

FERNANDEZ-KELLY, M. (1983) For We Are Sold: I and My People. Albany: State University of New York Press.

GERRY, C. (1978) "Self-employed proletarians in an informal factory: the case of Cali's garbage dump." World Development 6, 9-10: 1173-1185.

Ministerio de Desarollo Economico (1982) Manual de los sistemas especiales de importación-exportación "Plan Vallejo." Bogota, Colombia.

NASH, J. and M. FERNANDEZ-KELLY (1983) Women, Men and the International Division of Labor. Albany: State University of New York Press.

PALACIOS, M. (1980) Coffee in Colombia, 1850-1970. Cambridge: Cambridge University Press.

PRATES, S. (1983) "Cuando el sector formal organisma el trabajo informal." Dissertation prepared for the working group on employment and unemployment, Calasco-Recife.

PORTES, A. (1985) "The informal sector and the world-economy: notes on the structure of subsidized labor," pp. 53-62 in M. Timberlake (ed.) Urbanization in the World-Economy. New York: Academic.

———and L. BENTON (1984) "Industrial development and labor absorption: a reinterpretation." Population and Development Review 10, 4.

PORTES, A and J. WALTON (1981) Labor, Class and The International System. New York: Academic Press.

SAFA, H. (1981) "Runaway shops and female employment: the search for cheap labor." Signs 7, 2.

———(1984) "Female employment and the social reproduction of the Puerto Rican working class." International Migration Review XVIII, 4.

SASSEN-KOOB, S. (1984) "Notes on the incorporation of Third World women into wage-labor through immigration and off-shore production." International Migration Review XVIII, 4.

TRUELOVE, C. (1981) "A review of the constraints affecting development activities in the Cauca Valley." Unpublished manuscript presented to Appropriate Technology International, Washington, DC.

WARD, K. (1984) Women in the World-System. New York: Praeger.

PART II

STATE, ECONOMY, AND CRISIS

STATE RESPONSES TO THE GREAT DEPRESSION, 1929-1934:
Toward a Comparative Analysis of "Revolutionary" Mexico and "Nonrevolutionary" Colombia

Richard Tardanico
Florida International University

How does state making differ in revolutionary and nonrevolutionary settings? What are the consequences of its differences, not just for domestic sociopolitical and economic structures but also for their relations with worldwide patterns of capital accumulation and geopolitics? Recent comparative studies have examined these questions, which previously had received little serious attention (see Eckstein, 1982; Gereffi and Evans, 1981; Skocpol, 1979; Trimberger, 1978). The questions open up a promising line of inquiry as we strive to understand the historical foundations and present-day tendencies of the political economy of the Caribbean Basin.

Mexico and Colombia are major actors in the Caribbean Basin today. Both nations border on the region; thus neither is fully enveloped by its social, cultural, economic, and political networks. Yet their governments have exerted regional influence through the Contadora Group and other channels, and, of course, neither's foreign affairs can be understood without reference to the regional presence of the United States. Interwoven with their external commonalities are internal commonalities, too. Mexico and Colombia occupy extensive, mountainous, and highly regionalized territories. In the context of economic dependence, regionalism surfaces in the forms of uneven national development and centrifugal political tensions that pull against the reins of central authority. Civilian leadership has held these reins, though strengthened armies and domestic crises have spawned some concern over growing military leverage. The governments of Mexico and Colombia sit atop diversified economies. A key commodity—petroleum in Mexico and coffee in Colombia—has headed their respective formal exports, and in both cases informal exports—labor and drugs in Mexico, drugs in Colombia—figure prominently; but manufacturing, oil and mining, agriculture, commerce, and services all account for significant shares of the Mexican and Colombian economies. Underpinning the gamut of shared national traits is pronounced social inequality. Still another commonality—popular, if disunited, unrest—is therefore no surprise (Arrubla et al., 1982; Bagley, 1984; Kline, 1983, 1985; Levy and Székely, 1986; Newell and Rubio, 1984).

The fact remains that fundamental differences characterize Mexico and Colombia as well. Confrontation with its northern neighbor has been a crucial element of Mexico's post-independence history, and since the late nineteenth century Mexico has served as a leading site of U.S. investment. In this context Mexican-U.S. discord over Central America is nothing new; even before the Revolution, Mexican leadership attempted to counter U.S. influence in the area. With the Revolution (1910-1940) this strategic interest became interwoven with populistic ideology and institutions and state centralization. Mexico's surging petroleum earnings of the late 1970s to early 1980s, which reinforced its position as the largest, most industrialized economy in the Caribbean Basin, boosted the state's ability to offset North American dominance and to neutralize leftist critics at home by supporting populistic nationalism in the Caribbean zone and beyond (Bagley, 1984; Meyer, 1975). In contrast, only recently has Colombia aligned with populistic nationalism in the Caribbean Basin and the wider Third World. And its current domestic reformism is no stable, longstanding feature of government policy. Unlike Mexico, Colombia has never been a leading site of North American investment; and though the Caribbean represents a significant part of its history, the Andes have dominated Colombian society, economy, and politics. Hence, with the dramatic exception of Panama, Colombia has not shared Mexico's fundamental worries over U.S. expansionism. Its loss of Panama notwithstanding, reliance on coffee exports to North America solidified Colombian-U.S. relations.

So have Colombia's disputes with Nicaragua, Cuba, and Venezuela, as well as the combination of oligarchic rule and threats from below. Lagging far behind Mexico in state centralization, national development, and petroleum resources, Colombia lacks the former's institutional and material base for sustaining active foreign initiatives (Arrubla et al., 1982; Kline, 1983, 1985; Teaster, 1985).

The above suggests the interconnection of differing tendencies and capacities in external affairs with differing patterns of internal relations between state and society. This interconnection raises questions about the comparative roles of Mexican "revolutionary" state making and Colombian "nonrevolutionary" state making in the emergence of the Caribbean Basin as a zone of the world capitalist order. In the context of Mexico's preexisting advantages of economic and governmental dynamism, the two countries began the twentieth century with weakly integrated, oligarchic states that increasingly derived their economic and fiscal sustenance from metropolitan capital and markets. Not that the Revolution subsequently erased all traces of this arrangement in Mexico; as we shall see, new-regime actions were often anything but revolutionary, and they built upon old-regime legacies of social inequality, authoritarian politics, and economic dependence. By the 1940s, however, Mexico possessed a highly centralized, mass-incorporating state, whose leadership had broken the political back of the old-regime oligarchy and undercut the independence of foreign investors. Thus, the revolution had established the institutional foundations not just for government stability but additionally for the emergence of a large, diversified national bourgeoisie (see Hamilton, 1982; Meyer, 1973). In Colombia, though, very little had changed. The state had assumed greater authority, but it neither approximated Mexico's in scale nor challenged the power of the traditional upper classes. The oligarchy, then, remained in charge; nevertheless, its intensified factionalism debilitated the state and, given the concurrent sharpening of interclass conflict, unleashed some 20 years of nightmarish, widespread violence. By no means did Colombia rival Mexico's economic transformation during this period, and formal efforts to end *La Violencia* promoted "oligarchic democracy" and perpetuated the state's comparative weakness in Latin American perspective (see Kline, 1983; Oquist, 1980).

This chapter attempts to shed light on these divergent paths of state building by comparing government responses in "revolutionary" Mexico and "nonrevolutionary" Colombia to the onset of world economic crisis, 1929-1934. The 1920s had been a decade of transnational capitalist expansion, marked by the widening sphere of U.S. diplomatic-military and economic influence. This process encompassed conflict and accommodation regarding the continued incorporation of the emerging "Caribbean Basin" into the U.S. orbit. Such conflict and accommodation had accompanied economic growth and infrastructural modernization in Mexico and Colombia, including steps toward the strengthening of government tools for encouraging national development. With the end of expansionary conditions at the global and domestic levels came possibilities for the redefinition of state/class and state/state relations. How did Mexican and Colombian authorities respond to economic crisis? How did their responses contribute to the comparative unfolding of Mexican and Colombian state/class structures and linkages with the world political economy? These questions form the core of the following analysis.

COLOMBIA

Background: Colombia
in Historical Perspective

During the nineteenth century Colombian politics increasingly centered on intra-elite strife over the socioeconomic organization of the country and the desirability of export growth. This strife pitted the Liberal party, the prime supporter of socioeconomic modernization and export growth, against the Conservative party. Restricted export earnings, which came to revolve around coffee, conjoined with minimal metropolitan investment to limit Colombia's ties with the world economy, to preclude national integration, and to keep the Liberals from establishing political hegemony. As political conflict fostered rigid party alignments and society became more diversified, intense factionalism appeared within the ranks of Liberals and Conservatives alike. Factions representing equivalent interests arose in both parties, thereby allowing for complex interparty alliances. Elites dominated the two parties, which nonetheless were multiclass in composition, with party loyalty coming to be inherited along family, community, and regional lines. Such loyalty intensified as intra-elite competition turned more violent and governance turned more exclusivistic. These trends culminated in the War of a Thousand Days (1899-1902) (Bergquist, 1978; Oquist, 1980: chap. 2; Palacios, 1980: chap. 1).

Conservatives headed the twentieth-century Colombian state until 1930. Yet the end of civil war and the spread of coffee cultivation shifted the focus of intra-elite contention; the basic issue had now become how best to attain export growth. Reflecting this bipartisan consensus was the incorporation of Liberals into governance, though their position became more and more marginal. The administrations of the period adopted a series of modernizing policies, including military reforms, fiscal and monetary reorganization, transport development, and minimal industrial tariffs, and the loss of Panama (1930) did not deter leadership from seeking to normalize diplomacy and commerce with the United States. Beginning in 1910 booming coffee exports sparked general economic expansion. After World War I the normalization of Colombian-U.S. relations touched off the "Dance of the Millions," as over $200 million in U.S. credits poured into Colombia, and it leaped from among the lowest to fifth among Latin American countries in amount of U.S. investment. The main targets of credit and investment were petroleum and export-import infrastructure; coffee production, which now ranked second in the world to Brazil, remained almost entirely under local ownership, thus generating funds for reinvestment in commerce, finance, and industry. Foreign trade underlay rising government revenues and budgets, and economic expansion promoted the integration of the upper classes' regional cliques, primarily those of Bogotá, Antioquia, and Valle. But indicative of the persistence of both weak central authority and oligarchic factionalism was the marked degree of regional and local authority over taxation and spending. So too were rampant corruption and the worsening fiscal deficits of the late 1920s. Another aspect of Colombia's decentralized state structure was the absence of a strong national army, a characteristic that dated from the era of independence (Bergquist, 1978: chaps. 9-10; Cruz Santos, 1966: chaps. 3-6; Palacios, 1980: 198, 201-209; Rippy, 1931: chaps. 6-8; Thorp and Londoño, 1984: 82-92).

The extension of coffee farming stabilized the Colombian state in part by fostering economic integration of the oligarchy's regional factions. It did so as well because local ownership of coffee production and the spread of smallholdings provided extra-government channels for personal advancement, solidified points of elite/mass political convergence, and minimized receptiveness to nationalist and radical appeals (Bergquist, 1978: 257-262). Increasingly, however, a scarcity of land for coffee expansion and a shortage of rural labor incited localized conflicts between landlords and peasants. Meanwhile, proletarianization led to strikes. The most violent of these occurred in the foreign-owned banana and oil enclaves, though underdevelopment and regionalization restricted the labor movement's size and cohesion. Overlaying interclass struggle was mounting interparty competition. The Liberal party took advantage of the Conservative party's rigidity and repression in the face of popular unrest by articulating a platform that attracted significant urban working-class support. This platform contributed to the declining militancy of the labor movement as a whole (Melo, 1982: 85-90; Oquist, 1980: 82-84, 89-102; Palacios, 1980: 175-179, 196-197; Rippy, 1931: chap. 9).

State Policy and
World Crisis, 1929-1934

It is clear that coffee exports and U.S. investments instigated Colombia's economic and fiscal growth of the 1920s. In the second half of 1928, though, the inflow of foreign capital fell drastically. Thereafter coffee prices dipped, markedly so by late 1929. Petroleum and bananas headed the other exports that joined coffee in crisis. From 1928 to 1931-1932 the value of Colombian exports tumbled by 58%, with the money supply dropping by 49% and government income by 45%. Plunging government income and expenditure forced major cutbacks in public works programs, and, as urban unemployment rose and aggregate demand slumped, the downturn extended to construction, transportation, and manufacturing. Many workers who lost jobs in export agriculture, public works, and other urban-industrial activities returned to the countryside, thereby intensifying competition for land and counteracting the agrarian labor shortage of the mid-1920s. A fundamental aspect of the Colombian experience is that a large portion of coffee producers were smallholders whose income hardly exceeded subsistence level; just partially exposed to the market's vagaries, these farmers escaped much of the Great Depression's impact. We shall see that, under the aegis of the landowning/merchant bourgeoisie that controlled the sector's financing, marketing, and large estates, coffee production soon increased in compensation for the low prices that would plague the commodity throughout the decade. In contrast with the rest of the economy, food production for the domestic market, which had seriously declined in the 1920s, began to surge ahead (Ministerio de Hacienda y Crédito Público, República de Colombia, 1931: 13-17; Ocampo, 1984; Palacios, 1980: 212-214; Thorp and Londoño, 1984).

Colombia's economic instability of the late 1920s hastened political realignment within the oligarchy. Factionalism, of course, characterized the Conservative and Liberal parties alike. And it must not be forgotten that, despite multiclass memberships, the two parties were instruments of the oligarchy, with political maneuvering often involving crosss-party alliances. The Conservative party's principal factionalist tensions of the late 1920s were not at all surprising in view of the decade's economic development and class conflict. At bottom, these tensions divided the party's progressive wing of landowner/merchants and industrialists— groups that had gained considerable impetus in the 1920s—from its reactionary wing of traditional landowners. One source of divisiveness within the Conservative party was the progressive wing's quest to modernize the state apparatus, which, in spite of some reforms, remained very decentralized and organized along patronage lines. Contention over this point, which was interlaced with the persistent regionalism of the dominant classes, intensified as economic and fiscal crisis led to heightened competition over a shrinking government budget. So did contention over the desirability of more flexible state policy to confront economic crisis, increased unemployment, food shortage, and mass unrest. In splitting the Conservative party, these and other points of divergence enabled the Liberal party, whose platform appealed to workers, peasants, artisans, students, and professionals, to forge a bipartisan coalition of Colombia's modernizing elite. Led by the financial bourgeoisie of the Liberal party, this coalition aimed to restabilize class relations and to free socioeconomic resources for coffee-based national development. The Liberals ended the Conservative's longstanding dominance by winning the presidential election of 1930 (Mejía, 1982: 140-144; Melo, 1982: 97-100; Palacios, 1980: 208-211, 213-214).

Heading the peaceful transition to Liberal dominance was the presidency of Enrique Olaya Herrera (1930-1934). By no means did Olaya, a moderate liberal, envision anything approximating the restructuring of state, society, and economy. A former functionary in conservative governments, he ensured a smooth transition by appointing by bipartisan cabinet, by respecting decentralized political arrangements, and by proclaiming that agriculture would remain the heart of the Colombian economy. Olaya did speak mildly of social justice, but, consistent with his previous service as a Colombian diplomatic representative in Washington, D.C., and as a lawyer for U.S. oil firms, he proclaimed that the state would continue to seek massive foreign investment. That the new administration did not challenge the Colombian status quo and its relations with metropolitan interests was, therefore, no surprise. It must be recognized that, besides Olaya's own political moderation, broader pressures for sweeping change were minimal. For one thing, peasant conflicts and movements were localized, and, in spite of militant beginnings, organized labor failed to transcend the political limitations imposed by a highly regionalized and underdeveloped economy. Not to be overlooked either was popular attachment to the Conservative and Liberal parties, including the latter's special appeals to the masses in the 1920s, as well as the extent to which Colombians, rather than foreigners, owned the nation's productive resources. These political and economic conditions also kept middle-class nationalism in check while channeling the sector's leftist currents into compromises and opportunism within the Liberal party. Dependence on metropolitan capital and trade combined with the coalitional structure of the Olaya government to limit the reformist inclinations of the Liberal oligarchy (Bergquist, 1978: 256-262; Cruz Santos, 1966: chap. 7; Dix, 1967: 81-82; Garcia, 1978: 185-187; Oquist, 1980: 85; Melo, 1982: 98-99; Rippy, 1931: 197).

So, as the Olaya regime assumed office, it intended to address Colombia's economic crisis by adhering to the orthodox approach of encouraging U.S. direct investments and loans while promoting coffee exports and enhancing the economy's import capacity. During its first year or so, the government pursued this strategy most basically by stressing prompt payment on the external debt. Given reduced foreign investment and import-tax revenues as well as the continuation of fiscal and monetary orthodoxy, this priority was decidely contractionary; it ensured that Colombian interests, rather than metropolitan capital, absorbed the brunt of the shock associated with economic crisis (see Ministerio de Hacienda y Crédito Público de Colombia, 1932: 41; Ocampo, 1984: 127-130; Thorp and Londoño, 1984: 96-97). Linked with this priority were other measures that underlined the state's determination to remain in good standing with foreign investors. For the most part, government policy was consistent with the recommendations of American economist Edwin W. Kemmerer who, in line with his commission's plan of the previous decade, proposed fiscal and monetary guidelines that served international interests. Continued payment on the external debt was one of these recommendations, as were tax reforms, decreased public spending, maintenance of the gold standard, monetary deflation, minimal tariffs, and other orthodox policies (Cruz Santos, 1966: chaps. 6 and 7; Ministerio de Hacienda y Crédito Público, República de Colombia, 1931: 31-39).

From 1929 to 1931 severe price deflation accompanied Colombia's sharp drops in foreign reserves, central bank bills in circulation, and money supply (Ministerio de Hacienda y Crédito Público, République de Colombia, 1931, 1932; Ocampo, 1984: 127-128). Monetary policy, however, remained conservative, one reason being widespread fear of major currency depreciation like that of the War of a Thousand Days (Ocampo, 1984: 125-126; Thorp and Londoño, 1984: 96). Nevertheless, the political leverage of the nation's regional and local upper classes and bosses, along with the consequently decentralized structure of the Colombian state, made monetary and fiscal policy more complicated than initially apparent. In this respect, departmental and municipal governments defaulted on debt obligations even as the federal government resisted default and maintained the exchange rate. Indicative of federal authority's weakness was the fact that departmental and municipal governments often undertook autonomous public works projects and only later informed federal officials of the subsidies required. Local groups even obtained international loans to finance their undertakings (Thorp and Londoño, 1984: 96-97; see also Cruz Santos, 1966: 237-238, 242-243; Ocampo, 1984: 127-130). The Olaya government did minimally attempt to extend federal authority through fiscal reforms, the reorganization of customs operations, the coordination of public works projects, increased tariffs, and the like (Cruz Santos, 1966: 238-250, 261-264; Ministerio de Hacienda y Credito Público, República de Colombia, 1931, 1932). Indeed, tariffs represented the sole true anticyclical initiative of the administration's first year, with agriculture and industry alike benefiting from the tariff code enacted in May 1931. Still, because mild tariffs had already been a feature of national policy, this code was regarded as congruent with orthodoxy (Ocampo, 1984: 130).

A clear example of the administration's pro-United States stance was its petroleum policy. Colombian petroleum policy had never been articulated firmly, having vacillated between mild nationalism and efforts to attract metropolitan firms. Their complaints over land titles and other aspects of government regulation had picked up in 1928 when, in the setting of oil controversy, the Ministry of Industries proposed that the petroleum industry be declared a public utility and called for its stricter supervision. In so doing the ministry raised the possibility of planning to augment the nation's share of profits, to set up semiofficial enterprises, and to prepare for Colombian ownership of pipelines (Rippy, 1931: 148-149). But the Olaya presidency's Law of 1931 proved extremely generous to foreign companies. Among other things, it exempted petroleum exploration, extraction, production, and machinery from national, departmental, and municipal taxes, and granted up to 50,000 hectares per concession. Similar treatment was accorded to other enclave activities, such as those of the United Fruit Company. By accommodating such enterprises, the state reinforced not only Colombia's economic and political disarticulation but also its subordination to metropolitan capital (see Garcia, 1979: 188-189; Latorre, 1937).

In view of the absence of substantial statist intervention in the economy, it is not hard to guess the early course of the Olaya government's policy toward peasants and workers. We have already seen that many newly unemployed urban workers returned to the countryside. There they contributed to mass struggles over land tenure and labor conditions. Some rural movements became well organized; such movements, whose political organization sometimes involved external support by such groups as the National Union of the Revolutionary Left and the Communist Party, were most likely to benefit from the regime's piecemeal agrarian reform. Overall, though, limited class consciousness and the lack of overarching organization left peasants vulnerable to political manipulation and repression, a situation that encompassed traditional Conservative/Liberal rivalry. Similar conditions restricted the leverage of urban labor, with the nationalism unleashed in 1933 by Colombia-Peru border tensions further dampening labor militancy. Not to be neglected, however, is the fact that the continuation of many federal, departmental, and municipal public works programs responded in part to pressures from below, and that, among other measures, the federal government subsidized private firms to employ extra workers. Nonetheless, consistent with the Olaya presidency's alignment with international capital and the Colombian oligarchy, it never did carry out significant land and labor reforms (Cruz Santos, 1966; 243-247; Mejía, 1982; 155-158; Oquist, 1980: chap. 3; Thorp and Londoño, 1984: 97).

We have noted, in sum, that despite the weakened leverage of foreign capital and the domestic upper classes as a result of the Great Depression, the administration's initial policies did not attempt to centralize the state's machinery as a means of bolstering its power, redistributing wealth, and stimulating nationalist development. On the contrary, the administration conserved the state's alliance with U.S. interests and the oligarchy, thereby conserving as well the state's decentralized structure and weakness.

Yet pressures for statist intervention did gather steam. They emanated not just from the ranks of the popular classes, but from the state apparatus and the upper classes, too. Regarding the upper classes, a key source of such pressure was the Colombian Federation of Coffee Growers (FNCC). The FNCC originated as a nineteenth-century association of landowners dedicated to liberal economic principles. In the 1920s it developed under leadership by major landowners and politicians of Bogotá and Antioquia as a loosely structured, extraparty association, whose income came from a modest coffee export tax. Its purpose was to advance the economic and political interests of large and small coffee growers. Typifying the ambiguities inherent in the decentralized machinery of the Colombian state, the FNCC evolved as a legally private entity that, in actuality, was a quasi-public institution. Between 1929 and 1935 it became a hierarchically structured tool of large producers and exporters that began pressing for expansionary credit policy, including the establishment of an agrarian bank (Ocampo, 1984: 130-131; Palacios, 1980: 217-226; Thorp and Londoño, 1984: 99-100).

The FNCC's pressures coincided with those of several former ministers of finance and a congressional commission for expansionary banking measures. But what initiated the regime's break with orthodoxy was the sterling devaluation of September 1931, which dictated the introduction of exchange controls and in turn rendered superfluous orthodox monetary and fiscal policy. The government expanded its economic presence by founding the Agrarian Bank, the Central Mortgage Bank, and the Colombian Credit Corporation, and by directly intervening in the sugar industry. Not until early 1933, however, did the government suspend payments on the external debt; and, given the economy's continued orientation to the United States, it did so only because of fiscal pressures associated with Colombia-Peru border tensions. These tensions may have contributed to increased public expenditures, part of which were underwritten by the central bank, though the recovery of export prices was the prime factor. Under persistent pressure by the FNCC, the administration finally devalued Colombia's currency in September 1933 (Ocampo, 1984: 130-133; Thorp and Londoño, 1984: 99-101; see also Cruz Santos, 1966: 250-259; Ministerio de Hacienda y Crédito Público, Republica de Colombia, 1932, 1933, 1934; Palacios, 1980: 214-222).

By 1934 economic resurgence was evident. The import-substitution industry played a leading role, with gold production—which attracted considerable foreign capital—likewise booming and coffee exports increasing significantly (Ocampo, 1984: 120-124; Thorp and Londoño, 1984: 99-102). As regards coffee exports, the FNCC became a very powerful organization, not only successfully resisting penetration by foreigners but also serving to consolidate the leverage of the coffee bourgeoisie within the national government. As Marco Palacios (1980: 215) observes, the government's responses to the world crisis reflected "the dominance of the coffee-exporting group. It would not be an exaggeration to state that macro-economic orientation was based on the interests of this group." Devaluation and protective tariffs did accelerate the growth of the import-substitution industry. Nevertheless, Colombia's sectoral shift toward industry, and the concurrent diversification of the bourgeoisie, represented the continuation of a trend begun in the 1920s under the stimulus of coffee prosperity. Indeed, credit legislation and public spending on economic development were geared to commercial agriculture. Such policies, as well as tax reforms, did signify political realignment within the dominant classes insofar as they pressured the traditional landowning elite to modernize production (Garcia, 1978: 189-191; Ocampo, 1984: 137-141; Palacios, 1980: 214-216; Thorp and Londoño, 1984: 101-102).

In summary, what we see is that in 1931-1934 the Olaya regime promoted capital accumulation not by challenging but by consolidating Colombia's alliance of state, oligarchy, and metropolitan capital. By no means, then, was Colombia an "autonomous" state (see Hamilton, 1982; Skocpol, 1979); on the contrary, it remained a decentralized instrument of the nation's oligarchy. True, important steps had been taken toward the rationalization of the state's machinery. What these represented, however, was the continued ascendance of the oligarchy's modernizing segments—above all the financial bourgeoisie linked to coffee production and trade—which sought to foster national development by enchancing Colombia's dependent participation in the global division of labor.

Political and economic modernization picked up under the subsequent presidency of Alfonso López Pumarejo (1934-1938). A leading Colombian banker, López directed a campaign of state building and economic development that responded to the interests of the financial bourgeoisie and its associated coffee, merchant, and industrial entrepreneurs. His "Revolution on the March" drew inspiration from such sources as Mexico's revolutionary constitution and Cardenista reforms, the Peruvian *Apristas*, and U.S. "New Deal" and "Good Neighbor" policies. In the context of such international currents, Colombia's own popular-nationalist pressures led López and his clique to recognize the need to counterbalance the power of the reactionary oligarchy by centralizing state authority. Doing so meant intensified efforts toward labor and agrarian reform, educational expansion, bureaucratic reorganization, fiscal reform, transportation development, restricting the privileges of foreigners, and the like (Dix, 1967: 82-89; Mejía, 1982: 155-165).

Much of this campaign remained on paper. In fact, the regime did little on behalf of labor and peasants, a fundamental reason being resistance by the industrial and agrarian bourgeoisie. Having failed to establish mass-incorporating bulwarks against the reactionary upper classes, Colombia made only minimal progress toward government centralization and economic integration. Given continued intra- and interparty factionalism, the modernizing campaign began to unravel politically, with manufacturers and landowners alike opposing reforms. By 1946 the Liberal party's hegemony had ended, and with the return of Conservative rule came intensified intra- and interclass conflict. In the setting of a weak, decentralized state, such conflict took the form of *La Violencia*. Hence, as such states as Mexico and Brazil undertook aggressive programs of economic transformation that guided them into the "semiperiphery" of the world capitalist order, Colombia remained shackled by oligarchic traditionalism and widespread strife (Dix, 1967: 89-98; Kline, 1983: chaps. 3-5; Mejía, 1982: 149-183; Oquist, 1980: chaps. 3-6).

MEXICO

Background: Mexico in
Historical Perspective

In the late nineteenth and early twentieth centuries massive European and North American investments underwrote Mexico's regionalized, export-led prosperity and its long-lasting dictatorship of Porfirio Díaz (1876-1911). Eventually, however, enclave development, exclusionary government, and preexisting social patterns spawned reform movements and uprisings that crosscut Mexico's class, nationalist, regionalist, and personalist interests. These forces, in the setting of economic recession, diminishing European influence, and diplomatic tensions with the United Sates, toppled the eroding dictatorship in 1911, and led to the definitive collapse of the Porfirian state structure in 1914. The ensuing civil war centered on three armies whose respective constituencies were the northern reformist/nationalist bourgeoisie, the northern frontier's heterogeneous proletariat, and the south-central peasantry. Emerging victorious in 1916-1917 was the army of the northern bourgeoisie, in part because its leadership promised major social reforms and coopted a segment of organized labor (Córdova, 1973: chaps. 2-4; Meyer, 1973, chaps. 1-2).

A coup ushered in the presidencies of Alvaro Obregón (1920-1924) and his hand-picked successor Plutarco Elías Calles (1924-1928), which represented the northern bourgeoisie. They faced not only a disrupted economy but also internal and external resistance. Within Mexico, they encountered the economic weakness and political regionalism of the revolutionary bourgeoisie itself, as well as the decentralizing pressures of powerful warlords, the insurgent rural poor, and the old-regime upper classes. Internationally, the nationalism of the presidents clashed with the post-World War I economic and geopolitical expansionism of the United States, especially in regard to North American ownership of the bulk of Mexico's vital petroleum and mining resources (Córdova, 1973: chaps. 2-4; Meyer, 1973: chaps. 2-3). The state-making tactics of Obregón and Calles addressed these obstacles in two ways. First, they stressed the selective use of social reforms to extend and solidify the government's domestic support. Second, they demonstrated willingness to accommodate their nationalism to the realities of U.S. dominance.

Selective reformism enabled Obregón and Calles to take advantage of the pressures by, and disunity of, the popular classes. By implementing limited reforms and by manipulating revolutionary symbols, the administrations incorporated the heads of key segments of the urban and rural masses into the state apparatus. Hence the administrations fostered intraclass competition among the poor while transforming coopted groups into centrally directed weapons against remaining sources of internal opposition, which themselves were politically fragmented. The political and economic necessity of extending the new regime's authority over the economy's urban-industrial sector—above all, foreign oil and mining companies—led the governments to sponsor the consolidating of the Regional Confederation of Mexican Workers (CROM). Yet the governments were careful to circumscribe the leverage of CROM, and organized labor in general, by cultivating to a lesser degree the support of the National Agrarian Party (PNA). Pragmatic populism played a decisive part in the centralization of power. As mentioned above, it reinforced the disunity of the lower classes as a whole. Further, the state builders could encourage worker and peasant militancy as a means of extending federal authority over native propertied interests and regionalist bosses. Alternatively, the state builders could restrain the allied masses in order to promote economic recovery and mollify powerful domestic opponents (Brading, 1980; Carr, 1981; Córdova, 1973: chaps. 5-6; Meyer, 1973: chaps. 2-4; Tardanico, 1984).

Despite the predominance of North American capital in Mexico's export enclaves, competing interests within the United States lessened the willingness of its State Department to intervene militarily on behalf of big business. Taking advantage of U.S. pluralism, Obregón and Calles created significant latitude of action in their dealings with metropolitan investors. For example, they undertook, with some success, to increase the tax burden of petroleum and mining enterprises. At any given time, however, they generally targeted either petroleum or mining, not both. And though Calles enacted important legislation to regulate foreign investors as a whole, the two administrations combined nationalist policies with other measures to attract metropolitan capital. Underlying this careful mixture of nationalism and collaborationism were the equally pragmatic mass-inclusionary policies of Obregón and Calles. Just as new-regime leadership could use the coopted masses to oppose or appease domestic rivals, so too could it either mobilize them against foreign enterprises or else control them in order to forestall economic and military reprisals as well as encourage metropolitan investments (Bernstein, 1964: parts III-IV; Meyer, 1977: chaps. 4-6; Smith, 1972: chaps 5-9; Tardanico, 1983).

In sum, selective reformism stabilized and fortified the new state. By extending their authority over the lower classes, the governments undercut much of the independence of military and civilian bosses and the Mexican oligarchy, and to a lesser extent they buttressed the state against foreign opposition. In the process they began to centralize and modernize the army and civilian bureaucracy, thereby complementing their efforts to solidify the state's tax base and to deemphasize military spending in favor of expenditures on roads, irrigation, a federal banking system, and so on. Yet by 1928 the new state was just partially consolidated. Lower-class resistance had not been entirely overcome, and a fragile political balance characterized relations between central authority and provincial bosses. Government stability was all the more precarious because, given foreign ownership of the oil and mining enclaves, it hinged above all on the absence of U.S. armed intervention.

Concurrently, economic recovery stalled and state executives faced new challenges in the forms of a military revolt, a counterrevolutionary peasant uprising, and a crisis of presidential succession. These external and internal pressures—together with the growing wealth and conservatism of many "revolutionary" elites—led Calles to proclaim the failure of reformist and nationalist policies (Meyer, 1973: chaps. 3-4; Krauze, 1977; Loyola Díaz, 1980; Smith, 1972: 250-259).

State Policy and
World Crisis, 1929-1934

From 1929 to 1934 the Mexican state, and its succession of Calles-dominated presidencies, remained domestically based on a loosely woven coalition of military and civilian bosses. Still divided by personalist ambitions and regionalist loyalties, their tenuous unity depended on a common interest in consolidating the power and wealth that they had accumulated since the old regime's demise. For the most part, then, they continued to resist the building of a state apparatus that could encroach upon their provincial bases of power (Cornelius, 1973; Garrido, 1982; Medín, 1982).

Calles's founding of the National Revolutionary Party (PNR) in 1928-1929 addressed the fragility of the new-regime state. By integrating military generals as individual members along with leaders of state-level organizations and labor and peasant associations into a national political machine, the PNR provided institutional channels for the mediation of disagreements. The PNR was particularly important at the time of its founding, for the assassination of Obregón, the crisis of presidential succession, and a military uprising in 1927 had seriously jeopardized the ruling coalition at all levels. Not a highly centralized structure, the PNR was viewed by military and civilian leaders as a temporary expedient to survive the political crisis; by no means did they intend to surrender power to the national administration. Nevertheless, the mere fact that new-regime elites provisionally assented to join such a body reflected the extent of their political and economic gains of the previous decade. They had simultanteously gained a stake in a national state capable of defending their privileges, whether the threat be posed by competing elites or the masses. But in more fully incorporating them into the state apparatus, the PNR served state administrators as an instrument for the management of divergent interests. It enabled administrators to undercut further the autonomy of military and civilian bosses, thereby allowing Calles to dominate national politics during the next six years through a series of puppet presidents (Cornelius, 1973: 385-402; Garrido, 1982: chaps. 2-3; Medín, 1982).

The onset of world crisis deepened the economic downturn already affecting Mexico. From 1929 to 1932 the value of Mexican exports fell by 65%, with money supply declining by 60% and government revenue by 34%. Sharply reduced export earnings led to widespread unemployment in mining, petroleum, and henequen, and government cutbacks left many civilian employees and soliders without work. The general decline in purchasing power led to serious unemployment among railroad and manufacturing workers, too, with the value of manufacturing falling by about one-third. Not surprisingly, traditional agriculture was least affected by international crisis, and diminished food production for domestic sale was a consequence not of the depression but of rural counterrevolutionary warfare and climatic conditions. Compounding the problem of unemployment was the repatriation of some 400,000 Mexican workers from the United States (Cárdenas, 1984; 224-230; Córdova, 1980: 81-85; Fitzgerald, 1984; Hamilton, 1982: 115; Ortiz Rubio, 1931).

In considering the state's response to world crisis, we must remember that the new regime's architects had made significant progress toward government centralization. We must also remember, though, that the tactical flexibility of the state making elite had decreased not only because of domestic unrest, economic recession, and Mexican-U.S. tensions, but additionally because of the growing wealth and conservatism of new-regime leadership. Of further relevance is the fact that prior to the Great Depression, Mexico's state makers had espoused the ideals of liberal capitalism; even as they expanded the state's regulatory powers, the administrations had sought merely to establish preconditions for the development of indigenous private enterprise (Córdova, 1973: chaps. 5-6; Cornelius, 1973: 395-406, 417-419; Meyer, 1977: 126-140; Wilkie, 1970: chap. 3).

A fundamental concern of federal leadership was to minimize the depression's impact on government revenues (see Ortiz Rubio, 1930-1932). As long as officials remained committed to private enterprise and orthodoxy (Fitzgerald, 1984: 254-260; Gaxiola, 1938: chap. 9; Pani, 1936: 337-345; Shelton, 1964: 134-141), their options were twofold: They could impose a heavier fiscal burden on foreign and local firms, or by reducing taxes and introducing other incentives they could try to cushion the downturn's impact on business profits and state finances.

The first option, of course, could have galvanized bourgeois opposition. Oil and mining companies in particular could have responded to tax hikes with further production cutbacks, thus exacerbating economic and fiscal crisis while reducing Mexico's petroleum supply (see Bernstein, 1964: chap. 16; Meyer, 1977: 9-13, 141-142). Nationalist measures, moreover, could have jeopardized conciliatory Mexican-U.S. diplomacy. Indeed, active U.S. diplomatic support had played a significant role in the official resolution of the counterrevolutionary rebellion and the quelling of a serious military revolt. Still, in 1929 the U.S. government began to lay the groundwork for its "Good Neighbor" posture toward Latin America, and it announced its unwillingness to go beyond arbitration on behalf of North American oil firms in Mexico. What is more, Mexican leadership could potentially act, as its predecessors of the 1920s had done, to gain the backing of metropolitan bankers by pledging a portion of increased petroleum and mining taxes to renewed payments on the external debt, whose terms were being renegotiated (Cornelius, 1973: 416-417; Meyer, 1976: 57-66, 177-178, 217; Meyer, 1977: 9-13, 141-142).

Even as federal revenue plunged, tax policy did not challenge foreign investors and the local dominant classes. Fiscal concessions, as well as concessions regarding nationalist regulation, were granted to petroleum and mining firms, and several petroleum firms contributed loans to the Mexican government. But, in respondings to economic crisis, state tax and monetary policies benefited leading industrial, landed, and commerical interests as a whole (Bernstein, 1964: chap. 16; Dulles, 1961: 501; Meyer, 1977: chap. 7). For instance, increased tariffs afforded protection to manufacturers and domestically oriented commercial landowners alike (Ortiz Rubio, 1931: 543, 554-555), whereas both international segments of the bourgeoisie in general gained from the devaluation of the peso and the enactment of expansionary monetary reforms in 1932. As Mexico went off the gold standard, the new exchange rate profited exporters, and it complemented tariff policy by affording additional protection to locally produced commodities for domestic sale. Devaluation and monetary reforms fostered a price recovery that, in a political climate unfavorable to the masses, boosted the income of metropolitan and Mexican businesses at the expense of the lower classes (see Bernstein, 1964: 168; Córdova, 1980: 87-121; Cornelius, 1973: 404-406; Dulles, 1961: 507-517; Gaxiola, 1938: chap. 9; Pani, 1936: 337-338; Warman, 1976: 176-177).

So, instead of reviving the pragmatic nationalism of prior administrations, the Callista elite emphasized tax and monetary policies—and, as we shall see, labor and agrarian measures—which did not disturb the close association between Mexican and North American investors. Hence, the Callistas ignored or neutralized emerging popular-nationalist sentiment both within and outside the state organization, including labor and peasant bosses, small business groups, intellectuals, government technocrats, and such anti-Callista elites as interim president Emilio Portes Gil (1928-1930) (Meyer, 1977: 146-147; Portes Gil, 1964: chaps. 8-9; Wionczek, 1964: 40-54). But the economic downturn and conservative federal response did not reverse the previous decade's momentum toward strengthened central authority; the precedent of power-centralizing tactics combined with deteriorating economic conditions to promote the continued, if piecemeal, extension of federal regulation. For example, in 1930 the state loosened a number of restrictions on mining production, but in doing so it bolstered government authority to close unsafe mines, tightened control over registry of titles and commercial transactions, and empowered officials to review company books (Bernstein, 1964: 174-175). Meanwhile, new taxes, as well as the heightened importance of fiscal incentives, augmented state leverage over the bourgeoisie. So did currency devaluation, monetary reforms, and the strengthening of the central bank. Likewise important were continued, if reduced, spending on economic infrastructure and preliminary efforts to lower public utility rates. Perhaps most important of all was the Labor Code of 1931, which expanded central authority over capital and labor alike (Córdova, 1980: 97-121; Dulles, 1961: 504; Ortiz Rubio, 1931: 556-557; Shelton, 1964: 137-140; Wionczek, 1964: 53).

What was the role of the lower classes in the regime's quest to guarantee political stability and to reinvigorate the economy? Consistent with their pro-capital stance, the Callistas undertook to weaken and destroy the most threatening popular organizations and to curtail social reforms. Regarding urban labor, the government continued to withdraw support from CROM. Thus, it ended CROM's federal financing and favored competing union groups through PNR patronage, control over arbitration officials, outright repression, and the like. Government actions further disunified organized labor and rendered it all the more vulnerable to declining real wages and nonenforcement of labor laws. Regarding the peasantry, the Callistas drastically reduced land redistribution, dismantled the countryside's radical political machines, and disarmed rural militias. To these ends they replaced radical bosses with loyal officials, caused political splits in militant rural blocs, incorporated agrarianist armies into federal reserves units, and even divided communal landholdings so as to further disorganize peasant militias. Within the PNR they ousted militant rural opposition while coopting rival factions, and the federal army cooperated with wealthy landowners to defeat agrarianists who persisted in armed struggle. As of the early 1930s, then, the rural masses found themselves without independent leadership and more politically disunified than ever (Córdova, 1980: 81-160; Cornelius, 1973: 405-406, 413, 418-419; Falcón, 1978; Loyola Díaz, 1980: 140-146; Medín, 1982: 59-60, 95-103; Portes Gil, 1964: chap. 8).

To summarize, the Callistas responded to the onset of economic crisis not by reorganizing the Mexican status quo and its external linkages, but by preserving the wealth and privileges of the dominant classes and metropolitan capital. This response paralleled that of the Colombian state. What set the Mexican case apart, however, was its revolution, the political role of the masses, and the existence of an official party, which together delimited the short- and long-range consequences of global crisis for Mexico's state/class relations and world economic standing. We have observed that with the collapse of the Porfirian order and the mobilization of segments of the lower classes, new-regime leadership used tactical populism both to neutralize the masses and to transform their key factions into bulwarks against foreign interests, old-regime elites, and contending bosses. The process of revolutionary destruction and reconstruction differentiated Mexico from its Latin American counterparts, for it undermined the legitimacy of traditional institutions of land and labor and eliminated the rural oligarchy from formal participation in the making of government policy. Even as state managers assumed a more openly pro-business stance during the economic downturn, political inclusion of mass leadership remained vital not only to the authority and stability of the national state but also to the personal leverage of Calles and his clique. The Callistas therefore promoted within the PNR moderate reformists while ejecting radical bosses and dismantling independent popular organizations. Thus, the establishment of an offical party within a quasi-populistic framework reinforced the post-1920 impetus toward centralized authority, a trend encompassing the limited fiscal, monetary, and economic interventions of 1929-1932. With the beginning of economic recovery, how did this mode of domination influence the subsequent development of Mexico's sociopolitical institutions and relations with metropolitan interests?

The Mexican economy rebounded in 1933-1934. The value of production in many sectors, including manufacturing, came to equal or exceed pre-Depression peaks, and unemployment diminished. Mining and petroleum participated in this upswing but lagged well behind previous highs. This was especially true of petroleum, which, in spite of its continuing economic and political importance, had been in decline since the early 1920s (Cárdenas, 1984: 230-237; Solís, 1970: 90, 97-99).

During this period a new popular-nationalist coalition emerged as a powerful challenge to the Callistas. In the context of Mexico's revolutionary experience and the rise of statist experiments in the Soviet Union, the United States, and Europe, this coalition arose from a number of sources. One of these was the previous decade's growth of small manufacturers and merchants, who now faced intensified competition from privileged Mexicans and foreigners. These groups joined forces with intellectuals and government technocrats—whose own growth had been associated with state building and developmental programs—in a movement for nationalization of the utilities industry. Concurrently, technocrats and intellectuals, in seeking to ensure an adequate, low-priced supply of domestic fuel, began proposing the nationalization of the oil industry, too. In 1933 several labor unions—all former members of CROM—united as the General Confederation of Mexican Workers and Peasants (CGOCM), which stressed revolutionary Marxism and independence from the state as well as short-term economic gains (Córdova, 1980: chap. 4; Cornelius, 1973: 430; Hamilton, 1982: 113-115; Wionczek, 1964: 34-35).

Resurgent populistic nationalism coincided with the weakening of Calles's control over contending elites within the PNR who, for reasons of ideology and opportunism, sought to reinvigorate government commitment to the Revolution's principles. By taking advantage of their autonomous influence within the central party, such moderate agrarianists as Emilio Portes Gil and Lázaro Cárdenas organized formidable constituencies of their own among anti-Callista elites, PNR officials, and reformist leaders. This movement managed to nominate Cárdenas as the PNR's presidential candidate. In addition, it formulated a far-reaching official platform for the new presidency that, in emphasizing large-scale social reforms and strict regulation—though not wholesale exclusion—of foreign capital, represented an updated version of the revolutionary constitution. Ironically, then, the official party,

which Calles had brilliantly conceived and molded both to stabilize the
new state and to serve his personalist aspirations, had become the focal
point of serious political opposition. But, even as a major confrontation
was in the making, the widening split between Callistas and Cardenistas
did not challenge the state's basic legitimacy. Reflecting state-making
developments since the Revolution, this rift centered on programmatic
and personalistic disagreements *within* the new-regime elite and the
state's institutional channels; and by no means were the two factions
polarized on the entire range of issues. Calles recognized Cárdenas's
widespread support within the PNR. He consequently assented to the
presidential nomination and party platform while likely assuming that
as "supreme arbiter" he could coopt Cárdenas and minimize reformist
measures (Cornelius, 1973: 429-430, 430-438; Garrido, 1982: 145-165;
Hamilton, 1982: 117-122; Medín, 1982: 129-144).

Not unexpectedly, the interim Callista presidency of Abelardo
Rodríguez accommodated mounting dissidence by carrying out some of
the proposed measures. In 1933 the regime laid the legal groundwork for
direct federal intervention in the production and distribution of oil and
electricity, and the next year it founded Petromex, a semiofficial
enterprise. New legislation established a commission for mineral
development and a system of national mineral reserves. The regime
complemented these undertakings by founding two credit agencies, one
for financing public works and the other as a kind of investment bank.
The creation of labor and agrarian departments, as well as the
formulation of an agrarian code, augmented central authority in these
crucial spheres. And, by increasing the income tax while introducing
new taxes, the administration reinforced the state's fiscal underpinnings
(Bernstein, 1964: 175-181; Gaxiola, 1938: parts II and III; Rodríguez,
1933-1934; Meyer, 1977: 146-157; Shelton, 1964: 140-141; Wionczek,
1964: 38-60).

Even as the schism crystallized within the PNR, Calles could
realistically hope to minimize the political independence and reformist
success of the Cardenistas only as long as Mexico's array of populistic
forces remained disunified. This situation changed during Cárdenas's
presidential campaign of 1934 and first year in office. He openly
encouraged state-sponsored mobilization of labor and peasants toward
the goals enunciated in the party platform. Cárdenas did name several
Callistas to the presidential cabinet, but he placed loyal officials in many
key military and civilian posts. Given this broadened and strategic
backing, the president responded to Calles's harsh public criticism of

June 1935 by decisively replacing remaining Callista officials with Cardenistas. A new ruling coalition was provisionally in place (Cornelius, 1973: 429-450; Hamilton, 1982: 122-128; Medín, 1982: chap. 7).

The Cárdenas administration (1934-1940) consolidated the new coalition by bringing peasants and workers under its direct authority. Central leadership undermined the remaining political autonomy of the rural upper classes—including metropolitan investors—by supporting peasant militancy, by redistributing land on a large scale, by increasing farming credits and technical assistance to the agrarian masses, and by unifying the latter into a hierarchy of groupings under the aegis of the official party and Cárdenas himself. Simultaneously, the government boosted its leverage over major commerical and industrial entrepreneurs—again including international business—by promoting the mobilization of labor, which made significant gains in working conditions, wages, and benefits. The CGOCM and independent unions founded the National Committee for Proletarian Defense and later the Confederation of Mexican Workers, the political lever by which Cárdenas incorporated labor into the central party. As in agriculture, the advance of federal authority over industry and commerce occurred most dramatically in the form of expropriation, the most important case being the petroleum nationalization of 1938. And not to be forgotten is the fact that state-directed popular militias constituted a strategic counterpoise to anti-reformist military threats (Cornelius, 1973: 448-473; Hamilton, 1982).

These mass-inclusionary tactics were consistent with Mexico's basic state-making actions of the 1920s; and reformist and developmental policies both utilized and fortified the state machinery and economic infrastructure erected by the new-regime leadership of 1920-1934. In building upon these foundations, Cárdenas ensured that peasants and workers remained organized separately and directly under central supervision. Hence, besides offsetting the power of domestic and foreign opponents, popular incorporation further subordinated the lower classes to national authority (see Cornelius, 1973; Hamilton, 1982; Meyer, 1973).

Mexico's revolutionized state structure underlay its subsequent breakthrough into the semiperiphery of the world economy. Mexican officials employed the state organization to direct the masses against domestic and foreign interests whose wealth and power had limited the effective authority of the new regime and the development of the national bourgeoisie. At the same time, however, officials used their

centralized powers to minimize popular militancy, thus improving
government's capacity to attract local and international investment.
Mexico was not alone among Latin American countries in advancing
into the world's semiperiphery. Yet the Mexican state has proved
remarkably stable and comparatively adept not just in restricting
metropolitan intrusion into key economic activities, but likewise at
channeling metropolitan capital into the economy's retarded sectors.
Further, post-1940 governments, in their efforts to maintain political
legitimacy and to negotiate with U.S. interests, have commonly invoked
Mexico's symbols and ideology of social revolution in siding with
popular-nationalist campaigns in the Caribbean Basin and elsewhere in
the underdeveloped world.

CONCLUSION

This chapter began by posing two questions: How does state making
differ in revolutionary and nonrevolutionary settings? What are the
consequences of its differences, not just for domestic sociopolitical and
economic structures but also for their relations with worldwide patterns
of capital accumulation and geopolitics?

It is clear that in responding to the onset of world crisis Mexican and
Colombian policies were similar. The Great Depression weakened the
domestic upper classes and U.S. capital alike, thereby favoring statist
measures to stimulate national development by redistributing wealth at
home and redefining linkages with metropolitan interests. Yet, during
the initial years of crisis, neither state's leadership undertook large-scale
campaigns of social reform, political centralization, and economic
nationalism; on the contrary, their initial policies were conservative, as
leadership sought to generate recovery not by transforming but by
preserving preexisting class arrangements, state structures, and foreign
relations. "Nonrevolutionary" Colombia did stick with monetary
orthodoxy and external debt payments longer than "revolutionary"
Mexico, (see Cárdenas, 1984; Fitzgerald, 1984; Ocampo, 1984; Thorp
and Londoño, 1984). Ironically, though, Mexico's labor and agrarian
policies of 1930-1933 may have been more actively conservative than
Colombia's; as Colombia underwent transition from Conservative to
Liberal hegemony, Mexican authorities dismantled many populistic
gains associated with the Revolution.

Nonetheless, even as neither state challenged the domestic and
international status quo, a fundamental difference was that Mexico's

revolutionary experience had galvanized popular-nationalist forces. These forces underlay the power of the Callista elite; doing away with them would have undermined both the state apparatus and the Callista elite itself. Not that the Callistas could have done away with them. With the demise of the Porfirian state, the rural and urban masses had become an integral feature of Mexico's political landscape, and, along with the previous decade's growth of nationalist entrepreneurs and government fuctionaries, they imposed formidable constraints upon state-building options. Such was not the case, of course, in Colombia. The crucial difference was that while Mexico's reactionary oligarchy had been eliminated from active participation in governance, Colombia's retained its powerful role. Indeed, Mexican peasants and workers had been coopted by an authority-centralizing, revolutionary clique; but cooptation of the Colombian masses reinforced the Conservative and Liberal parties of its decentralized, oligarchic state, and, given Colombia's weaker state, more retarded economy, and less conflictual relations with the United States, its middle classes and government functionaries were much less capable than Mexico's of opposing this arrangement. In Mexico, then, the state's conservative response to the onset of world crisis unleashed a resurgence of populistic nationalism that further centralized the new-regime state, definitively undermined the old-regime oligarchy, altered the terms of metropolitan investment, and promoted large-scale capitalist accumulation. Colombia experienced a milder form of populistic nationalism that culminated not in statist and capitalist transformation like Mexico's, but rather in oligarchic reaction, political chaos, and a comparatively traditional relationship with foreign capital. As noted in this chapter's introduction, the impact of revolution in Mexico and its absence in Colombia has continued to manifest itself in the comparative dimensions of their present-day sociopolitical crises and involvement in the regional crises of the Caribbean Basin.

REFERENCES

ARRUBLA, M. et al. (1982) Colombia, Hoy (8th ed.). Bogotá, Colombia: Siglo Veintiuno Editores de Colombia.
BAGLEY, B. M. (1984) "The politics of asymmetrical interdependence: U.S.-Mexican relations in the 1980s," pp. 141-159 in H. M. Erisman (ed.) The Caribbean Challenge: U.S. Policy in a Volatile Region. Boulder, CO: Westview.

BERGQUIST, C. W. (1978) Coffee and Conflict in Colombia, 1886-1910. Durham, NC: Duke University Press.

BERNSTEIN, M. D. (1964) The Mexican Mining Industry, 1890-1950. Albany: State University of New York Press.

BRADING, D. A. [ed.] (1980) Caudillo and Peasant in the Mexican Revolution. Cambridge: Cambridge University Press.

CÁRDENAS, E. (1984) "The Great Depression and industrialization: the case of Mexico," pp. 222-241 in R. Thorp (ed.) Latin America in the 1930s: The Role of the Periphery in World Crisis. New York: St. Martin's Press.

CARR, B. (1981) El movimiento obrero y la política en México, 1910/1929. Mexico, DF: Ediciones Era.

CÓRDOVA, A. (1973) La ideología y la revolución Mexicana. Mexico, DF: Ediciones Era.

———(1980) La clase obrera en la historia de Mexico: en una época de crisis (1928-1934). Mexico, DF: Siglo Veintiuno Editores.

CORNELIUS, W. A. (1973) "Nation building, participation, and distribution: the politics of social reform under Cárdenas," in G. A. Almond et al. (eds.) Crisis, Choice, and Change: Historical Studies of Political Development. Boston: Little, Brown.

CRUZ SANTOS, A. (1966) Economía y hacienda pública (vol. 2) Bogotá, Colombia: Ediciones Lerner.

DIX, R. (1967) Colombia: The Political Dimensions of Change. New Haven, CT: Yale University Press.

DULLES, J.W.F. (1961) Yesterday in Mexico: A Chronicle of the Revolution, 1919-1936. Austin: University of Texas Press.

ECKSTEIN, S. (1982) "The impact of revolution on social welfare in Latin America." Theory and Society 11, 1: 43-94.

FALCÓN, R. (1978) "El surgimiento del agrarismo Cardenista—una Revisión de las teses populistas." Historia Mexicana 27, 3: 333-386.

FITZGERALD, E.V.K. (1984) Restructuring through the Depression: The State and Capital Accumulation in Mexio, 1925-1940," pp. 242-265 in R. Thorp (ed.) Latin America in the 1930s: The Role of the Periphery in World Crisis. New York: St. Martin's Press.

GARCIA, A. (1979) "Colombia: medio siglo de historia contemporánea," pp. 178-230 in P. Gonzáles Casanova (ed.) América Latina: historia de medio siglo. Vol. 1: América del sur. Mexico, DF: Siglo Veintiuno Editores.

GARRIDO, L. J. (1982) El partido de la revolución institutionalizada: la formación del nuevo estado (1928-1945). Mexico, DF: Siglo Veintiuno Editores.

GAXIOLA, F. J. (1938) El Presidente Rodríguez (1932-1934). Mexico, DF: Editorial Cultura.

GEREFFI, G. and P. EVANS (1981) "Transnational corporations, dependent development, and state policy in the semi-periphery: a comparison of Brazil and Mexico." Latin American Research Review 16, 3: 31-64.

HAMILTON, N. (1982) The Limits of State Autonomy: Post-Revolutionary Mexico. Princeton, NJ: Princeton University Press.

KLINE, H. F. (1983) Colombia: Portrait of Diversity. Boulder, CO: Westview.

———(1985) "New directions in Colombia?" Current History 84: 65-68, 83.

KRAUZE, E. (1977) Historia de la revolución, período 1924-1928: la reconstrucción económica. Mexico, DF: El Colegio de México.

LATORRE, L. F. (1937) Doce leyes y otros parlamentarios. Bogotá, Colombia: Editorial Minerva.

LEVY, D. C. and G. SZÉKELY (1986) "Mexico: challenges and responses." Current History 85: 16-20, 37.

LIEUWEN, E. (1968) Mexican Militarism: The Political Rise and Fall of the Revolutionary Army, 1910-1940. Albuquerque: University of New Mexico Press.

LOYOLA DÍAZ, R. (1980) La crisis Obregón-Calles y el estado Mexicano. Mexico, DF: Siglo Veintiuno Editores.

MEDÍN, T. (1982) El minimato presidencial: historia política del Maximato, 1928-1935. Mexico, DF: Ediciones Era.

MEJÍA, A. T. (1982) "Colombia: siglo y medio de bipartidismo," pp. 102-185 in M. Arrubla et al. (eds.) Colombia, Hoy. Bogotá, Colombia: Siglo Veintiuno Editores de Colombia.

MELO, J. O. (1982) "La república conservadora (1880-1930)," pp. 52-101 in M. Arrubla et al. (eds.) Colombia, Hoy. Bogota, Colombia: Siglo Veintiuno Editores de Colombia.

MEYER, J. (1973) La revolución Mejicana, 1910-1940. Barcelona, Spain: DOPESA.

——(1976) The Cristero Rebellion: The Mexican People Between Church and State. Cambridge: Cambridge University Press.

MEYER, L. (1975) "Continuidades e innovaciones en la vida política Mexicana del Siglo XX: El antiguo y el nuevo régimen." Foro Internacional 16, 1: 37-63.

——(1977) Mexico and the United States in the Oil Controversy, 1917-1942. Austin: University of Texas Press.

Ministerio de Hacienda y Crédito Público, República de Colombia (1931-1934) Memoria. Bogotá, Colombia: Imprenta Nacional.

NEWELL G., R. and L. RUBIO, F. (1984) Mexico's Dilemma. Boulder, CO: Westview.

OCAMPO, J. A. (1984) "The Colombian economy in the 1930s," pp. 117-143 in R. Thorp (ed.) Latin America in the 1930s: The Role of the Periphery in World Crisis. New York: St. Martin's Press.

OQUIST, P. (1980) Violence, Conflict, and Politics in Colombia. New York: Academic.

ORTIZ RUBIO, P. (1951) "Informes presidenciales, 1931-33," pp. 118-171 in La hacienda pública a traves de los informes presidenciales. Mexico, DF: Secretaría de Hacienda y Crédito Público.

PALACIOS, M. (1980) Coffee in Colombia, 1850-1970. Cambridge: Cambridge University Press.

PANI, A. (1936) Mi contribución al nuevo régimen, 1910-1933. Mexico, DF: Editorial Cultura.

PORTES GIL, E. (1964) Autobiografía de la revolución Mexicana. Mexico, DF: Instituto Mexicano de Cultura.

RIPPY, J. F. (1931) The Capitalists and Colombia. New York: Vanguard Press.

RODRÍGUEZ, A. (1951) "Informe presidencial, 1933-1934," pp. 572-94 in La hacienda pública a traves de los informes presidenciales. Mexico, DF: Secretaría de Hacienda y Crédito Público.

SHELTON, D. H. (1964) "The banking system: money and the goal of growth," pp. 111-190 in R. Vernon (ed.) Public Policy and Private Enterprise in Mexico. Cambridge: Harvard University Press.

SKOCPOL, T. (1979) States and Social Revolutions. Cambridge: Cambridge University Press.

SMITH, R. F. (1972) The United States and Revolutionary Nationalism in Mexico, 1916-1932. Chicago: University of Chicago Press.

SÓLÍS, L. (1970) La realidad económica Mexicana. Mexico, DF: Siglo Veintiuno Editores.

TARDANICO, R. (1983) "México revolucionario, 1920-1928: capitalismo transnacional, luchas locales y formación del nuevo estado." Revista Mexicana de Sociología 45, 2: 375-405.

———(1984) "Revolutionary Mexico and the world economy: the 1920s in theoretical perspective." Theory and Society 13, 6: 757-772.

TEASTER, J. B. (1985) "Strife From Left and Right slows Colombia's efforts at peace." New York Times (November 29): 8.

THORP, R. and C. LONDOÑO (1984) "The effect of the Great Depression on the economies of Peru and Colombia," pp. 81-116 in R. Thorp (ed.) Latin America in the 1930s: The Role of the Periphery in World Crisis. New York: St. Martin's Press.

TRIMBERGER, E. K. (1978) Revolution From Above. New Brunswick, NJ: Transaction Books.

WARMAN, A. (1976)... Y venimos a contradecir: los campesinos de Morelos y el estado nacional. Mexico, DF: Ediciones de la Casa Chata.

WILKIE, J. W. (1970) The Mexican Revolution: Federal Expenditure and Social Change. Berkeley: University of California Press.

WIONCZEK, M. (1964) "Electric power: the uneasy partnership," pp. 19-110 in R. Vernon (ed.) Public Policy and Private Enterprise in Mexico. Cambridge: Harvard University Press.

Chapter 7

COFFEE AND POLITICS IN CENTRAL AMERICA

Jeffery M. Paige
University of Michigan

To even the casual visitor the differences among the Central American republics are striking. Indeed, it would be difficult to find three political systems anywhere in the world that differ among themselves as much as do those of contemporary Guatemala, Nicaragua, and Costa Rica. The first is a "garrison state" of relentless ferocity and medieval barbarism (Aguilera, 1982; Aguilera and Romero, 1981; Americas Watch, 1983; Amnesty International, 1981; Torres-Rivas, 1980); the second, a revolutionary regime evolving to some as yet undefined version of socialism (Black, 1981; Carl, 1984; Collins, 1982; Gorman, 1981; Nolan, 1984; Vargas Llosa, 1985); the third, a tropical welfare state with one of the few genuinely democratic political systems in Latin America (Bell, 1971; Rosenberg, 1983; Seligson, 1980; Torres-Rivas, 1975; Vega, 1981, 1982). These differences are even more surprising when one considers the many characteristics shared by all

AUTHOR'S NOTE: I would like to acknowledge the kind assistance of David Kaimowitz of the Centro de Investigaciones y Estudios de la Reforma Agraria in Managua and José Angel Castillo Mora of the Oficina del Café in San Jose. I am also grateful for the cooperation of the Dirección General de Estádistica y Censos in Guatemala City and the Empresa Nicaragüense del Café in Managua. All conclusions expressed in this chapter are my own and these individuals and institutions bear no responsibility for them.

Central American Republics: a common Hispanic culture, a common religion, a common colonial history, and involvement in common political struggles as late as 1855. All of the five principal Central American republics (Costa Rica, Guatemala, Honduras, Nicaragua, and El Salvador) were part of the colonial Captaincy General of Guatemala; all participated in the ill-fated empire of Augustín Iturbide; all were involved in the Central American Federation and other nineteenth century attempts at union; all united to defeat William Walker and his filibusters (MacLeod, 1973; Woodward, 1985; Wortman, 1982). All share a common isthmian location that has facilitated domination by outside powers—first Spain, then Great Britain and Germany, and finally, the United States. All are small peripheral export economies that have depended since colonial times on the export of one or two agricultural commodities; and in four of the five countries (Costa Rica, Guatemala, Nicaragua, and El Salvador) one agricultural export—coffee—dominated their economies from the last half of the nineteenth century until approximately 1950 (Cardoso, 1975; Torres-Rivas, 1971). With the exception of Honduras where bananas, not coffee, ruled until after World War II (Morris and Ropp, 1977; Posas, 1981), the political economy of Central America in the late nineteenth and early twentieth centuries is largely the political economy of coffee cultivation and export.

Despite these similarities, differences among the Central American republics were apparent by 1821 (Torres-Rivas, 1975: 9) and, to a lesser extent, as early as 1650 (MacLeod, 1973: 307). In each of the four principal exporting countries coffee developed in ways that both reflected and accentuated the varying political and economic structures inherited from the colonial past. These countries faced the revolutionary crisis of the 1970s and 1980s with political systems dominated by traditional oligarchies whose wealth derived, to a greater or a lesser extent, from coffee cultivation, processing, and export. It was not coffee alone that created the tensions leading to revolution, but it was coffee that created the political structures with which the Central American republics, with varying degrees of success, tried to cope with revolution. It is beyond the scope of this chapter to trace the historical development of individual Central American coffee export economies even though the rapid accumulation of research findings on Costa Rica (Cardoso, 1977; Hall, 1978, 1982; Seligson, 1975, 1980; Stone, 1982), Guatemala (Biechler, 1970; Cambranes, 1980, 1982; Dominguez, 1970; McCreery, 1976, 1980; Montenegro, 1976; Mosk, 1955; Nañez, 1961, 1970), El

Salvador (Aubey, 1968-1969; Browning, 1971; Colindres, 1976, 1977; Kerr, 1977; Menjívar, 1980; Trujillo, 1981), and even poorly documented Nicaragua (Delgado, 1961; Gariazzo et al., 1983a, 1983b; Keith, 1974; Radell, 1964; Wheelock, 1980) makes such a review overdue. Instead, the Central American coffee export economies will be examined as they existed at the midpoint of the twentieth century just prior to the economic transformations that would create the preconditions for the contemporary crisis. The goal is not to account for the origins of the revolutionary crisis itself but to account for the differing responses of the coffee elites of Costa Rica, Guatemala, Nicaragua, and El Salvador to the challenge posed by growing demands for political power from below. In Costa Rica, the coffee elite was swept aside with surprising ease, and political power passed to new social groups in a democratic political order (Bell, 1971; Stone, 1980, Seligson, 1980). In El Salvador the coffee oligarchy clings to power with extensive American assistance in the face of a vigorous and long-entrenched revolutionary movement (Baloyra, 1982; Dunkerly, 1982; Montgomery, 1982). In Nicaragua, a popular revolution swept to power with the assent and even the active assistance of some members of the traditional elite (Black, 1981; Gilly, 1980; López et al., 1980), and in Guatemala, the coffee oligarchy and their allies in business and the military have imposed a counter-revolutionary government on a revolutionary society (Aguilera, 1982; Aguilera and Romero, 1981; Jonas and Tobis, 1974). It is the contention of this chapter that these differing elite responses can in large part be accounted for by differences in the organization of coffee production in each country, and that these differences in organization in turn shaped the class base of the elite, the character of their lower-class opponents, and the terms of the conflict between them. The Central American coffee oligarchs developed their industry in political and social systems that were already distinct. The solutions to the fundamental problems of land tenure, production, labor recruitment, processing, and export available to each elite were, therefore, different and the nature of their solutions set the direction of economic and political life for more than a century after the rise of the coffee export economies. The coffee growers' associations formed by members of these elites or the governments they controlled also left behind detailed statistical portraits of their industries. It is this statistical record that forms the basis of the following comparative analysis of the Central American coffee economies.

THE ORGANIZATION OF PRODUCTION

Each of the Central American coffee elites had to solve four fundamental problems common to coffee production everywhere: (1) acquisition and control over land, (2) organization and rationalization of production, (3) mechanization and finance of processing, and (4) finance and control over exports. Transport, roasting, soluble coffee manufacture, distribution, and retail sales were always controlled by agents of the importing nations (Fischer, 1972: 50-51; Wickizer, 1943: 55-56; Sivetz and Foote, vol. 2: 279), but the first four steps involved varying degrees of participation by Central American nationals or by European immigrants taking up permanent residence in the region. Control over land, production, processing, exports, or over some combination of these steps provided Central American coffee growers, both immigrant and national, with important sources of wealth and political power. Nevertheless, Central American coffee growers differed considerably among themselves in their ability to solve problems of land, production, processing, and export, in the nature of the solutions they adopted, and in the effect of their solutions on their ultimate political positions. To understand both the economic and political behavior of the Central American coffee elite requires some under-standing of the problems facing them at each stage of the coffee production process.

Land

Control over land is not only an obvious prerequisite for any kind of agricultural activity including the production of coffee, but it also can be in itself an important source of power and wealth. Possession of an estate in Central America even now—but more so in the recent past—implied possession of seignorial rights over the rural population resident on or near the estate and, as a result, almost complete control of this population's political allegiance (Pansini, 1977: 18-21; Stone, 1982: 109-110; Wheelock, 1980: 33). This kind of social and political power exists even if no coffee is grown, and even inefficient, unprofitable producers may be politically influential through their control over labor or voting blocs. Possession of land has, in turn, always depended more on access to political than to economic power. Privileged Central Americans and European immigrants used this power to acquire coffee lands, and coffee wealth to acquire political power. State power was used by the Central American coffee elites to expropriate the extensive lands held by the Church and indigenous communities in Guatemala (Cambranes, 1982: 18; McCreery, 1976: 456-457; Torres-Rivas, 1975: 48-49); by indigenous communities and municipal governments in El Salvador (Browning, 1971: 174-175; Kerr, 1977: 7; Menjívar, 1980: 86-87); by indigenous communities and the national government in Nicaragua (Delgado, 1961: 38; Wheelock, 1981: 109); and by the national government in Costa Rica (Hall, 1982: 34-35; Stone, 1980: 99). Even in Costa Rica, where the colonial heritage was weakest, two-thirds of the major nineteenth-century coffee growers were descendants of only *two* colonial families (Stone, 1980: 191). In Guatemala much coffee production passed rapidly into the hands of German immigrants who enjoyed preferential citizenship rights and official favor (Nañez, 1970: 19-20, 23-25). In El Salvador privileged urban groups and government officials became the first planters and were quickly joined by European immigrants attracted by the coffee boom (Browning, 1971: 168-169; Menjívar, 1980: 129, 131). In Nicaragua the coffee estate evolved from the colonial hacienda and Europeans and North Americans were granted extensive concessions (Delgado, 1961: 38; Niederlein, 1898: 51-52; Wheelock, 1980: 32). The consolidation of control over coffee lands formed an enduring base of political power for the coffee elites throughout Central America, although the amount of land and the strength of seignorial control varied considerably among the four major coffee-producing nations. The Central American coffee elites also varied considerably in their ability to convert control over land and people into agricultural wealth through the rationalization of the next stage in the coffee cycle—production.

Production

Land secured, the Central American planters devoted themselves to coffee production with varying degrees of technical sophistication and productivity. All Central American planters were confronted with the fact that coffee production (as opposed to processing) admits of little or no mechanization in cultivation and none whatsoever in harvesting. El Salvadoran planter J. Hill's observation in the 1930s that the maximum number of coffee beans harvested per worker per day could not exceed approximately 40,000 (Hill, 1936: 424) is as true today as it was in 1930, or for that matter, in 1830. Attempts to mechanize the harvest process, notably in Brazil (Holloway, 1974: 61), have never met with much success and machinery is even more difficult to use in the rugged terrain of Central American coffee farms. Furthermore, in every Central American producing country except Nicaragua coffee beans are now, and always have been, picked with the utmost care one bean at a time to protect the quality of the fine washed "milds" produced in the region (Duque, 1938: 41-45; Sivetz and Foote, 1963, vol. 1: 50; Wellman, 1961: 365-366; Jamaica Coffee Industry Board, 1959: 17). Since the peak harvest period in Central America tends to be short (a month or less) planters experience an acute need for massive amounts of hand labor at a critical point in the production cycle. Cultivation, weeding, and pruning also are not mechanized although chemical herbicides and unshaded, tightly spaced plantings have begun to reduce the demand for labor in the preharvest period (Jamaica Coffee Board, 1959: 7-11; Wellman, 1961: 198-200). The limited prospects for mechanization and the corresponding need for hand labor, particularly at harvest, committed Central American planters to a continuous search for large pools of cheap labor and severely limited their ability to substitute capital for labor in the production process itself. Paradoxically, this worked to the advantage of Central American nationals as it lowered capital requirements for entry in the industry and made it possible for Central Americans with land or political influence but little cash to rise to positions of prominence in coffee production.

Although capital could not be profitably invested in machinery, productivity could and was vastly increased in some areas by investment in the condition of the coffee trees themselves. Productivity per unit area of bearing tree can be increased substantially by planting newer and higher-yielding varieties such as Bourbon in the 1940s and 1950s and Caturra today; by increasing the density of plantings; by making use of organic or chemical fertilizers; by planting nitrogen-fixing plants; by using chemical weed killers; by the application of pesticides and fungicides; and by careful pruning to maximize yield and minimize effort during harvest (Dominguez, 1970: 134-196; Sivetz and Foote, 1963, vol. 1: 30-37; Wellman, 1961: 191-351). Because the difference between high- and low-yielding varieties, fertilized and unfertilized fields, or pruned and unpruned trees can be as much as 50% for each innovation, the combined effect on yields can be substantial. As denser, higher-yielding groves are easier to harvest, there are likely to be savings at harvest as well as during cultivation and weeding. Furthermore, the more attention devoted to scientific cultivation practices the healthier the plants, and the less the need to expend labor on replanting diseased groves or fighting epidemics of plant blight or insect infestation. Inasmuch as the coffee plant is subject to a remarkable variety of diseases, this is an important cost consideration for a planter. The net effect of these innovations is to increase substantially both the productivity of the land per unit area and the productivity of labor per unit weight of coffee harvested. Although capital cannot be profitably invested in machinery, it can be profitably invested in a standing tree crop with a productive lifetime of approximately 5-25 years. In the case of coffee cultivation, capital literally grows on trees.

Given the substantial gains in both productivity and profitability that can be realized through scientific cultivation, a technological imperative of considerable force drives planters in the direction of capital-intensive rationalized production. This has in fact been the outcome unless—as has frequently been the case in Central America—political or social factors have blocked rationalization of the industry. To the degree that capital is invested in scientifically managed coffee groves, the planter becomes more and more an agrarian capitalist and less and less a seignorial landowner. The returns on this invested capital or the principal itself can be used to expand production or to diversify into other agricultural sectors or into finance or industry. Financial power can, of course, be translated into political power so that the successful scientific coffee grower gains an additional source of influence beyond that granted by ownership of the land itself and control over the people who live on it. But the power is different in substance and the political goals of a nascent class of agrarian capitalists are not likely to be identical to those of a traditional seignorial elite with little disposable capital other than the land itself. As one moves downstream in production sequence to processing and export, agrarian capital gradually changes into industrial and financial capital, respectively, and the economic base of the coffee elite, as well as their economic interests, correspondingly shift.

Processing

Under Central American conditions, processing, unlike production, can be extensively mechanized and therefore the capital requirements are considerably greater in processing than in production. Furthermore, fully rationalized processing requires an elaborate physical plant so that the capital is less agrarian than industrial. Harvested coffee beans begin to ferment almost immediately and if the crop is not to be lost, it must be processed within 8 to 36 hours after picking (Sivetz and Foote, 1963: 54; Wellman, 1961: 370). Whatever form the processing takes, it must remove the seeds of the coffee berry—the source of coffee as a beverage—from the surrounding organic material. Each coffee berry consists of an outer skin surrounding a thick pulp that constitutes the greater part of the mass of the berry. Surrounding the seeds are a thick, sticky substance known as mucilage, a paper-like membrane called the parchment, and a thin coating called the silver skin. In Central America, the unprocessed berries are usually referred to as cherries (*cereza*), and coffee in this state is said to be *en cereza*. The parchment membrane is called *pergamino* and partially processed coffee with the skin pulp and mucilage removed is said to be *en pergamino*. Threshed beans with parchment and silver skin removed ("green" coffee in English) are referred to by the Spanish word for gold, *oro*. Processing must dispose of the skin and pulp, separate the mucilage from the parchment, and strip off the parchment and silver skin without contaminating or damaging the beans themselves. As the dry green coffee bean is relatively fragile and has an active affinity for a variety of contaminants, processing can be complex.

In general, two major approaches have evolved to solve the problem of removing the bean from the berry and in the coffee trade these approaches are called "dry" and "wet" processing (Sivetz and Foote, 1963: 55-57; Wellman, 1961: 370-374; Wickizer, 1943: 41-45). In the dry method, coffee may be processed without elaborate machinery simply by drying the harvested berries on an open patio or even on hard, dry ground and then threshing the hardened fruit. The threshing can be done with a technology as simple as driving cattle across the dry ground or pounding the dried fruit against a hollow stump with a stick. Quality control is, however, difficult to achieve with the dry method and this problem is particularly acute in moist climates such as those prevailing in most of the Central American coffee zone. As a result, the production of high-quality coffee in Central America depends on the much more elaborate technology of wet processing. In this system, the outer shell and pulp are first removed by mechanical means, and the mucilage is allowed to ferment until it can be washed away. The beans are then dried in the open or by mechanical dryers and then mechanically threshed to remove the parchment and silver skin membrane. Although wet processing can be carried out through relatively simple procedures such as depulping the beans by stamping on them barefoot and removing the mucilage by hand washing, considerable efficiencies can be gained by the use of power-driven machinery. The range of applicable technology is considerably greater in wet than in dry processing, and in Central America, processing plants have ranged from rudimentary hand-driven wooden devices of local manufacture (Keith, 1974: 92; Radell, 1964: 51-52) to elaborate, power-driven industrial installations (Instituto Centroamericano de Administración de Empresas, 1981: 6-11; Morrison and Norris, 1954: 318-322).

Because the capital requirements of a large, technologically sophisticated wet process plant are substantial and have been so since industrial processing technology was developed at the end of the nineteenth century, the owners of coffee-processing plants (called *beneficios* in Spanish America) are industrial capitalists using an agricultural raw material rather than agriculturalists. It is, of course, entirely possible for a coffee producer to integrate downstream into processing, and in fact many large producers in Central America have owned their own processing plants (Baloyra, 1982: 25; Dominguez, 1970: 264; Hall, 1982: 87; Radell, 1964: 25). But whether or not the processing plant is owned by a producer, the capital requirements of this industrial technology imply not only a different but substantially larger base of economic power than that provided by coffee production alone. In addition, most coffee processors purchase additional coffee from other growers to realize economies of scale; this in turn may lead them to make advances to other growers and hence assume the role of banker. It is not uncommon in Central America for large processing plants to provide the capital for banks and production; processing and banking activities often overlap in coffee production (Habib, 1958: 138; Hall, 1982: 45; Slutsky and Alonso, 1971: 21-22; Wheelock, 1980: 144-145). Similarly, a processor possesses a fund of capital that may allow diversification into other agricultural activities or into industry, tourism, or real estate (Colindres, 1976: 471; Nañez, 1970: 385-410; Stone, 1982: 147-351). To the degree that a coffee elite is involved in processing, its economic base and political interests will tend to diverge further from those of a traditional landowning elite.

Export

Export is the stage of the coffee cycle that demanded the most capital and it is also the area where foreigners have had their greatest impact on the Central American industry. The exporter not only must purchase the crop in Central America and hold it until eventual sale to European or American importers, but also must be part of an elaborate international trading and financial network. At this point, financial and mercantile considerations vastly outweigh purely agricultural concerns, and although exporters may be involved in production, they are often principally financial intermediaries. Exporters may become involved in financing the entire coffee system through advances as, for example, occurred with English capital in Costa Rica (Hall, 1982: 45-46) or German capital in Guatemala (Biechler, 1970: 36). Nevertheless, throughout Central America, many of the largest producers and processers did become involved in export and in El Salvador this pattern was particularly pronounced (Colindres, 1976: 471; Sebastián, 1979: 950-951). Although in many cases production, processing, and export were often controlled by the same individuals or family groups, the differing financial and technical requirements of the export phase of the coffee-production cycle provide an additional base for differentiation of Central American coffee elites.

Moving downstream from the point of production to the point of sale through control over land, production, processing, and export, capital requirements, entrepreneurial and managerial skills, prospects for diversification, and association with purely financial activities all change markedly. The industrial and financial capital and skills required in the downstream stages have given Europeans and North Americans a distinct advantage in export and, to a lesser extent, processing whereas Central American nationals have used their better political connections to gain control over land and production. In Guatemala, for example, by the 1930s, although German growers controlled only 25% of the plantations, they accounted for almost two-thirds of production and an even larger percentage of exports (Biechler, 1970: 36-37). As Biechler (1970: 36) notes, "To a significant extent, coffee ceased to be a national activity." In Nicaragua, all coffee exports were controlled by a subsidiary of two American banking houses allied with the Nicaraguan national bank, and it was not until the 1950s that Nicaraguan nationals had any direct role in exports (Wheelock, 1980: 144). In Costa Rica, foreigners exercised relatively little direct control over production, but as late as 1935 almost a third of the processers in Costa Rica were either foreigners or descendents of immigrants who arrived in Costa Rica after 1840, and these grand processers—many of whom were also exporters—controlled 44% of the national harvest (Hall, 1982: 53). Even in El Salvador, where national capital was strongest, international trading firms such as Curaçao

(Dutch) and Nottlebohm (German) controlled a major portion of exports (Asociación Cafetalera de El Salvador 1940: 192-199). Nevertheless, the relatively low capital requirements for entry into at least the production phase of the coffee cycle provided Central Americans with a source of national wealth and a possible point of entry into processing and export. But the coffee elites of Costa Rica, Guatemala, Nicaragua, and El Salvador differed markedly in their ability to exploit the opportunities provided by coffee and in their relative dominance over each phase of the coffee production sequence. These differences at each stage—land acquisition, production, processing, and export—are clearly evident in the detailed statistical record accumulated by coffee growers and their governments. This statistical record provides us not only with a portrait of the differences among the four coffee systems but also reveals important differences in the economic base of each of the ruling coffee elites in the early twentieth century.

EMPIRICAL ANALYSIS

Analysis of the coffee production sequence suggests two very different bases of political power for Central American coffee elites. Control over land and tight seignorial restrictions over people resident on it provide a source of military or political influence, but may or may not be associated with great financial or industrial power. Control over production, processing, and export, on the other hand, ensures some degree of industrial or financial power but does not guarantee the control over land and people, which has been the traditional base of oligarchic dominance throughout Latin America. In fact, to the degree that rationalized coffee cultivation requires clearing resident workers from the subsistence plots and substituting wage for bound labor, the two forms of power may not be entirely compatible. Although in Central America the two bases of power can be and have been combined, the coffee elites differ sufficiently among themselves in their dependence on either control over land, coffee, and people or control over production technology, processing, and export, to require the consideration of each potential base of elite power separately.

Control over Land, Coffee, and People

There is little disagreement among authors writing about Guatemala (Biechler, 1970: 109, Cambranes, 1982: 19; Montenegro, 1976: 144;

Nañez, 1970: 81) or in official statistical sources (Guatemala, Dirección General de Estadística, 1953: 5; 1971: 245, 248) about the absolute domination of Guatemalan coffee land and production by large estates. Similarly, there is little disagreement about the domination of a planter oligarchy over land and production in El Salvador (Browning, 1971: 179; Colindres, 1976: 470-471; Sebastián, 1979: 950-951), although comparative analysis of the substantial differences between the two systems has received less attention (Cardoso, 1975; Torres-Rivas, 1971). There is, however, considerable debate about the true distribution of land and production and the relative size and importance of the large estate in the cases of both Costa Rica and Nicaragua. For Costa Rica the opposing positions are most forcefully stated by Carolyn Hall (1982) and Mitchell Seligson (1975, 1980), although Hall's position has been argued by Cardoso (1977) and Torres-Rivas (1975) and Seligson's work builds on that of Moretzsohn de Andrade (1967). Hall argued that Costa Rican coffee landownership and production have been dominated by smallholders, and that estate production is of less relative importance and the estates themselves are smaller than elsewhere in Central America. Seligson contends that the rise of coffee production transformed the traditional smallholding pattern of Costa Rican agriculture and led to dominance by large estates, unequal land distribution, and the growth of a landless proletariat. Jaime Wheelock, in his influential work *Imperialismo y Dictadura* (1980), argues that the Nicaraguan coffee estate was simply an extension of patterns of colonial agriculture and that large manorial units dominated coffee production. In Wheelock's view, Nicaragua differs from El Salvador in the technical development of coffee production and processing but not in the importance of the large estate. Baumeister (1982), on the other hand, has proposed a model of the Nicaraguan agrarian economy suggesting that Nicaragua, like Costa Rica, is an exception to the Latin American pattern of large estate dominance and that smallholders and what he calls a bourgeoisie *chapiolla*, or small employer strata, were the most important factors in prerevolutionary Nicaraguan coffee production.

   The outcomes of both of these debates have implications that go far beyond the coffee economy. In the case of Costa Rica, the prominence of smallholders has long been seen as an important support for democracy (Bell, 1971: 6; Merz, 1937: 288; Torres-Rivas, 1975: 70), and in Nicaragua the absence of a class of large estate owners in coffee should weaken resistance to the revolutionary program of the Sandinistas (Baumeister, 1982: 48). As is often the case in such debates, there is more than a little truth in both positions, and in part the continued discussion reflects the more varied internal structure of coffee production in Costa Rica and Nicaragua as opposed to Guatemala and El Salvador. In all four countries, however, an accurate assessment of the true distribution of land and production requires a consistent and sociologically meaningful definition of estate and smallholder production. As Gariazzo et al. (1983b: 22) have pointed out, smallholding and estate production are sociological class categories, not simply size of holding intervals. The relationship between size of coffee holding and class position is complex and depends on the intensity, technical development, and social organization of production. Given the high value and labor intensivity of the crop, even relatively small holdings can create a substantial class division between the dominant landowners and their estate and migrant harvest laborers. Furthermore, the class position of a coffee grower is tied more closely to the area in coffee than to the total size of holding and the latter index is likely to be particularly misleading when coffee cultivation is combined with cattle raising or other extensive agriculture.

In order to provide a basis for systematic comparison among the four major Central American coffee producers as well as to decide among the competing images of class structure in Costa Rica and Nicaragua, it is necessary to have both a definition of class position in coffee cultivation and a metric defined in terms of coffee areas reported in Central American coffee censuses. The system used here is based on those developed by Ricardo Falla for research in the Department of Jinotega, Nicaragua, described to Gariazzo et al. (1983b: 28) and by the Centro de Investigaciones y Estudios de la Reforma Agraria (n.d.) for Nicaragua as a whole. Because the focus of this study is on elite composition, an additional distinction has been introduced to include important differences in the organization of estate production evident in the abundant descriptive literature on individual estates (Bratton, 1939; Cardoso, 1977; Comité Interamericano de Desarrollo Agrícola, 1965; Gariazzo et al., 1983b; Hall, 1978; Instituto Centroamericano de Administración de Empresas, 1977, 1981; Morrison and Norris, 1954; Nañez, 1970; Pansini, 1977; Villegas, 1965).

Falla (Gariazzo et al., 1983b: 28-29) distinguished three important types of producers in Jinotega: *agricultores fuertes* (strong farmers); *agricultores medianos* (medium farmers); and *campesinos ricos* (rich peasants). Strong producers controlled 50 to 100 manzanas (1 manzana = .69 hectare) of coffee, but did not themselves participate in production or management. Instead, they employed administrators who directed the activities of from 10 to 20 to sometimes as many as 60 permanent laborers as well as a much larger number of harvest workers. Medium farmers managed their estates directly and sometimes took part in specialized cultivating activities. They employed a smaller number of workers, the majority of them temporary, and controlled from 10 to 49 manzanas of coffee. Rich peasants had from 3 to less than 10 manzanas of coffee and worked the farm themselves, aided by family members and a few hired temporary laborers. The system developed by the Centro de Investigaciones y Estudios de la Reforma Agraria (CIERA) in Nicaragua is similar to Falla's, although the ranges of coffee area intervals are slightly different and, significantly, CIERA terms producers with more than 65 manzanas of coffee *latifundistas y gran burguesia* (large landholders and grand bourgeoisie) rather than using Falla's "strong farmer" term for the corresponding category. CIERA also identified an additional "poor peasant" category (5 manzanas of coffee or less), which defines those cultivators too poor to support themselves solely by coffee growing. Most "poor peasant" coffee cultivators are forced to search for outside employment often, although not invariably, on other, larger coffee farms. The category system for smaller growers adopted for this study combines the Falla and CIERA systems and defines the following groups according to their functional class position as measured by the amount of coffee they control: *sub-family farmers* who control from 0 to 4.9 manzanas of coffee are assumed to be too poor to support themselves from their farms and can, therefore, be thought of as part-time mini-farmers and part-time wage laborers; *family farmers* who control from 5 to 10 manzanas of coffee are assumed to be able to support themselves in coffee cultivation largely through their own and their family's labor; *small employers* who control from 10 to 49.9 manzanas are assumed to rely on permanent and harvest wage laborers rather than family members for most labor, to manage their farms themselves, and to participate in some specialized cultivation tasks.

It is apparent from both the Falla and CIERA definitions and from studies of individual estates that a producer with from 50 to 99.9 manzanas of coffee who employs from 10 to as many as 60 resident laborers and perhaps as many as 300 harvest laborers is, both functionally and socially, a member of the agrarian upper class. In a region of impoverished family farmers and landless laborers, the owner of even such a seemingly modest estate can be a political and social power to be reckoned with. An estate studied by Gariazzo et al. (1983b:

61-65) in Diriamba, Nicaragua, for example, had 80 manzanas of coffee and employed a year-round labor force of 2 resident and 20 day laborers and a harvest labor force of more than 80. The owner, a widow, lived in a seignorial, although somewhat decrepit, villa and her children had all managed to attain managerial or professional positions outside agriculture. She was a relative by marriage of a prominent member of the prerevolutionary oligarchy who had been a close associate of the Somozas. Her late husband had been a shareholder in a major Nicaraguan beer bottler and, although she no longer received income from the shares, it is clear that the family's interests extended outside agriculture. Socially and politically, her family was clearly part of the prerevolutionary Nicaraguan aristocracy. Similarly, the owner of a Costa Rican estate of approximately the same size (75 manzanas in coffee; 14 permanent and 200 to 300 harvest workers) was a thirteenth-generation descendent of the conquistador, Juan Vazquez de Coronado, owned several other estates, as did several other members of her family, and maintained a lifestyle that could only be called sumptuous. Both her father and her brother had held influential posts in the Costa Rican national government (Curridabat interview, Costa Rica, Feb. 1, 1984). As these examples make clear, in both Nicaragua and Costa Rica, it is possible for a family to achieve a position of national, social, and political prominence with a coffee estate much smaller than the vast coffee domains of São Paulo or the smaller but still sizable estates of Guatemala. In both examples the owner or her family owned additional estates so that the actual economic base of both families is considerably broader than ownership of a single estate in the 50 to 100 manzana range would suggest. Such concentrated ownership is, however, the rule, not the exception in Central America, so that the actual concentration of coffee land and production is much greater than the distribution by size of individual holdings would indicate. Analysis of the detailed ownership listings in the 1910 Nicaraguan coffee census (República de Nicaragua, 1910) suggests that multiple owernship was common especially among large growers. The same pattern is found in Costa Rica (Hall, 1982: 53, 86, 110) and El Salvador (Colindres, 1976: 471).

Nevertheless, it is also clear that relatively few growers at this level control the financial resources associated with vertical integration from production to processing to export. Neither the Nicaraguan nor the Costa Rican estate described above had its own *beneficio* and neither estate owner was involved directly in exports. In general, control of larger amounts of coffee land is associated with both processing and export activity; smaller estate producers, despite their social and political prominence, typically lack the resources for such activities. As a result, an additional distinction was made between *estate* producers who control a farm with between 50 and 99.9 manzanas in coffee and *integrated producers* who control a farm with 100 manzanas or more in coffee. An estate producer typically will employ an administrator to oversee the day-to-day operations of the estate and to supervise the work of a large number of resident and harvest wage laborers. Although the ownership of such an estate, combined as it frequently is with ownership of other such estates, provides the owner with an upper-class lifestyle and the leisure in which to enjoy it, it will not typically be associated with processing, export, or financial activities in the coffee industry. Owners of estates with 100 manzanas or more in coffee, on the other hand, will typically own their own processing plants, will often control an exporting firm, and will usually own numerous other large estates. Such owners will also possess the financial resources to diversify into other agricultural activities or into industry, finance, or real estate, and these resources together will almost certainly assure national political and economic power. In Guatemala, for example, the German immigrant Erwin Paul Dieseldorf, the largest land owner in the Department of Alta Verapaz, controlled 25 coffee estates with a total area of almost 60,000 manzanas of which 694 were planted in coffee. He processed all his own coffee to the parchment stage; acquired one of four plants in the Alta Verapaz for the final processing of parchment coffee; and became one of Guatemala's largest exporters, accounting for some 11,000 quintales (1 quintal = 46 kilograms) of his own and other's coffee in 1936-1937 (Nañez, 1970: 81, 153, 163, 228). Juan Rafael Mora used his and his family's ownership of several coffee estates in nineteenth-century Costa Rica to control 8% of total national exports in 1845 and 16% of national processing capacity in 1850. In 1850 he became president of Costa Rica and in 1858 his attempt to form a bank independent of other coffee processors who, then as now, financed the Costa Rican crop, led to a coup d'etat in 1859 and his eventual execution by firing squad (Hall 1982: 45, 51; Stone, 1982: 197, 387). Adolfo Bernard, the Nicaraguan "Sugar King," owned estates of 123, 50, and 65 manzanas in coffee in the Department of Carazo and estates of 50, 60, and 90 manzanas in Granada in 1910, and their combined production accounted for 2% of the Nicaraguan total. Although he owned two processing plants and extensive sugar interests, he did not become involved in exports (Calculated from data presented in República de

Nicaragua, 1910). In El Salvador in 1940, the Meardi family owned 12 processing plants and exported coffee under more than 60 different brand names (calculated from data presented in Asociación Cafetalera de El Salvador, 1940: 183-199). The economic and political role of such major integrated producers is clearly much greater than that of estate producers not involved in processing or export, although both groups are clearly fractions of the same aristocratic class. It would, of course, be preferable to use direct measures of total holdings, processing plant ownership, and export activity but Central American coffee data are seldom presented in a form that would make such measures possible. Thus possession of at least one estate with 100 manzanas or more in coffee will be used as an indirect indicator of an integrated producer.

The distinction between estate and integrated producer in combination with the earlier distinctions among smaller growers yields five functionally defined class positions in Cental American coffee production—sub-family, family, small employer, estate, and integrated producer. Table 7.1 shows the distribution of coffee area and production by class position for each of the four major Central American coffee producers for periods as close to the 1950s as available data permit. It should be kept in mind that the area intervals used to define class position always refer to area in coffee, not to the total area of the holding. Idiosyncracies of reporting and the absence of information on area in coffee for some countries make comparisons difficult. An effort therefore has been made to approximate the five-category system defined by area in coffee for each country, even if this requires some estimation of data. (A detailed description of the estimation procedures used in Tables 7.1-7.4 may be obtained by writing this author directly.)

The data in Table 7.1 make it possible not only to clarify some of the issues raised in the debates over coffee and class in Costa Rica and Nicaragua, but also to compare the class systems of each of the Central American coffee producers. Three major conclusions can immediately be drawn by inspection of Table 7.1. First, concentration of both land and production is notably greater in Guatemala than it is anywhere else in Central America. Not only are coffee area and production in Guatemala more concentrated than in Costa Rica or Nicaragua, they are also much more concentrated than in oligarchic El Salvador. Approximately two-thirds of both Guatemalan coffee area and production are controlled by integrated producers and an additional 17% is controlled by estate producers. Family and sub-family producers are so inconsequential that little systematic data is collected on them, and the

TABLE 7.1

Coffee Area and Production for Costa Rica (1955), Nicaragua (1957-1958), El Salvador (1940, 1957-1958), and Guatemala (1966-1967) by Class Position of Producers

Class Position	Farm Area in Coffee	Costa Rica (1955)		Nicaragua (1957-1958)		El Salvador (1940)		Guatemala (1966-1967)	
		Number of Farms	Percentage of Total Area	Number of Farms	Percentage of Total Area	Number of Farms	Percentage of Total Area	Number of Farms	Percentage of Total Area
		Coffee Area in Manzanas							
Sub-family	0-4.9	19,049	33.6	5,762	11.4	9,768	----	25—	----
Family	5-9.9	1,775	14.2 } 47.8	2,059	13.1 } 24.5	----	---- } 18.9	30,000	---- } 11.6
Small employer	10-49.9	979	22.1	1,256	22.6	1,322	27.4	606	4.6
Estate	50-99.9	101	8.6	314	19.2	263	16.4	1,148	17.2
Integrated producer	100+	83	21.6 } 30.6	212	33.6 } 52.8	192	37.3 } 53.7	636	66.5 } 83.7
Totals		21,987	100.1	9,603	99.9	11,545	100.0	----	99.9
Total area		80,574		123,253		117,216 (1940) 178,070 (1957-1958)		330,900 (1964)	

Class Position	Farm Area in Coffee	Costa Rica (1955)		Nicaragua (1957-1958)		El Salvador (1957-1958)		Guatemala (1966-1967)	
		Yield	Percentage of National Production	Yield	Percentage of National Production	Yield	Percentage of National Production	Yield	Percentage of National Production
		Coffee Production in Quintales of Green Coffee							
Sub-family	0-4.9	5.6	29.5	1.2	3.5	7.4	----	----	----
Family	5-9.9	5.7	12.7 } 42.2	2.7	9.3 } 12.8	----	---- } 13.5	----	---- } 13.1
Small employer	10-49.9	5.9	20.3	3.9	22.9	10.7	28.4	12.8	7.3
Estate	50-99.9	7.3	9.8	4.3	21.3	12.5	19.7	8.6	17.1
Integrated producer	100+	8.2	27.7 } 37.5	4.9	42.9 } 64.2	11.9	38.4 } 58.1	7.6	62.4 } 79.5
Totals		$\bar{X} = 6.5$	100.1	$\bar{X} = 3.9$	99.9	$\bar{X} = 10.6$	100.0	$\bar{X} = 6.6$	99.9
Total produced		522,998		474,683		1,891,201		2,188,517 (1964)	

SOURCES: Costa Rica: Costa Rica Dirección General de Estadística y Censos (1957: 101, 230); Nicaragua: Nicaragua Dirección General de Estadística y Censos (1961: 7); El Salvador: Asociación Cafetalera de El Salvador (1940: 26); El Salvador Dirección General de Estadística y Censos (1961: 51); Guatemala: Biechler (1970: 109); Guatemala Dirección General de Estadística (1953: 5; 1971: 245, 248).

small-employer stratum is of little greater importance. In Guatemala, the dominance of the large estate in coffee production is almost complete.

Second, Nicaragua and El Salvador show almost identical levels of concentration in both coffee area and production. Estate and integrated producers control approximately 53% of total coffee area in both countries and these two classes of large growers actually control a greater proportion of production in Nicaragua (64.2%) than in El Salvador (58.1%). Contrary to the view of Baumeister, Nicaragua is not an exception to the pattern of estate dominance in Latin American agriculture. The data in Table 7.1 indicate that Nicaragua more closely resembles El Salvador, a country with a well-deserved reputation for oligarchic dominance, than it does Costa Rica. Only approximately 500 of some 9600 coffee farms in Nicaragua in 1957-1958 accounted for half of the coffee area and almost two-thirds of total production. The small-employer stratum, although considerably more important than in Guatemala, is actually less important in Nicaragua than in El Salvador. The data in Table 7.1 do not show that Baumeister's bourgeoisie *chapiolla* was the dominant factor in prerevolutionary Nicaraguan coffee production. In neither Nicaragua nor El Salvador do the numerous smallholdings of family and sub-family farmers make any substantial contribution to production; they control less than a quarter of the coffee area in Nicaragua and less than 20% in El Salvador. On the basis of the coffee-class structure in Nicaragua and El Salvador revealed in the data in Table 7.1, similar patterns of oligarchic dominance would be expected in both countries. Despite these similarities in land ownership and production, the two coffee systems diverge substantially in production techniques, processing technology, and national control over exports so that in fact the economic basis and the political behavior of the two coffee elites have been very different.

Although the national-level Nicaraguan data presented in Table 7.1 provide little support for the Baumeister hypothesis, and examination of the internal structure of the Nicaraguan coffee economy indicates that, as might be expected, there is an element of truth in his argument. Table 7.2 presents data organized by the same five class categories used in Table 7.1 although they are, in keeping with Nicaraguan census practices, defined in terms of production rather than area in coffee (assuming 1957 yields).

The data in Table 7.2 reveal three different regional coffee systems in Nicaragua. The original center of Nicaraguan coffee production, the

TABLE 7.2
Distribution of Production by Class Position of Producers for Nicaragua, 1910 and 1957

Managua / Regions III-IV / Carazo

Class Position	Production (QQ)	Managua 1910	Managua 1957	Regions III-IV 1910	Carazo 1957
Sub-family	10	.0	.3	.2	.6
Family	10 < 40	.4 } .4	.9 } 1.2	3.5 } 3.7	3.7 } 4.3
Small employer	40 < 200	11.3	7.1	21.4	15.0
Estate	200 < 500	33.9	21.1	22.7	22.5
Integrated producer	≥ 500	54.3 } 88.2	70.5 } 91.6	52.1 } 74.8	58.3 } 80.8
Total percentage		99.9	99.9	99.9	100.1
Total produced		67,440	81,004	47,187	119,087
Percentage of nation		38.8%	17.1%	27.1%	25.1%

Matagalpa / Region VI / Jinotega

Class Position	Production (QQ)	Matagalpa 1910	Matagalpa 1957	Region VI 1910	Jinotega 1957
Sub-family	10	1.1	1.8	.3	5.3
Family	10 < 40	3.1 } 4.2	9.9 } 11.7	3.5 } 3.8	14.1 } 19.4
Small employer	40 < 200	19.2	30.9	18.8	23.5
Estate	200 < 500	33.1	24.7	24.7	21.3
Integrated producer	≥ 500	43.5 } 76.6	32.7 } 57.4	52.7 } 77.4	35.8 } 57.1
Total percentage		100.0	100.0	100.0	100.0
Total produced		18,444	116,734	16,484	65,894
Percentage of nation		10.6%	24.6%	9.4%	13.9%

Estelí / Region I / Nueva Segovia

Class Position	Production (QQ)	Estelí 1910	Estelí 1957	Region I 1910	Nueva Segovia 1957
Sub-family	10	5.7	18.1	14.7	9.4
Family	10 < 40	11.1 } 16.8	40.7 } 58.8	33.9 } 48.6	21.5 } 30.9
Small employer	40 < 200	48.0	11.6	40.7	64.5
Estate	200 < 500	35.2	29.6	10.8	4.6
Integrated producer	≥ 500	--- } 35.2	--- } 29.6	--- } 10.8	--- } 4.6
Total percentage		100.0	100.0	100.1	100.0
Total produced		2,341	4,476	2,322	15,535
Percentage of nation		1.3%	.9%	1.3%	3.3%

SOURCE: República de Nicaragua (1910), calculated from census listing. Nicaragua, Dirección General de Estadística y Censos (1961: 7).

Departments of Managua and Carazo (Regions III and IV in revolutionary Nicaragua), contributed more than half of national production according to the 1910 Coffee Census. In these departments the degree of concentration in 1957 actually exceeded that of Guatemala, and although it increased slightly after 1910, it always has been very high. In Matagalpa and Jinotega (Region VI), on the other hand, estate and integrated producers controlled less production, although the overall distribution was similar to that of El Salvador in the 1950s. As the data on percentage of national production by department indicate, Region VI was the most dynamic sector of the Nicaraguan coffee economy. The leading producing department shifted from Managua in 1910 to Matagalpa in 1957. Gariazzo et al. (1983a: 4) indicate that these trends continued in the 1960s and 1970s. It is also significant that the small-employer stratum increased its share of total production in Region VI between 1910 and 1957, whereas the estate sector lost ground. As there is no reason to believe that these trends have not continued, the Region VI data lend some support to Baumeister's ideas on the importance of the small bourgeoisie in Nicaraguan coffee production. Wheelock's model, on the other hand, fits the Managua-Carazo region best (Wheelock is himself the scion of two distinguished Managua-Carazo coffee growing families), and there is also a substantial estate sector in Region VI where he conducted his field research on the large coffee farm.

The departments of Estelí and Nueva Segovia (Region I) contributed a small share of national coffee production but showed a class structure dramatically different from that of the rest of Nicaragua or of the remainder of Central America. Smallholders and small employers dominated production in both 1910 and 1957 and increased their share in both departments in the intercensal period. The integrated producer stratum is absent in these departments, and the estate stratum has almost disappeared in Nueva Segovia, although it retains a sizable minority share of production in Estelí. By 1957 smallholders dominated production in Estelí and small employers in Nueva Segovia. Inasmuch as production has been expanding in both these regions, particularly in the period after 1957, once again it would appear that the estate sector is not the center of dynamism in the Nicaraguan coffee economy. The data from Region I provide some additional support for Baumeister's hypothesis, although this is a relatively minor coffee region.

The data in Table 7.2 indicate why Nicaragua is more difficult to characterize than the other Central American coffee systems. The coffee sector actually contains three different class systems: a Guatemala-like domination by large estates in Managua and Carazo; a Salvadoran-like estate structure in Matagalpa and Jinotega challenged by an expanding small-employer stratum; and a smallholder- and small-employer-dominated system in Estelí and Nueva Segovia, which has no exact duplicate elsewhere in Central America. The differing views of Wheelock and Baumeister, then, reflect both the differentiated and changing character of the Nicaraguan coffee system. Wheelock's view emphasizes the traditional estate system that formed the economic base of the Nicaraguan oligarchy in the period before World War II; Baumeister's model fits best the dynamic new sectors that emerged with the rapid expansion of export production in coffee and other crops in the post-War period. Although the cross-national comparison of Table 7.1 would simply categorize Nicaragua with El Salvador as a system dominated by an estate-based oligarchy, the internal data in Table 7.2 indicate that the Nicaraguan class system in coffee is considerably more complex. Because both revolutionary and counterrevolutionary forces are now engaged in armed competition for the support of Region VI coffee growers, the class structure of this area is of more than academic interest. Although the political implications of the Wheelock and Baumeister views are complex, it is clear that the success of the agrarian policies of the revolutionary government of which both analysts are a part will depend, in part, on an accurate analysis of the class structure of the Nicaraguan coffee economy.

The third conclusion suggested by the data in Table 7.1 is similarly mixed. There is considerable support for both Seligson's and Hall's views of the Costa Rican coffee system. It is clear that compared to El Salvador and Nicaragua, to say nothing of Guatemala, the smallholding farmers control a much more substantial share of coffee area and production and that the estate sector is correspondingly smaller. Smallholders are approximately twice as important in area and three times as important in production as they are in either Nicaragua or El Salvador and the estate sector is proportionately approximately a third less important in both area and production. Differences of this magnitude reflect profound differences in the political and economic power of the coffee elites of Nicaragua and El Salvador relative to those of Costa Rica, and tend to support Hall's contentions regarding the strength of smallholders and the weakness of the large estate in Costa Rican coffee production.

This conclusion must, however, be immediately qualified by noting that the most important smallholding class is *not* the family farmers but rather the sub-family farmers, who are not only much more numerous but control more production and area. Since in 1955 19,000 of the 22,000 coffee growers in Costa Rica fell into the sub-family category, Seligson might well contend that Costa Rican coffee farmers were a semi-proletariat of land-starved mini-farmers rather than an autonomous yeoman farmer class. The family farm is actually relatively insignificant in numbers, area, and production. Furthermore, a small number of large estates (184 of 22,000) control 30.6% of total coffee area and 37.5% of production. As Seligson contends, there is in fact a high degree of concentration in Costa Rican coffee production, although not so much as elsewhere in Central America. Although naive views of Costa Rica as the "Switzerland of Central America" will find no support from the data in Table 7.1, Hall's position does receive some support from the cross-national comparison. On the other hand, Seligson's image of a Costa Rica divided between a few large estates and a mass of proletarians is also supported by the data. But the situation is even worse elsewhere.

The data in Table 7.1 do not, however, provide support the idea that the dominance of an independent yeoman farmer class provides the economic base for Costa Rican democracy and Costa Rican excep-tionalism in Central America. Although comparison between Costa Rica and either Nicaragua of El Salvador as a whole gives the impression of relative smallholder dominance in Costa Rica, compar-ison with a region dominated either by smallholders, such as Estelí, or small employers, such as Nueva Segovia (see Table 7.2), indicates that estate and, especially, integrated producers are in a position to exert considerable economic and political power over a dispersed and improverished class of sub-family farmers. As the integrated producers also control the processing of the small farmer's crop, the dominance is even greater than the area and production data alone would suggest. The failure of the Costa Rican coffee oligarchy to impose a coffee dictatorship of the Salvadoran variety cannot be explained simply by family-farm dominance in coffee production.

The data in Table 7.1 provide not only a comparative portrait of the entire class structure of Central American coffee production, but also provide information that makes possible an assessment of the absolute economic and political strength of Central American coffee producers, both individually and as a class. Table 7.3 presents the information in Table 7.1 in a slightly different form to emphasize these differences. The data on mean area and mean production of estates with 100 manzanas or more in coffee by country provide indirect information about landed

TABLE 7.3

Mean Area and Mean Production of Estates with 100 Manzanas
or More Planted in Coffee, and Total Area and Total Production
of Estates with 50 Manzanas or More Planted in Coffee
by Country

| | Estate Area in Coffee | | | |
| | ≥ 100 Mz | | ≥ 50 Mz | |
Country	Mean Area (Mz)	Mean Production (QQ)	Total Area (1000 Mz)	Total Production (1000 QQ)
Costa Rica	210	1722	24.7	196.1
Nicaragua	195	955	65.1	304.8
El Salvador	228	2713	95.6	1098.8
Guatemala	342	2479	202.1	1278.3

SOURCE: Table 7.1. Guatemala area and production data based on average of 1950, 1964 census figures.

power—best measured by mean area—and wealth—best measured by mean production—of the average individual large estate owner in each country. Once again, Guatemala is unique. The extremely large mean coffee land area controlled by individual estate owners (342 manzanas) is almost 1½ times the mean size of large estates elsewhere in Central America. It is also notable that the optimum size of an estate seems to be approximately the same in Costa Rica, Nicaragua, and El Salvador— 200 manzanas. Contrary to Hall's view, Costa Rican estates are not markedly smaller than those of El Salvador and are in fact larger on average than those of Nicaragua. Comparison with Guatemala is, of course, misleading as in both overall distribution and average size of large estates it is an exceptional case.

The data on mean production indicate a distinctly different pattern of economic power. Salvadoran growers manage to produce more coffee per estate than Guatemalan growers despite the much smaller average area of coffee on their estates. Inasmuch as the Salvadorans are producing more coffee on less land, their efficiency and hence profitability and financial power should be greater than the approximately equal average production per estate in the two countries would suggest. The average production of large Costa Rican estates lags somewhat behind the average production of Salvadoran or Guatemalan estates, and the Nicaraguan integrated producers are the weakest in Central America by a considerable margin (half the production per estate of Costa Rica, approximately a third of that of Guatemala or El Salvador).

This pattern of efficiency, productivity, and economic strength of Salvadoran growers and inefficiency, backwardness, and economic weakness of Nicaraguan producers also appears in data on technology and processing still to be presented. Although the distribution of coffee land and production does not differ appreciably in the two countries, differences in productivity make the Salvadoran and Nicaraguan growers, respectively, the economic strong and weak classes of Central America.

The information on mean area and production for estates with more than 100 manzanas in coffee in the first two colums in Table 7.3 provides an index of the political and economic power of individual Central American coffee growers. The data on total area and production for all estates with more than 50 manzanas in coffee in the third and fourth columns of Table 7.3 provide an index of the absolute political and economic power of the coffee growing classes as a whole. Measured once again by control over land, the Guatemalan elite is in a class by itself. The total coffee area controlled by large growers in Guatemala is twice that of El Salvador, three times that of Nicaragua, and eight times that of Costa Rica. Total production, however, is almost as high in El Salvador as it is in Guatemala, even though Guatemalan growers as a class control twice as much land. Once again, the Salvadoran elite is distinguished by its greater productivity and efficiency. Nicaragua and Costa Rica lag far behind the region's two top producers in both total area and total production. Although both individually and as a class Costa Rican estate owners produce more coffee per unit area than do Nicaraguan growers, the total power of the Costa Rican elite as a whole—assessed in terms of either coffee land or production—is actually less than that of the Nicaraguan elite. The reasons for the relative weakness of the Nicaraguan and Costa Rican coffee elites are, however, different. The Nicaraguan elite was weak because it was inefficient; the Costa Rican elite was weak because it lost control over a substantial share of production to a class of smallholders.

It has been assumed throughout that control over land implies control over people, although it is clear that some forms of productive organization lead to more control over people than others, even if the same amount of land is involved. Table 7.4 assesses this idea directly by presenting the number of workers under administrative control by estate owners (resident or permanent workers) and the number under temporary control (harvest migrants) for the three Central American producers for which data are available. Data are from coffee censuses

TABLE 7.4

Number of Smallholders and Number of Resident and
Nonresident Workers Employed on Estates with
More than 50 Manzanas in Coffee in El Salvador (1940),
Guatemala (1942-1943), and Costa Rica (1935)

Category	El Salvador	Guatemala	Costa Rica
Smallholders	9,768	9,340	23,641
Resident adult males	27,396	76,767	— — —
Permanent workers	— — —	— — —	23,636
Harvest migrant (all workers)	231,710	142,941	— — —
Total harvest labor	310,000	350,000	75,000
Estate area (1000 Mz)	62.9	164.5	21.0
Estate production (1000 QQ)	784.4	895.2	194.7

SOURCES: El Salvador: Asociación Cafetalera de El Salvador (1940: 26, 34, 35, 39);
Guatemala: Guatemala Oficina Central del Café (1946: 87, 99, 109, 213); Biechler
(1970: 264); Costa Rica: Costa Rica Instituto de Defensa del Café de Costa Rica
(1935: 58, 59).

conducted in the period from 1935 to 1942. Data on labor force
organization are not presented in later censuses. It is clear from the data
in Table 7.4 that the Guatemalan coffee elite controlled approximately
three times as many resident laborers as did the Salvadoran elite, even
though Salvadoran production was only slightly less than Guatemalan.
The absolute difference in the size of populations controlled is actually
greater than these figures suggest because the families of resident
laborers usually lived with them on the estate. As families of permanent
workers could be mobilized to help in the harvest, the number of outside
harvest migrants is greater in El Salvador than in Guatemala. Nevertheless, the total harvest labor force including hired outsiders, permanent
workers, and the working members of their families is greater in
Guatemala (350,000) than in El Salvador (310,000).

The data in Table 7.4 support the assessment of the relative positions
of the Salvadoran and Guatemalan coffee elites suggested by the land
and production distribution data of Tables 7.1 and 7.3. Control over
more land does translate into control over more people, all other things
being equal. The comparative labor force data in Table 7.4 also indicate
that the El Salvadoran growers used their permanent labor force much
more efficiently because output per permanent worker is almost three
times higher in El Salvador than in Guatemala. The mechanical

limitations of hand picking restrict any such dramatic productivity differences in harvesting, however. Once again, the Salvadoran elite is distinguished by its vastly more efficient production system; the Guatemalan elite by its greater control over land and people in a relatively inefficient system.

The difference between El Salvador and Guatemala in control over people is actually much greater than the data in Table 7.4 suggest because control is qualitatively as well as quantitatively distinct in the two countries. Since its origins in the late nineteenth century, the Guatemalan coffee production system has been dominated by various forms of forced labor (Bingham, 1974; Cambranes, 1982; Garlant, 1968; Grieb, 1979; McCreery, 1983; Nanez, 1970) that have varied only in whether effective control was exercised by the state or individual planters. During the dictatorship of Jorge Ubico (1931-1944) the state required that the Indian population work a minimum of 100 or 150 days a year for either a private employer or the state and made state employment sufficiently onerous to compel labor in coffee (Grieb, 1979: 39). Both before and after this period, debt servitude and labor contractors under the control of estate owners provided labor with only the indirect involvement of the state in maintaining the legal structure that made these institutions possible. This system, which continues to function today, has been described in detail by Nañez (1970: 317-348), Pansini (1977: 9-21), and Schmid (1967: 181-204) among others. Typically, laborers were advanced money to estate owners but never managed to work off their debts and became permanently indebted. Because debts could be inherited by the beginning of this century, a distinct class of hereditary serfs (*colonos*) had developed on coffee estates and institutionalized serfdom (*colonaje*) had come to be sanctified in Guatemalan law and custom. In some particularly notorious cases, such as the Finca San Francisco owned by Enrique Brol (Anonymous, 1982; personal communication, James Birchfield, 1985), owners were able to rule like medieval dukes backed by squads of armed guards. Even progressive planters like Erwin Paul Dieseldorf intentionally acquired lands simply to control the labor of *colonos* resident on them and combined modern management techniques with medieval labor organization (Nañez, 1970: 317-348). Modern corporate farms like "El Pilar" studied by Pansini (1977: 14-21) used exactly the same legal forms as the most backward growers in remote interior regions. The resident *colono* labor force was supplemented by gangs of harvest migrants (*cuadrilleros*) who were recruited into fixed-term debt servitude by a system of advances (*habilitaciones*) controlled by unscrupulous labor contractors (*habilitadores*). These gang laborers were seldom able to work off all their debts and differed from the resident *colonos* principally in the fixed-term nature of their contracts and the absence of even the limited legal protection afforded the *colonos*.

This elaborate legal system of forced labor is not duplicated elsewhere in Central America, although varying degrees of extra-economic coercion such as the use of company stores in Nicaragua (Wheelock, 1980: 92), rural patrols in Salvador (Trujillo, 1980: 128), and estate housing or subsistence plots in Costa Rica (Stone, 1980: 110) were universal. Guatemala is unique not only in the numbers of people and vast amounts of land controlled by its coffee elite, but also in the elaboration of an institutionalized system of forced labor backed by both the informal armed power of the coffee planters and the formal armed power of the state. The observation of one North American visitor in 1908 that Guatemala had so many soldiers that it looked like a penal colony (Bingham, 1974: 105) is as true today as it was then. Backed by domination of Guatemala's most productive land, producing its most important source of wealth, and controlling a vast dependent population through state-sanctioned forced labor, the Guatemalan coffee elite became a political force that has no exact parallel in the other coffee-producing countries. Not even in El Salvador was such extensive control over land and people possible.

The Costa Rican data in Table 7.4 are not directly comparable with those of El Salvador and Guatemala because the 1935 Costa Rican coffee census reports the number or persons *working* on coffee estates, not the number of workers *resident* on the estates as in El Salvador or Guatemala. Because many Costa Rican coffee workers were day rather than resident laborers, the difference in reporting conventions may reflect real differences among the systems. Nevertheless, it is clear that the Costa Rican elite could not have controlled, at a maximum, more than a third of the number of workers resident on Guatemalan estates, and the actual number of resident laborers is probably considerably less. Comparison with the data on El Salvador is probably misleading for the same reason. The principal value of the data in Table 7.4 for Costa Rica is to indicate that the ratio of smallholders to hired laborers was much higher in Costa Rica than in either El Salvador or Guatemala, although the smallholders and hired laborers could, of course, be the same people. Nevertheless, it is clear that the Costa Rican elite faced a lower class divided by the ownership of small amounts of property. Class polarization was considerably more advanced in El Salvador and Guatemala than it was in Costa Rica. When the Costa Rican coffee elite eventually faced a challenge from rural workers, it came from workers in bananas, not coffee (Seligson, 1980: 49).

The analysis of land, coffee, and people demonstrates that Guatemalan and Salvadoran growers, both individually and as classes, were both relatively powerful but for different reasons. The Guatemalan coffee elite controlled more land and people and controlled the people more tightly than did any other coffee elite in Central America. Its power rested on the captive allegiance of its serfs and the armed force at its command. The Salvadoran planter elite became the most productive, efficient, and profitable in Central America. But it controlled fewer people and controlled them less securely. Its power was more financial than military, although it too used a captive state for its own purposes. The coffee elites of Nicaragua and Costa Rica gained neither the military and political power of the Guatemalans nor the financial power of the Salvadorans. Although control of Nicaraguan coffee land was as concentrated as it was in El Salvador, the Nicaraguan coffee elite never approached the productive efficiency of the Salvadorans and remained the least productive planter class in Central America. Its low level of productivity severely restricted its financial power. Although many Costa Rican growers controlled estates as large as any in Central America outside Guatemala, as a class they never gained the concentrated control over land and production achieved in El Salvador or Nicaragua. Instead, they shared this control with a persistent class of sub-family farmers. The coffee elites of Guatemala and El Salvador gained political and financial power, respectively. The elites of Costa Rica and Nicaragua failed to gain political or financial power, respectively. These differences are further accentuated by substantial differences in control over production technology, processing, and export.

Production, Processing, Export

The differences in production per unit area evident in Tables 7.1, 7.3, and 7.4 are based on substantial differences in the technology of production, and superiority in production tends to be associated with technical sophistication in processing as well. As might be expected from these data, El Salvador has been the traditional leader in production technology, followed by Costa Rica. Guatemala lags behind Costa Rica and is far behind El Salvador; Nicaragua is at or slightly behind the Guatemalan level. In processing, Costa Rica and El Salvador are the clear leaders with Guatemala close behind and Nicaragua trailing with remarkable low levels of efficiency for most of its history.

Table 7.5 presents three readily accessible indices of technical sophistication in production: *arabica* variety; fertilizer use; and density of plantings. By the 1950s Salvador had already made the transition from the traditional Central American varieties, Típica and Maragogipe, to the hardier and higher-yielding Bourbon strain. In 1957 more than two-thirds of Salvadoran coffee area was in modern varieties whereas the transition had hardly begun in either Nicaragua of Guatemala and extended to only approximately a third of the coffee area in Costa Rica. Although fertilizer use statistics by area are not available for El Salvador, the relative position of Costa Rica compared to Nicaragua and Guatemala is the same as in the variety subtable. In the 1950s organic or chemical fertilizers were used on 35.7% of the total Costa Rican coffee area. The corresponding figures for Nicaragua and Guatemala are 5.0% and 11.9%, respectively. Density of plantings was almost twice as great in Salvador as it was in Guatemala. The reliability of the Nicaraguan density data is questionable as it appears to be census practice to assume rather than count 1000 trees per manzana. The technical superiority of El Salvador is indicated most clearly in yields (expressed in *quintales* per *manzana*) for selected periods from World War II to the present (Table 7.6). For most of the period, Salvadoran yields are more than twice those of Guatemala or Nicaragua and substantially greater than those of Costa Rica. By 1978 government-sponsored technical development programs in Costa Rica had reversed the relative positions of El Salvador and Costa Rica and by 1980 Costa Rica was clearly in the lead. Still, for most of the period El Salvador had the highest yields not only in Central America but in all of Latin America and, with the exception of some relatively minor producers, the highest yields in the world (United Nations Food and Agriculture Organization, 1981: 184). By 1980 Costa Rica had assumed the lead in both Central and South America and, excepting minor procedures, had the third highest yield in the world (United Nations Food and Agriculture Organization, 1981).

The differences in production technology between El Salvador and Costa Rica, on the one hand, and Guatemala and Nicaragua, on the other, are pronounced and have been so for some time. In June 1937 the Colombian agronomist Juan Pablo Duque made a survey of Central American production for the Colombian coffee board, which was

TABLE 7.5
Distribution of *Arabica* Varieties, Fertilizer Use,
and Density of Plantings by Country, 1950-1957

Technical Index	Costa Rica 1955	Nicaragua 1957	El Salvador 1957	Guatemala 1950
Variety	*Percentage of Total Coffee Area*			
Typica	67.9 } 67.9	80.1 } 84.4	29.3 } 29.3	48.5 } 53.5
Maragogipe	---	4.3	---	5.0
Typica-Bourbon	---	---	---	32.1
Bourbon	16.4 } 32.1	15.4 } 15.5	58.8 } 70.7	14.3 } 14.3
Others	15.7		11.9	---
Total	100.0	99.9	100.0	99.9
Fertilizer Use	*Percentage of Total Coffee Area*			
Organic	10.4 } 35.7	2.0 } 5.0	---	6.6 } 11.9
Chemical	25.3	3.0	---	5.3
None	64.4	95.0	---	88.2
Total	100.0	100.0	---	100.1
		Number of Trees/Mz		
Density	---	1000	1258	635

SOURCES: Costa Rica: Costa Rica Dirección General de Estadística y Censos, (1957: 40, 42, 44, 233); Nicaragua: Nicaragua Dirección General de Estadística y Censos (1961: 11, 13, 18); El Salvador: El Salvador Dirección General de Estadística y Censos (1961: 3-5); Guatemala: Guatemala Dirección General de Estadística (1953: 7, 37, 71).

worried about increased competition. His description of the relative technical positions of the four Central American coffee systems (Duque, 1938), summarized in Table 7.7, is echoed in other cross-national surveys (Cardoso, 1975; Hearst, 1929; Jamaica Coffee Industry Board, 1959; Torres-Rivas, 1975) as well as in studies of the technical organization of individual systems (Browning, 1971; Dominguez, 1970; Gariazzo et al., 1983a, 1983b; Hall, 1978, 1982; Keith, 1974; Morrison and Norris, 1954; Nañez, 1970; Radell, 1964).

Although production technology has changed over the twentieth century, the relative positions of the four producers remained constant until the Costa Rican surge in the 1970s. Duque (1938: 41, 50) found that harvesting techniques were similar in Costa Rica, El Salvador, and Guatemala although more passes were made in Costa Rica. In Nicaragua, however, then as now, pickers strip or milk the branches of a mixture of ripe and unripe berries, leaves, twigs, buds, and other detritus damaging the trees, reducing yields and producing a low grade of coffee

TABLE 7.6

Yields in Quintales of Green Coffee per Manzana
for Selected Periods by Country

Period	Costa Rica		Nicaragua		El Salvador		Guatemala	
1942 or before	7.6	(1935)	6.1	(1910)	11.1	(1940)	6.3	(1942-
1948-1952	6.9		5.3		10.1		5.4	1943)
1961-1965	9.1		5.2		12.4		8.0	
1969-1971	13.2		6.9		17.1		8.3	
1978	17.8		9.2		16.7		9.7	
1980	21.2		9.0		14.7		9.5	

SOURCES: United Nations Food and Agriculture Organization (1981: 184; 1960:
129); Costa Rica Instituto de Defensa (1935: 59), Estadística y Censos (1965: 151);
Nicaragua: República de Nicaragua (1910: 644), Gariazzo et al. (1983: Appendix
Table 7); El Salvador: Asociación Cafetalera (1940: 26); Guatemala: Oficina Central,
(1946: 152, 194), Estadística (1971: 245, 248).

(Duque, 1938: 45; Hearst, 1929: 120; Playter, 1927: 26; Radell, 1964: 48).
It is not entirely clear why this practice has persisted in the face of
determined government and private efforts to suppress it, but it may be
related to the relative backwardness of Nicaraguan processing technology, which cannot produce higher grades of coffee no matter what
quality of harvested fruit is used as input (Keith, 1974: 92; Radell, 1964:
25, 51). In pruning, Costa Rica and El Salvador had a distinct advantage
as in most areas of Nicaragua and Guatemala the coffee bush was
allowed to grow freely with only maintenance cutting (Duque, 1938:
23-36). In Nicaragua the elaborate pruning system developed by the
progressive grower Arturo Vaughan ("*poda* Vaughan") is used on some
of the larger estates on the Carazo plateau but not elsewhere (Radell,
1964: 16). The distinct Costa Rican style of pruning, which encouraged
candelabra-like branching, had some success among progressive planters in Guatemala but was not generally adopted (Dominguez, 1970: 134,
138). In 1937 Duque (1938: 5) found a "great preoccupation" with the
use of chemical fertilizers in Costa Rica and the 1935 coffee census
found that 30 percent of Costa Rican coffee lands were fertilized (Costa
Rica, Instituto de Defensa del Café de Costa Rica, 1935: 59). This
compares with 5.0% of Nicaraguan and 11.9% of Guatemalan coffee
lands as late as the 1950s (Table 7.5). Duque (1938: 10) also found an
active interest in fertilizers in El Salvador as well as the extensive use of
the *izote* plant (*yucca* sp.) as a fertilizer supplement or substitute.
Nicaraguan growers used very little fertilizer then and, in substantial
areas of the country, very little now (Gariazzo et al., 1983b: 12). Duque

TABLE 7.7

Estimates of the Technological Organization of Central American Coffee Production by Juan Pablo Duque for the Colombian Coffee Board, June 1937

	Costa Rica	Nicaragua	El Salvador	Guatemala
Harvesting	Mature beans only	Stripping ripe and unripe beans, leaves	Mature beans only	Mature beans only
Pruning	Intense	Free growth	Intense but variable	Free growth
Fertilizer	"Great preoccupation with spreading the use of chemical fertilizers"	None	Izote (*Yucca* sp.) and mineral fertilizers	General use[a]
Transport	Ox carts, trucks	Trucks (Carazo); pack animals (Matagalpa-Jinotega)	Carts, trucks	Carts, trucks, pack animals, human bearers
Processing machinery	Imported, sophisticated; "constant preoccupation with improving processing plant"	Local, primitive	Imported, sophisticated; similar to Costa Rica	Imported, sophisticated (but lags behind Costa Rica and El Salvador)
Quality control	High	Nonexistent	High	High
Machine drying	Yes	No	Yes	Yes

SOURCE: Duque (1938).

a. Dominguez (1970: 167) reports that fertilizer use was confined to German planters and that "inorganic fertilizers were, broadly speaking, out of reach of all but the most prosperous of the planters." Data from the 1950 census reported in Table 7.4 show that no fertilizer was used on almost 90% of the coffee area.

also found substantial interest in fertilizer among Guatemalan planters, but Dominguez (1970: 167) reports that its use was confined to German planters and the data in Table 7.5 indicate that fertilizer use was not widespread in the 1950s. Costa Rican and El Salvadoran planters used the most advanced techniques of harvesting, pruning, and fertilization. Nicaragua used the most primitive methods in all three areas, and Guatemala used advanced techniques in harvesting only.

Transportation technology was most highly developed in El Salvador and Costa Rica where good roads made it possible to use ox carts and later trucks to quickly bring harvested berries from farm to processing plant (Duque, 1938: 40, 47-48; Hearst, 1929: 42-44; Seligson, 1982: 34). The primitive transportation network of North Central Nicaragua made even the use of oxcarts difficult and much coffee was moved on the back of mules. Roads were better in the Managua-Carazo area but much of the crop was moved by mule or ox cart rather than by truck (Duque, 1938: 45-46; Radell, 1964: 27, 54). In Guatemala there were also regional variations but in general carts, pack animals, and—unique in Central America—human bearers were used to transport coffee (Biechler, 1970: 18; Duque, 1938: 50; Nañez, 1970: 251-253). In the remote Alta Verapaz region, human bearers carried 100-pound bags of coffee as much as 40 miles (Nañez, 1970: 284). The poorly developed transportation system of Nicaragua severely restricted the development of processing technology because the harvested crop could not be brought to a central location quickly enough to avoid spoilage. In Guatemala, where most estates were large enough to afford their own processing plants, poor transportation did not restrict processing as severely but much coffee was still sold in the partially processed parchment stage (Biechler, 1970: 171-172).

Processing technology, too, was most advanced in Costa Rica and El Salvador, where imported European and North American power-driven equipment was extensively used in large industrial installations frequently located off the farm in cities or other central locations (Duque, 1938: 51; Hall, 1982: 50-51; Hearst, 1929: 139-140; Seligson, 1982: 34). European, especially German, growers in Guatemala were responsible for many of the technical innovations in the coffee industry worldwide, including development of the widely used "Guardiola" and "Okrassa" coffee dryers and the "Smout" and "Okrassa" shellers and polishers, but technological innovation ceased after World War I and the processing industry stagnated (Dominguez, 1970: 264-265). In the 1930s Duque (1938: 51) found that the processing industry in Guatemala trailed those of Costa Rica and El Salvador, and the gap is even wider today. In the Managua region of Nicaragua the development of processing was handicapped not only by poor transportation but also by a shortage of water, and before World War II as much as half of the crop was processed using the dry method. Even though by the 1950s 90% of the crop was wet processed, the shortage of water led to the improper washing of much of it. In Carazo, where transportation was better, the water shortage also led to improper washing although most of the crop was processed in centralized plants as in El Salvador and Costa Rica. In north central Nicaragua there was plenty of water but so few roads that partial wet processing was done with homemade equipment and much coffee was stored for weeks or months before being processed (Keith, 1974: 92; Radell, 1964: 24-26, 51). As a result, it was impossible to maintain quality standards in Nicaraguan coffee, whereas quality control was high in Costa Rica, El Salvador, and even in Guatemala.

Duque's observations on the superiority of Costa Rican and El Salvadoran processing technology are also supported by the data in Table 7.8 showing the number of processing plants in each of the four countries for the period from the late nineteenth century to the present. As a general rule, the smaller the number of plants, the greater their technological sophistication, the greater the number of farms served by a given processor, and the better the transportation system on which they depend. A small number of plants also indicates that they are industrial installations located off the farm, often in urban areas. Costa Rica and El Salvador have always had a relatively small number of processing plants—approximately 200 before World War II—and by 1972 the number declined to 114 in El Salvador and 83 in Costa Rica. The much greater number of processing plants in Nicaragua is a result of the large number of homemade wet-processing systems in the Matagalpa-Jinotega region. In Guatemala the large number reflects a decentralized, large estate-based processing system. Since in the 1950s El Salvador and Guatemala processed approximately equal amounts of coffee; the average Salvadoran plant processed more than 10 times as much coffee as the typical Guatemalan plant and the scale of the facilities varies accordingly. In fact, El Salvador possesses what is said to be the largest processing plant in Central America, El Molino (Wellman, 1961: Plate 27). The relative numbers of Salvadoran and Costa Rican plants suggest that the scale of Costa Rican technology is similar. My own observation of plant operations in the Barba canton of Costa Rica substantiates this. Although El Salvador has traditionally been the leader in production technology, both Costa Rica and El Salvador have

TABLE 7.8
Number of Coffee-Processing Plants (*beneficios*)
for Selected Periods by Country

		Number of beneficios		
Period	Costa Rica	El Salvador	Nicaragua	Guatemala
1888-1910	256	---	423	---
1940-1942	221	207	---	4243
1950-1957	---	---	1263[a]	1334[a]
1972	114	83	---	---

SOURCES: Costa Rica: Stone (1982: 256), Instituto de Defensa (1935: 59), Seligson (1975: 24); Nicaragua: República de Nicaragua (1910, calculated from census listing), Estadística y Censos (1961: 25); El Salvador: Asociación Cafetalera (1940: 183-191, calculated from listing of *beneficios*), Castenada (1977); Guatemala: Oficina Central (1946: 146), Estadística (1953: 80).
a. Data for farms producing 200 QQ or more of coffee berries in Guatemala only. For comparative purposes the Nicaragua total includes only farms producing 40 QQ of green coffee or more (5 QQ of berries yields approximately 1 QQ of green coffee).

highly developed processing systems. In fact, the Costa Rican coffee elite, as Hall (1982: 52-53) and Seligson (1975: 24-25) both argue, is largely an elite of coffee processors, not producers.

Given the substantial economic gains to be realized through scientific cultivation and industrial processing, it might be asked why all the Central American countries did not follow the path of El Salvador and later Costa Rica toward the full rationalization of both production and processing. For Nicaragua the answer, as Wheelock (1980) has demonstrated, is to be found in the politics of intervention. In 1910 Nicaragua took its first coffee census—a remarkably detailed document. In 1912 the United States Marines arrived, not to leave again until 1933. Their war against Augusto Cesar Sandino was fought in the heart of the Matagalpa-Jinotega coffee belt, and there is little doubt that the intervention stopped the rationalization and expansion of production in what later would become Nicaragua's most dynamic coffee zone. It was not until the 1950s that expansion resumed in this region. Nicaragua did not not take another coffee census until 1957. The intervention also deprived the coffee elite of control over exports, which passed into the hands of American banks.

In Guatemala, United States intervention involved bananas not coffee (Jonas and Tobis, 1974; Schlesinger and Kinzer, 1982) and estate size was certainly large enough to generate capital for modernization. The failure to rationalize the industry is clearly related to the temptations of forced labor and and a racist legal structure. With labor virtually free for the taking, thanks to state-enforced debt servitude, and the Indian population with almost no protection from planter land grabs, there was little incentive to rationalize production. Land costs remained vastly lower in Guatemala than in Costa Rica (Cardoso, 1977: 175; Stone, 1980: 96) and wage levels were the lowest in Central America (Duque, 1938: 58; Hearst, 1929: 125). Indeed, what is surprising about Guatemala is not how little rationalization of production took place, but how much. But it took place almost entirely among German planters who were more closely tied to world capitalism than to the extractive society of colonial Guatemala. Once the Germans were expropriated during World War II, the Guatemalan coffee elite reverted to doing what it had always done best—living in luxury on the tribute of a captive Indian population. Technological innovation stopped and planters and their allies in the military devoted themselves to the rationalization not of coffee production but of state terror.

Costa Rica lagged behind El Salvador in production technology but not in the industrialization of processing. Although the elite of integrated producers rapidly modernized and large estates such as Aquiares, studied by Morrison and Norris (1954), or Concavas, studied by Hall (1978), were models of productive efficiency, the yield figures for smaller growers (see Table 7.1) indicate that they were slow to rationalize production. The small growers remained captives of the processing-plant owners until the economic crisis of the depression, when the establishment of the *Instituto de Defensa del Café* shifted some measure of control to the state. After the 1948 revolution, the *Oficina del Café* pushed through a technical development program that substantially benefited the small growers and caused Costa Rican yields to exceed those of El Salvador by the 1970s (Hall, 1980: 153, 159; Seligson, 1975: 28). As long as the impoverished sub-family coffee farmers of Costa Rica were under the unrestricted control of the coffee-processing elite, they lacked both the capital and the technical knowledge necessary to rationalize production. The failure of the small producers to modernize without state intervention is another indication of the unequal distribution of wealth and power in the Costa Rican coffee system.

In El Salvador the complete rationalization of production and processing early in the century enabled the coffee elite to move downstream into export and thereby gain control of what Sebastián (1979: 950-951) calls the "power pyramid" of coffee land, processing, and export. The data in Table 7.9 show this pattern as it existed in 1940 according to the first Salvadoran coffee census (Asociación Cafetalera de El Salvador, 1940: 183-199).

TABLE 7.9
Number of Coffee-Processing Plants (*beneficios*)
and Number of Legal Export Trademarks held by
Largest Holders in El Salvador in 1940

Holders of Largest Number of beneficios			Holders of Largest Number of Export Brands		
Family or Company	beneficios	Export	Family or Company	Export	beneficios
Meardi	12	60	Meardi	60	12
Daglio	8	17	Alvarez	22	4
Sol Millet	7	5	Curaçao Trading	19	1
Guirola	7	6	de Sola	18	6
de Sola	6	18	Daglio	17	8
Salaverría	5	6	J. Hill	16	1
Alfaro	5	5	Goldtree-Liebes	9	2
Caceres	5	–	Delpech	8	1
Bonilla	5	–	Meza Ayau	7	1
Regalado	4	6	Nottlebohm Trading	7	2
Alvarez	4	22	Dueñas	6	4
Magaña	4	–	Guirola	6	7
Duenas	4	6	Morán	6	1
Lima	4	4	Matamoros	6	1
			Regalado	6	4
			Salaverría	6	5
			Vides	6	1

SOURCE: Asociación Cafetalera de El Salvador (1940: 183-199).

The census lists the names of the owners of all processing plants in the country as well as the holders of all export licenses listed by export brand names. Although the number of export brands is only an approximate measure of export activity, the listing of owners by name makes the 1940 census a particularly valuable source on the overlap in processing and export in El Salvador. The left half of Table 7.9 lists by family surname the number of processing plants and export brands controlled by families with four or more processing plants. It is clear from these data that almost all large processers were also active exporters. The right half of Table 7.9 lists by family name the number of export brands and processing plants controlled by those families and companies with the largest number of registered export brands. It is clear from these data that the most active exporters were, for the most part, also owners of large numbers of *beneficios*. The exceptions to this generalization are largely international trading firms like Curaçao or

Nottlebohm, who are primarily buyers, not processors. Still, with these exceptions the names on both lists represent a who's who of the Salvadoran oligarchy (see Aubey, 1968-1969; Baloyra, 1982; Colindres, 1977). The power pyramid of coffee processing and export in El Salvador conferred power over other export crops, especially cotton and sugar, and frequently control in finance and industry as well. Torres-Rivas (1982) has called the Central American elite a "three-footed beast" with one foot in export agriculture, one in finance, and one in industry. No coffee elite in Central America fits this description better than the Salvadoran. An elite of fully integrated producers controlled the coffee system and much else as well.

The most dramatic contrast to the fully integrated production system and powerful coffee elite of El Salvador is the case of Nicaragua. The Nicaraguan coffee elite achieved neither the rationalization of coffee production nor hegemonic power in Nicaraguan economy or society. Table 7.10 presents a list of individuals who might have been the founders of the Nicaraguan coffee oligarchy if U.S. intervention, civil war, and the rise of the Somoza dynasty had not undermined their economic and technical power and denied them a political opening. The table shows the 11 largest growers in the Department of Carazo as they were recorded in the 1910 coffee census (República de Nicaragua, 1910) on the eve of the 1912 United States intervention. In 1910 Carazo was not only the department with the second largest (after Managua) produc-tion, but also possessed relatively favorable growing conditions and tech-nologically progressive planters. The largest producer was Arturo Vaughan (misspelled Vaugham in the census), the developer of the system of pruning that bears his name. His leading position was due not to his control over a large area in coffee but rather to his complete rationalization of production. His yields of 22.5 *quintales/manzana* actually exceed the national average of Costa Rica, Latin America's technological leader, in 1982. Vaughan might be taken as typical of the Salvadoran-type integrated producer who might have formed, along with other technologically progressive planters, the nucleus of a Nicaraguan coffee oligarchy. Vaughan's estate, San Francisco, is still owned by his family and is in production today; the current owner, also named Arturo, has diversified to become one of Nicaragua's largest egg producers.

But it was not the descendants of Arturo Vaughan and other technologically sophisticated producers, such as Carlos Wheelock in nearby Managua, who became the masters of Nicaragua. Instead, it was

TABLE 7.10
Principal Producers in the Department of Carazo, 1910

Producer	Estates	Area (Mz.)	Production (QQ)	Total Area	Total Production	Number beneficios
Arturo Vaugham	San Francisco	222	5000	222	5000	1
Jose E. Gonzalez	La Providencia	240	1200	590	4000	2
	Monte Cristo	175	1500			
	La Palmera	175	1300			
Adolfo Benard	San Dionisio	123	1300	238	2200	1
	Santa Rosa	50	500			
	San Francisco	65	400			
Rappaccioli	El Paraiso	145	1000	330	2000	2
(Vincente Y Hnos.)	El Pochoton	100	400			
	La Moca	85	600			
Fernando Chamorro	La Amistad	90	800	210	1700	2
	El Brasil	120	900			
Teodoro Tefel	Chilamatal	305	1500	305	1500	1
Vincente Rodriquez	Santa Cecilia	100	1100	175	1450	1
	San Ramiro	75	350			
Jose Ig. Gonzalez	San Jorge	60	600	160	1400	1
	Las Delicias	100	800			
Ignacio Baltodano	El Brasilito	180	1100	180	1100	1
Jose M. Siero	Santa Gertrudis	56	600	146	900	0
	Andalucia	90	300			
Anastasio Somoza	Santa Julia	5	50	94	730	2
	El Convoy	14	80			
	El Porvenir	75	600			

SOURCE: República de Nicaragua (1910: 666-671). Based on census listing of all individual producers for Carazo in 1910.

the son of the eleventh largest producer in Carazo, whose yields were only a third (7.8 quintales/ manzana) of those of Arturo Vaughan, and who did not control sufficient land to be included in the "integrated producer" class in this study. The rise of Anastasio Somoza as ruler of Nicaragua and its largest coffee producer was, of course, based on international power politics, not coffee wealth. Anastasio Somoza García was sufficiently impoverished to have worked as a used car dealer in the United States, and he gained his political prominence in part through his command of English (Millet, 1977: 51). It would take a revolution to bring to power the coffee-growing Wheelock family in the person of Jaime Wheelock, a member of the FSLN (*Frente Sandinista de Liberación Nacional*) since 1969 and currently Nicaraguan Minister of Agriculture. But Wheelock's policies for the reorganization of coffee production are as far as could be imagined from the dreams of oligarchs, Nicaraguan or Salvadoran.

Some members of the 1910 Carazo planter elite owned their own processing plants (Table 7.10), yet none owned as many as members of the Salvadoran elite; in fact, Carazo coffee-processing technology was in a prolonged state of arrested development because of a shortage of water. Exports were, of course, controlled by American banks in partnership with the Nicaraguan national bank. Two families of Carazo planters listed in Table 7.10, the Rappacciolis and the Baltodanos, did become major factors in exports in the 1950s, but by then they had fallen behind their counterparts in El Salvador and Costa Rica in accumulating export-based economic power. Furthermore, their ability to diversify into areas of the economy or even expand their coffee holdings was limited severely by the dominance of Somoza family interests. Technologically backward in both production and processing, deprived of control over exports, and hemmed in by the Somozas, the Nicaraguan coffee elite never completed the transition from estate to integrated producers. If the Salvadoran coffee oligarchy rested on a power pyramid of coffee, processing, and export, the Nicaraguan coffee economy was a pyramid without a base.

CONCLUSIONS: COFFEE AND POLITICS

The empirical analysis has demonstrated that each of the four principal Central American coffee producers except Nicaragua gained a relative advantage in one phase of the production process: Guatemala, in land and people; El Salvador, in production; and Costa Rica, in processing. The relative positions of the four producers circa 1940 are shown in Figure 7.1, where an X represents a relative advantage in the development of one phase of the production sequence. The Guatemalan elite, particularly in its national sector, was characterized by large estates, large amounts of land under estate control, and large numbers of people under tight seignorial restrictions. Estates owned by Guatemalan nationals were never characterized by rationalized production technology and, before World War II, processing and exports were largely controlled by Germans. Salvadoran coffee estates did not match those of Guatemala in size of number of people under direct control. Indeed, the Salvadorans substituted migratory harvest for resident labor, gaining economic efficiency by surrendering a substantial measure of the kind of political control exercised by the Guatemalan elite. But the Salvadoran producers became for much of the century the most efficient in the world, and this substantial technical advantage translated into control over both processing and export. As Figure 7.1 indicates, Salvadoran producers moved downstream to control completely the coffee-production process from field to wharf; they thereby became the only fully integrated producers in Central America. The Costa Rican elite never managed to separate a persistent class of mini-farmers from their tiny coffee fields. Instead they moved downstream into processing, which gave the elite indirect economic control over the mini-farmers but lost them any claim to the political hegemony exercised by the Guatemalans. Their control over advanced processing technology led in turn to control over export. But the Costa Rican processing-export complex lacked the key element in the Salvadoran power pyramid—control over coffee land and production. In Nicaragua none of the elements of the Salvadoran pyramid emerged. Hobbled by the United States' intervention and dynastic rule, the Nicaraguan elite failed to carve out a distinct base of economic power in any phase of the production process.

These differences in both the nature and the strength of the economic base of the Central American coffee elites generated both differing elite structures and differing forms of social and political behavior. Table 7.11 presents lists of the members of the "oligarchies" of Nicaragua, Guatemala, and El Salvador (no comparable data were available for Costa Rica) constructed by researchers with other interests. An X next to a family name indicates that the family fortune was or is based on coffee wealth. Although the measure is a crude one and the definitions of

	Guatemala	El Salvador	Costa Rica	Nicaragua
Land	X			
Production		X		
Processing		X	X	
Export		X	X	0

Figure 7.1: Bases of Power by Stage of the Production Process for the Coffee Elites of Guatemala, El Salvador, Costa Rica, and Nicaragua, circa 1940

oligarchy differ somewhat in the various sources noted in Table 7.11, a clear pattern emerges.

As might be expected, the Salvadoran coffee elite dominates the Salvadoran oligarchy, with the fortunes of approximately two-thirds (19 of 30) of its families based on coffee wealth. In Guatemala, where the oligarchy derived its wealth from commerical and industrial activity as well as from coffee, the proportion of coffee families is lower but still substantial (11 of 20). In Nicaragua only 5 of the 21 members of Wheelock's (1980: 188) "financial oligarchy" came from families whose wealth was based primarily on coffee. The list is heavily weighted toward the pre-coffee colonial cattle-raising elite (Cardenal, Chamorro, Sacasa, Pellas) and the post-coffee cotton barons (Montealegre, Reyes, Lacayo). Of the Carazo growers listed in Table 7.10 only the families of Tefel, Baltodano and Gonzales make it onto Wheelock's list, and Anastasio Somoza Debayle is, of course, a special case. Arturo Vaughan is nowhere to be seen despite his family's continued economic activity in Nicaragua. Coffee brought great economic power to the Salvadoran elite, lesser but still substantial power to the Guatemalan elite, and very little power to the Nicaraguan elite. In the case of Costa Rica, Stone (1982: 351) argues that coffee planters were an important, but far from the only, source of capital for other sectors of the economy. His data suggest that in economic power, the Costa Rican elite falls somewhere between the Guatemalan and Nicaraguan elites and probably closer to the former. It should be kept in mind that Table 7.11 lists members of the economic elite only and therefore understates the immense political power granted to the coffee barons of Guatemala through their control of serfs and armed men. But it further emphasizes the difference in the base of power of the Salvadoran and Guatemalan elites.

The diverse political fates of these four coffee elites who have dominated Central American society and politics for more than a

TABLE 7.11
Coffee and Elite Structure in Nicaragua, Guatemala, and El Salvador

Nicaragua Family	Coffee Wealth	Guatemala Family	Coffee Wealth	El Salvador Family	Coffee Wealth
Alvarez		Abularch		Alvarez	X
Arguello Téfel	X	Alejos	X	Batarse	
Baltodano	X	Arenales		Battle	X
Chamorro Benard		Aycinena		Bernheim	X
Chamorro Cardenal		Bouscayrol	X	Borgonovo	X
Fernandez Hollman		Castillo	X	Deininger	X
Frawley		Cofiño	X	De Sola	X
Gonzalez	X	Cordon	X	Dueñas	X
Hollman		Dorion		Escalón	X
Knoepffer	X	Granai		Frenkel	
Lacayo Terán		Herrera	X	Freund	X
Matheson	X	Ibargüen		Gadala Marfa	
Montealegre		Kong	X	Goldtree-Liebes	X
Osorio Peters		Matheu		Guirola	X
Pellas Chamorro		Novella		Hasbun	
Pereira		Sinibaldi	X	Hill	X
Reyes Cardenal		Skinner Klee	X	Magaña	X
Reyes Montealegre		Toriello	X	Mathies	X
Sacasa Guerrero		Weissenberg	X	Meza Ayau	
Teran		Zimieri		Nasser	
Villa				Poma	
	5/21		11/20	Quiñonez	X
				Regalado	X
				Safie	
				Schwartz	X
				Siman	
				Sol Millet	X
				Vairo	
				Wright	X
				Zablah	
					19/30

SOURCE: Nicaragua: Wheelock (1978: 188); Guatemala: Jonas and Tobis (1974: 216-251); El Salvador: Aubey (1968-1969: 272-276); Coffee holdings based on these sources and Republica de Nicaragua (1910), Colindres (1976: 471), and Asociación Cafetalera (1940: 183-199).

century closely correspond to the strength and character of their economic base. In Nicaragua a revolutionary movement rising from the hills of the Matagalpa-Jinotega coffee zone overwhelmed a government without a base in a weakened coffee oligarchy. In the end, even if the Nicaraguan coffee oligarchs had wanted to form a united front with Somoza, they lacked the economic and political power to do so. Although some joined him, many others—or their sons—joined the opposition. The very wells from which Somoza drew his strength—his total control over Nicaraguan economy and society—fatally weakened his natural allies in the coffee oligarchy. The United States' intervention in the 1920s and 1930s destroyed just that social group that has proved to be its most loyal ally in Guatemala and El Salvador in the 1970s and 1980s—the coffee oligarchy. In Guatemala the coffee elite and, increasingly, its allies in the military have used the immense repressive apparatus of a forced-labor society to fend off continual challenges from below, although with increasing difficulty. The Salvadoran coffee elite, the strongest economic force in Central America, paradoxically finds itself in sufficient difficulty to require extensive outside military aid. It also was forced to weather the only mass Communist insurrection in Latin American history in the *matanza* of 1932. Displaced subsistence farmers converted into agricultural wage laborers, first in coffee then later in cotton, have become a revolutionary rural proletariat driven by the fires of desperation. How long the Guatemalan oligarchy stands is a matter of debate, but it is clear that El Salvador would fall tomorrow without United States military aid. By surrending seignorial control over its labor force, the Salvadoran elite gained economic power but may have lost its life as a political entity. Finally, in Costa Rica, the coffee elite found to its great amazement that it had been pushed from political power by a revolution that it had originally backed in the hope of protecting its economic and political position. Its impotence in the face of the challenges of the 1948 revolution and the rising Costa Rican middle and working classes may have come as a shock to a class that had been ruling the country without interruption since the rise of the coffee export economy in the mid-nineteenth century. But it is not at all surprising, considering the relatively meager economic and political resources on which its power rested. In Costa Rica, El Salvador, Guatemala, and Nicaragua coffee has shaped history for more than a century. It has also in fundamental ways shaped the political challenges of the present and the political possibilities of the future.

REFERENCES

AGUILERA, G. (1982) "Estado militar y lucha revolucionaria en Guatemala." Polémica 6: 12-25.

———and J. ROMERO (1981) Dialéctica del terror en Guatemala. San José: Editorial Universitaria Centroamericana.

Americas Watch (1983) Creating a Desert and Calling It Peace. New York: Author.

Amnesty International (1981) Guatemala: A Government Program of Political Murder. London: Author.

Anonymous (1982) "La toma de Nebaj." Polémica 3: 36-43.

Asociación Cafetalera de El Salvador (1940) Primer censo nacional del café. San Salvador: Author.

AUBEY, R. T. (1968-1969) "Entrepreneurial formation in El Salvador." Explorations in Entrepreneurial History 6: 268-285.

BALOYRA, E. (1982) El Salvador in Transition. Chapel Hill: University of North Carolina Press.

BAUMEISTER, E. (1982, October) "Notas para la discusión de la cuestión agraria en Nicaragua." Presented at the Third Congress of Nicaraguan Social Sciences, Managua.

BELL, J. P. (1971) Crisis in Costa Rica. Austin: University of Texas Press.

BIECHLER, M. J. (1970) "The coffee industry of Guatemala: a geographic analysis." Ph.D. dissertation, Michigan State University.

BINGHAM, J. (1974) "Guatemalan agriculture during the administration of President Manuel Estrada Cabrera 1898-1920." Master's thesis, Tulane University.

BLACK, G. (1981) Triumph of the People. London: Zed Press.

BRATTON, S. T. (1939) "El Pacayal: a coffee finca in Guatemala." Journal of Geography 38, 2: 45-50.

BROWNING, D. (1971) El Salvador: Landscape and Society. Oxford: Oxford University Press.

CAMBRANES, J. C. (1980) "Sistemas de producción agrícola latifundio-minifundio: el cultivo de café en Guatemala." Mesoamérica 1, 1: 286-295.

———(1982) "Café sangriente." Polémica 3: 18-31.

CARDOSO, C.F.S. (1975) "Historia económica del café en Centroamérica (siglo XIX)." Estudios Sociales Centroamericanos 4, 10: 9-55.

———(1977) "The formation of the coffee estate in nineteenth century Costa Rica," pp. 162-202 in K. Duncan and I. Rutledge (eds.) Land and Labour in Latin America. Cambridge: Cambridge University Press.

CARL, B. V. (1984) "How Marxist is Nicaragua? A look at the laws." Crime and Social Justice 21-22: 116-127.

CASTENEDA, H. (1977) "El café en El Salvador." Unpublished manuscript, Instituto Centroamericano de Administración de Empresas, Managua.

Centro de Investigaciones y Estudios de la Reforma Agraria (n.d.). Las clases sociales en el agro. Managua: Author.

COLINDRES, E. (1976). "La tenencia de la tierra en El Salvador." Estudios Centroamericanos 31, 335/336: 463-472.

———(1977) Fundamentos económicos de la burguesía Salvadoreña. San Salvador: Universidad Centroamericana.

COLLINS, J. C. (1982) What Difference Could a Revolution Make? San Francisco: Institute for Food and Development Policy.

Comité Interamericano de Desarrollo Agrícola (1965) Tenencia de la tierra y desarrollo socio-económico del sector agrícola: Guatemala. Washington, DC: Panamerican Union.

Costa Rica Dirección General de Estadística y Censos (1957) Censo agropecuario, 1955. San José: Author.

——(1965) Censo agropecuraio, 1963. San José: Author.

Costa Rica Instituto de Defensa del Café de Costa Rica (1985) "El instituto levanta el censo cafetalero del país: resumen general de la república." Revista del Instituto de Defensa del Café de Costa Rica 3, 14: 58-74.

DELGADO, S. (1961) "El café en la economía nacional." Revista Conservadora 2, 13: 38-41.

DOMINGUEZ, M. (1970) "The development of the technological and scientific coffee industry in Guatemala 1830-1930." Ph.D. dissertation, Tulane University.

DUNKERLY, J. (1982) The Long War: Dictatorship and Revolution in El Salvador. London: Junction Books.

DUQUE, J. P. (1938) Informe del jéfe de departamento técnico sobre su viaje de estudio a algunos países cafeteros de la Amética Central, Federación Nacional de Cafeteros de Colombia. Managua: Asociación Agrícola de Nicaragua.

El Salvador Dirección General de Estadística y Censos (1961) Compendio del segundo censo nacional del café. San Salvador: Author.

FISCHER, B. S. (1972) The International Coffee Agreement: A Study in Coffee Diplomacy. New York: Praeger.

GARIAZZO, A., E. INCER, D. DYE, and R. SOLEY (1983a) "El subsistema del café en Nicaragua." Presented at the Second Seminar on Central America and the Caribbean, Managua, February 9-12.

——(1983b) "Estrategía de reproducción económico-social de las pequeñas productores cafetaleros: casos de Matagalpa y Carazo." Unpublished manuscript, Instituto de Investigaciones Económicos y Sociales, Managua.

GARLANT, J. (1968) "Developmental aspects of Barrios' agrarian program, Guatemala, 1871-1885." Master's thesis, Tulane University.

GILLY, A. (1980) La nueva Nicaragua: antimperialismo y lucha de clases. Mexico, DF: Editorial Nueva Imagen.

GORMAN, S. M. (1981) "Power and consolidation in the Nicaraguan revolution." Journal of Latin American Studies 13, 1: 133-149.

GRIEB, K. J. (1979) Guatemalan Caudillo: The Regime of Jorge Ubico, Guatemala 1931-1944. Athens: University of Ohio Press.

Guatemala Dirección General de Estadística (1953) Censo cafetalero 1950. Guatemala: Author.

——(1971) Censo agropecuario 1964 (vol. 2). Guatemala: Author.

Guatemala Oficina Central del Café (1946) Informe cafetalero de Guatemala. Guatemala: Author.

HABIB, F. (1958) "The course and problems of an export economy: the case of El Salvador." Ph.D. dissertation, Duke University.

HALL, C. (1978) Formación de una hacienda cafetalera: 1889-1911. San José: Editorial Universidad de Costa Rica.

——(1982) El Café y el desarrollo histórico-geográfico de Costa Rica (3rd ed.). San José: Editorial Costa Rica.

HEARST, H. L. (1929) "The coffee industry of Central America." Master's thesis, University of Chicago.

HILL, J. (1936) "Raising coffee in El Salvador." Tea and Coffee Trade Journal 71, 12: 424.

HOLLOWAY, T. (1974) "Migration and mobility: immigrants and landowners in the coffee zone of São Paulo, Brazil 1886-1934." Ph.D. dissertation, University of Wisconsin.

Instituto Centroamericano de Administración de Empresas (1977) Finca "La Montana." Managua: Author.

————(1981) Finca "Santa Domingo." Managua: Author.

Jamaica Coffee Industry Board (1959) The Report on the Coffee Demonstration Tour of Costa Rica, El Salvador, and Guatemala, Oct.-Nov. 1958: Kingston: Author.

JONAS, S. and D. TOBIS [eds.] (1974) Guatemala. Berkeley, CA: North American Congress on Latin America.

KEITH, L. L. (1974) "Technology versus tradition: the modernization of Nicaraguan agriculture." Ph.D. dissertation, University of Kansas.

KERR, D. N. (1977) "The role of the coffee industry in the history of El Salvador." Master's thesis, University of Calgary.

LOPEZ, J., O. NUNEZ, C. F. CHAMORRO, and P. SERRES (1980) La caída del somocismo y la lucha sandinista en Nicaragua. San José: Editorial Universitaria Centroamericana.

McCREERY, D. J. (1976) "Coffee and class: the structure of development in liberal Guatemala." Hispanic American Historical Review 56, 3: 438-460.

————(1983) "Debt servitude in rural Guatemala: 1876-1936." Hispanic American Historical Review 64, 4: 735-759.

MACLEOD, M. (1973) Spanish Central America: A Socioeconomic History, 1520-1720. Berkeley: University of California Press.

MENJÍVAR, R. (1980) Acumulación originaria y desarrollo del capitalismo en El Salvador. San José: Editorial Universitaria Centroamericana.

MERZ, C. (1937) "Estructura social y económica de la industria del cafe en Costa Rica." Revista del Instituto de Defensa del Café de Costa Rica, 2, 32-33: 288-307.

MILLET, R. (1977) Guardians of the Dynasty. Maryknoll, NY: Orbis.

MONTENEGRO, C. R. (1976) "La explotación cafetalera en Guatemala 1930-1940." Thesis (licenciado), Universidad de San Carlos.

MONTGOMERY, T. S. (1982) Revolution in El Salvador: Origins and Evolution. Boulder, CO: Westview.

MORETSOHN de ANDRADE, F. (1967) "Decadencia do campesinato costarriquenho." Revista Geografica pp. 135-152.

MORRIS, J. A., and S. C. ROPP (1977) "Corporatism and dependent development: a Honduran case study." Latin American Research Review 12, 2: 27-63.

MORRISON, P. C. and T. L. NORRIS (1954) "Coffee production and processing on a large Costa Rican *finca*." Papers of the Michigan Academy of Science, Arts, and Letters 39: 309-322.

MOSK, S. A. (1955) "The coffee industry of Guatemala 1850-1918: development and signs of instability." Interamerican Economic Affairs 9, (Winter): 16-20.

NAÑEZ, G. (1961) "German contributions to the economic development of the Alta Verapaz of Guatemala 1865-1900." Master's thesis, Tulane University.

————(1970) "Erwin Paul Dieseldorf, German entrepreneur in the Alta Verapaz of Guatemala, 1889-1937." Ph.D. dissertation, Tulane University.

Nicaragua Dirección General de Estadística y Censos (1961) El Café en Nicaragua. Managua: Author.

NIEDERLEIN, G. (1898) The State of Nicaragua of the Greater Republic of Central America. Philadelphia: Philadelphia Commercial Museum.

NOLAN, D. (1984) The Ideology of the Sandinistas and the Nicaraguan Revolution. Coral Gables, FL: Institute of Interamerican Studies, University of Miami.

PANSINI, J. (1977) "'El Pilar,' a plantation microcosm of Guatemalan ethnicity." Ph.D. dissertation, University of Rochester.

POSAS, M. (1981) Luchas del movimiento obrero hondureño. San José: Editorial Universitaria Centroamericana.

PLAYTER, H. (1927) Nicaragua: A Commercial and Economic Survey. Washington, DC: Government Printing Office.

RADELL, D. (1964) Coffee and Transportation in Nicaragua. Field Work Report, ONR Contract 3656(03) NR 388 067. Berkeley: Department of Geography, University of California.

República de Nicaragua (1910) Censo cafetalero. Managua: Author.

ROSENBERG, M. (1983) Las luchas por el seguro social en Costa Rica. San José: Editorial Costa Rica.

SCHLESINGER, S. and S. KINZER (1982) Bitter Fruit. Garden City, NY: Doubleday.

SCHMID, L. J. (1967) "The role of migratory labor in the economic development of Guatemala." Ph.D. dissertation, University of Wisconsin.

SEBASTIÁN, L. (1979) "El camino económico hacia la democracia." Estudios Centroamericanos 35, 372/373: 947-960.

SELIGSON, M. (1975) Agrarian Capitalism and the Transformation of Peasant Society: Coffee in Costa Rica. Special Studies Series, No. 69, Council on International Studies, State University of New York at Buffalo.

———(1980) Peasants of Costa Rica and the Development of Agrarian Capitalism. Madison: University of Wisconsin.

SIVETZ, M. and H. E. FOOTE (1963) Coffee Processing Technology (2 vols.). Westport, CT: Avi Publishing.

SLUTZKY, D. and E. ALONSO (1971) Quien es quien en la caficultura nacional. San Salvador: Universidad de El Salvador.

STONE, S. (1982) La Dinastía de los conquistadores. San José: Editorial Universitaria Centroamericana.

TORRES-RIVAS, E. (1971) Interpretación del desarrollo social centroamericano. San José: Editorial Universitaria Centroamericana.

———(1975) "Síntesis histórico del proceso político," pp. 9-18 in E. Torres-Rivas et al. (eds.) Centroamérica Hoy. México, DF: Siglo Veintiuno Editores.

———(1980) "Vida y muerte en Guatemala: reflexiones sobre la crisis y la violencia política." Foro Internacional 20, 4: 549-574.

———(1982) "State making and revolution in Central America." Lecture given at the Center for Research on Social Organization, University of Michigan, November 19.

TRUJILLO, H. (1981) "La formación del estado en El Salvador." Estudios Sociales Centroamericanós 10, 28: 117-131.

United Nations Food and Agriculture Organization (1960) Production Yearbook, (vol. 14). Rome: Author.

———(1981) Production Yearbook (Vol. 34). Rome: Author.

VARGAS LLOSA, M. (1985) "In Nicaragua." New York Times Magazine (April 28): 36.

VEGA, J. L. (1981) La formación del estado nacional en Costa Rica. San José: Instituto Centroamericano de Administración Pública.

———(1982) Poder político y democracia en Costa Rica. San José: Editorial Porvenir.

VILLEGAS, M. (1965) Mi lucha por el Café de Guatemala. Guatemala: Tipografía Nacional.

WELLMAN, F. (1961) Coffee: Botany, Cultivation, and Utilization. London: Leonard Hill Books.

WHEELOCK, J. (1980) Imperialismo y dictadura: crisis de una formación social (5th ed.). México, DF: Siglo Veintiuno Editores.

WICKIZER, V. D. (1943) The World Coffee Economy with Special Reference to Control Schemes. Stanford, CA: Food Research Institute.

WOODWARD, R. L. (1985) Central America: A Nation Divided. Oxford: Oxford University Press.

WORTMAN, M. L. (1982) Government and Society in Central America, 1680-1840. New York: Columbia University Press.

Chapter 8

SANDINISTA RELATIONS WITH THE WEST:
The Limits of Nonalignment

Robert P. Matthews
Center for Latin American Caribbean Studies
New York University

A nation's foreign policy is both a reflection of its domestic ideals and a design for asserting its sovereignty and national interests. Inasmuch as sovereignty is the first requisite of an independent state, Nicaragua was regarded by the Sandinistas in 1979 as a good deal less than a nation. U.S. policy over the past 80 years had repeatedly frustrated Nicaraguan aspirations for self-determination. Thus, at the core of Sandinista ideology are the twin tenets of nationalism and anti-imperialism.

Except for the special case of Puerto Rico, Nicaragua's history is unique in the degree to which the United States has controlled that country's political destiny. Washington's reward for the sponsoring of Somoza and his praetorian National Guard was a loyalty to U.S. regional and global objectives that Somoza used to boast was second to

AUTHOR'S NOTE: This chapter was originally prepared for presentation at the World-Systems Conference, "Crisis in the Caribbean Basin: Past and Present," Tulane University, New Orleans, March 28-30, 1985. Portions of the chapter appeared in "The Limits of Friendship: Nicaragua and the West" in the May/June issue of NACLA's *Report on the Americas (Sandinista Foreign Policy: Strategies for Survival).*

none. This included the strategic use of Nicaraguan territory for CIA-sponsored interventions such as those launched against the Jacobo Arbenz government in Guatemala (1954) and Fidel Castro in the Bay of Pigs invasion (1961). The symbiotic relationship between U.S. administrations and the Somoza dynasty (1936-1979) gave an anti-imperialist cast to the struggle waged in the 1970s by the Sandinista Front for National Liberation (FSLN). The Nicaraguan Revolution, more than any other Latin American antidictatorial struggle, was by definition a movement for independence from the United States. The program of the FSLN aimed less at purely economic independence—U.S. direct investment was relatively low—than at recovering the national sovereignty that had so long been mortgaged to Washington's geopolitical goals.

The Sandinistas chose nonalignment as a logical response to Nicaragua's historic dependency on the United States. The policy reflects positions taken from the inception of the FSLN program in 1969 and in subsequent doctrinal statements. It is based on a strategy of "walking on four legs": developing a broad spectrum of relations with the Third World, Western Europe, the Socialist bloc, and the United States (Gorostiaga, 1984: 226-227). Nonalignment, although entailing an inescapable distancing of Nicaragua from the U.S. orbit, did not imply a Sandinista rejection of "correct" diplomatic and economic relations with Washington. Nor, as we will see, did it suggest severing military ties. Aware that Nicaragua's size, underdevelopment, and proximity to the United States made full independence an impossible short-term goal, the Sandinistas spoke of "diversifying dependency" in both the economic and military spheres. This strategy would accept aid from any quarter, as long as it came with no harmful conditions. Diversification would also lessen Nicaragua's vulnerability to trade and credit restrictions as instruments of foreign pressure. Thus, nonalignment, for the Sandinistas, was not only the international correlative of its domestic program of social transformation and a necessary expression of their desire to free Nicaragua from U.S. hegemony; it was, more pragmatically, a strategy for survival.

However, the FSLN understood all along that of its three fundamental principles—political pluralism, a mixed economy, and international nonalignment—it was only the last that concerned the United States. Throughout the twentieth century Washington had cared little for democracy in Nicaragua; nor had it greatly minded when Somoza squeezed out his own bourgeoisie and captured 40% of the productive sector for himself.

Nicaragua's decision to join the Non-Aligned Movement (NAM) in September 1979 was not in itself judged a threat to U.S. interests. Countries as diverse as Argentina, Peru, and Jamaica are members; Venezuela, Costa Rica, and even El Salvador have observer status. The problem is how Washington perceives a country's interpretation of nonalignment. A radical nationalist regime risks having its foreign policy regarded as a facade for Soviet-bloc alignment (Armstrong, 1985: 15-17). But radical nationalism and nonalignment is one thing in areas of lesser geopolitical significance and quite another in the Central American backyard. Peru, for example, has a greater debt to the Soviet Union for military aid than does Nicaragua; but a State Department official has said, "We accept the Peruvians claim that large-scale Soviet military supplies will not affect their independence. It is essentially the Peruvians' business" (Black and Matthews, 1985: 149).

Moreover, there is a fear that such a development so close to home would serve as a model for replication in neighboring countries and cast doubts on the credibility of U.S. power. In 1979 the quickening crisis in El Salvador heightened Washington's worry over the demonstration effect of the Sandinista revolution. The FSLN also had the misfortune to take power at a critical juncture in U.S. foreign policy, when liberalism was in retreat before the ascendant influence of the Right. In these political circumstances even a Sandinista pledge of neutrality or equidistance from the superpowers constituted an intolerable loss of U.S. influence in a region defined as a critical national security zone.

Despite these difficulties, the Sandinistas have made a genuine effort to maintain a nonaligned foreign policy from 1979 to the present. There is no substantive evidence that they ever desired to replicate the Cuban experience in international affairs, and indeed were counseled otherwise by Fidel Castro. Nor did signals from the Soviet Union encourage Nicaragua to ally itself with the Soviet bloc. After all, Cuba—prosperous by Nicaraguan standards—was costing the Soviets $4 billion annually.

On the other hand, U.S. strategy has rendered Nicaragua's goal of nonalignment ever more uncertain. Washington created conditions designed to drive the Sandinistas toward the Soviet bloc, then justified the policy as a legitimate response by declaring Nicaragua a Soviet beachhead and its nonalignment a canard. The Reagan administration was then able to shift the terms of the debate to an East-West plane where it held considerable leverage. Even a partial acceptance of the White House's Manichean visions of the Nicaraguan question has prejudiced that country's relations with Western Europe and Latin America. As U.S. attitudes hardened, Western support became more problematic even as the need for such backing became more acute. Although the current Republican administration soon settled on a policy of unconditional hostility, the objective conditions for its evolution were established during the final days of the Carter presidency.

SETTING THE MARGINS: U.S. POLICY
AND NICARAGUA'S MILITARY NEEDS

Congress finally approved Carter's $75 million economic aid package to Nicaragua, but only after a full year of political wrangling with conservatives on Capitol Hill. In its final form disbursement of the funds was conditioned on an unprecedented number of stipulations that clearly infringed upon Nicaraguan sovereignty. The Sandinistas were in no position to refuse the aid or negotiate the conditions; however, Washington had sent an unmistakable signal that future U.S. support would be uncertain at best (Jonas, 1982; LeoGrande, 1982).

This vital period in the evolution of Nicaraguan foreign policy was marked by the more crucial discovery that the United States was not going to supply military aid. The FSLN aimed, against all odds, to build a professional army with Cuban mentors and Western military aid. Washington, was approached within a month of the triumph. However, the mood of the increasingly conservative Congress simply would not permit bankrolling the Sandinista army under any circumstances (Washington Post, 1979). As seen in the fight over the economic aid bill, the FSLN's radicalism and historic ties with Cuba were enough to indict them. The issue of Cuban advisers was really secondary. The Cubans' presence effectively foreclosed the possibility of Nicaragua purchasing an adequate supply of arms from the United States or its Western allies.[1]

Over the next five years the nature of Sandinista military relationships would thrust itself to center stage in the conflict with Washington. Following its unsuccessful attempt in 1979 to secure military aid from the United States, Nicaragua spent two years exhausting other avenues of Western arms supplies. After 1981, under well-calibrated U.S.

military pressure, the Sandinistas were to become dependent on the Soviet Union for their military lifeline. Those ties in turn would prejudice Nicaragua's image as a nonaligned nation, serve in the campaign to discredit the revolution as "totalitarian," and determine the categorical limits on Western economic and diplomatic support.

The dead end of U.S. military aid, no matter how historically or structurally inevitable, had far-reaching implications for future Sandinista foreign policy. First, although tiny amounts of nonlethal sales trickled through the pipeline—$105,000 worth from 1979-1983—the Nicaraguans were effectively barred from purchasing arms commercially in the United States. In April 1981, Deputy Defense Minister Edén Pastora complained that Nicaragua had been forced to buy arms from the Mafia in Miami: "I talked to the CIA and they wouldn't help us. Legitimate arms dealers refused to sell us weapons" (Latin American Regional Report, May 1, 1981).

Second, the obverse of the military aid embargo on Nicaragua was a heavy U.S. military investment in the rest of Central America. The Reagan administration has consistently confused cause and effect, depicting this aid as a response to Nicaragua's "Soviet-sponsored build-up." Before late 1981 and the start of U.S. support for the *Contra* war during that year, Soviet-bloc military support for Nicaragua was not substantial. Washington's own estimates of the values of this aid are $5 million for 1979 and $6-7 million for 1980 (Edelman, 1985: 49-50). The U.S. military buildup, though sharply escalated under the Reagan administration, in fact was underway long before that. Its predecessor had set the ball rolling right after the Sandinista triumph.

U.S. military loans and grants to the Central American region soared from $2.7 million in FY 1979 to $130.4 million by FY 1983—the lion's share going to Honduras and El Salvador. Washington's military sales and aid to Central America in 1982 and 1983, in fact, exceeded that of the past three decades combined. Nicaragua's neighbors also began to arm themselves from other sources. In 1979, within months of the Sandinista victory, El Salvador, Honduras, and Guatemala all acquired new higher-performance aircraft. El Salvador received 18 Dassault Super Mystère B-2 fighter-bombers from Israel; Honduras received 9 of the same model. Guatemala bought 10 Brazilian T-23 *Uirapurù* trainers. Nicaragua, on the other hand, has not obtained a single combat aircraft to date (The Defense Monitor: 4-5; Latin American Regional Report, May 3, 1985).

The advent of the Reagan Administration brought a quantum leap in the role of Honduras. The country became not only a base for large-scale *Contra* attacks but also a platform for a series of joint military maneuvers designed to intimidate Nicaragua and rehearse the rapid deployment of U.S. forces in the region. U.S. military aid and ESF (Security Support) funds to Honduras jumped to $8.9 million in 1981, $68.1 million in 1982, and $90.3 million in 1983 (Central American Historical Institute, 1984).

The Carter Administration's ambivalence toward Nicaragua had given way to the incoming Republicans' full-blown hatred of the Sandinistas. Reagan came into office obsessed with Soviet-Cuban penetration of the Caribbean Basin and fearing that "the Nicaraguan base on the American continent will now facilitate a repeat of the new Nicaraguan revolutionary model." The Administration's attitude was laid out clearly in a 1980 report by the Committee of Santa Fe, a group of New Right academics and policy analysts. The report in turn had a major impact on that year's Republican National Convention platform, which read as follows:

> We deplore the Marxist Sandinista takeover of Nicaragua and the Marxist attempts to destabilize El Salvador, Guatemala and Honduras. We do not support U.S. assistance to any Marxist government in the hemisphere and we oppose the Carter Administration aid program for the government of Nicaragua.... We will return to the fundamental principle of treating a friend as a friend and self-proclaimed enemies as enemies, without apology.

Prefiguring the administration's later backing for the *Contras*, the Republicans added, "We will support the efforts of the Nicaraguan people to establish a free and independent government." The new administration delivered its verdict from the start: In a rigidly bipolar world, the Sandinistas were Marxists—enemies—and a danger to U.S. national security. Confrontation, rather than accommodation, was the correct policy. By implication, any Western government that helped the Nicaraguan regime would be the object of attack by Washington. Equally threatening to the United States would be any action by the West that might challenge the Republican thesis about the Sandinistas' true nature by proving that Nicaragua could indeed pursue a non-aligned course outside the Soviet bloc.

Thus, the third implication of the embargo on arms sales to Nicaragua was that Washington's mounting drive to isolate the Sandinistas would extend to pressure on alternative arms suppliers in Latin America and Western Europe. Nicaragua's experience was a striking contrast with that of Guatemala, which after a cutoff of military funds on human rights grounds in 1977 had continued to receive substantial shipments of arms from U.S. allies such as Israel, Belgium, and Brazil.

The point was driven home early. In September 1979 Tomás Borge, Nicaragua's Minister of Interior, declared that "we prefer the U.S. (arms) market, but if it is closed to us then we will have to seek another, possibly the European market." He named Belgium as the first choice (Foreign Broadcast Information Service, 1979). That same month, then Defenses Minister Bernardino Laríos set off on an arms-buying mission to Belgium, West Germany, Spain, Mexico, and Brazil. He returned empty handed (Washington Post, Sept 1, 1979).

TOUCHSTONE OF WESTERN LIMITS:
THE FRENCH CONNECTION

Any prospective arms supplier to Nicaragua would need to offer a number of characteristics: a substantial arms export market; enough political latitude from Washington to cope with U.S. displeasure; and sufficient confidence in its future stability to guarantee continuous supplies of ammunition and spare parts. Even then, Nicaragua's requests for arms were bedevilled by its inability to pay market rates. The largest arms suppliers to the Third World are the "Big Six"—the United States, the Soviet Union, France, Italy, Great Britian, and West Germany—who between them account for 88% of all arms sales to the Third World. Some distance behind are the smaller Western arms exporters: Norway, the Netherlands, Brazil, Israel, Sweden, Belgium, Switzerland, and Spain. Each of the Western members of the Big Six presented problems as a potential supplier for Nicaragua: West Germany had banned arms exports to "areas of tension" in 1977; Britain had elected the arch-conservative Thatcher government in May 1979; and Italy's Christian Democratic administration collapsed in March 1980, the latest in the country's notorious series of revolving-door governments. Only France remained, and its modest effort to test the limits of Washington's tolerance graphically illustrated the structural boundaries to the Sandinistas' effort to diversify their "military dependency."

By 1981 the pressure from Washington for its Western allies to toe the line on Central America was intense. One European diplomat commented that "It is a very, very delicate issue right now," and that governments had to "walk a thin line between their commitment to social justice and their desire for a working relationship with the United States" (New York Times, July 30, 1981). May had seen the election in France of François Mitterrand's Socialist government. Its relations with Nicaragua were cordial from the start. The official FSLN newspaper *Barricada* heralded Mitterrand's win as a major triumph for Nicaragua. In June, Foreign Minister Miguel D'Escoto visited Paris. As the year went on, Nicaragua lavished praise on France. Junta member Sergio Ramírez commented warmly on the growing closeness between the two nations; Daniel Ortega declared in Paris that "the Nicaraguan government has a total convergence with France on the situation in Central America" (Washington Post, July 14, 1982). Much like the government of Felipe González, which took power in Spain the following year, and in line with the position of the Socialist International (SI), Mitterrand aimed to balance a firm commitment to containment of the Soviet Union with a measure of sensitivity to North-South issues. In keeping with France's traditional distance from NATO and its experience with its former African colonies, Mitterand was suspicious of what the French call the "primary anti-communism" of Reagan's Washington. In particular, the French objected to the U.S. emphasis on building a strategic consensus of regimes to combat Soviet expansionism around the globe, and pointed to the Middle East as an example of the limitations of this policy. France believed instead that the East-West conflict must be won in the South, and argued that support for revolutionary forces was necessary to prevent their inexorable gravitation into the Soviet camp.

In late 1981 the Sandinistas' search for arms in the West finally bore fruit. Under a secret deal signed on December 21, 1981, France agreed to sell Nicaragua $15.8 million worth of military equipment, an idea that had arisen during D'Escoto's June visit to Paris. The deal included two Alouette-3 helicopters, two coastal patrol boats, 45 troop transport trucks, 100 helicopter-mounted STRIM 89 rocket launchers and 7000 rocket rounds. The agreement also provided for training 10 Nicaraguan pilots and 10 naval officers. The French stressed the *defensive* character of all this materiel, and the terms of the contract also expressly forbade resale or transshipment to a third party (New York Times, Jan. 9, 1982; Financial Times, March 10 1982).

The sale was in accord with France's belief that such deals would weaken Nicaraguan ties to the Soviet Union to the extent that they reduced the revolution's dependency on military supplies from the Soviet bloc. France made it clear that this had been a *Sandinista* initiative:

> When a country such as Nicaragua applies to France for aid," said one official, "it is often because it is seeking to escape dependency on one of the superpowers. . . . The fact that Nicaragua has shown the desire to ask France for aid is a prime indication that the Managua government has no desire to count entirely on Cuba and the Soviet Union to supply its defense needs" [New York Times, Jan. 9 1982].

The arms agreement, though the largest the Nicaraguans had so far received, should be put into perspective. It was not enough to radically recast the nature of the Sandinista military; but any more would have risked a major showdown with Washington. The dollar sum involved was only tiny in relation to other French arms transactions. France had recently concluded deals for $2.5 billion with Saudi Arabia and $1 billion with Egypt. A $1 billion arms deal with Iraq was in the pipeline. Then again, although France extended credit, the deal was a *sale*; Soviet-bloc military aid to Nicaragua was a donation.

Most disconcerting to the Sandinistas was the pressure exerted on France after the sale, and Mitterrand's reaction to it. Small though the deal was, Washington was outraged. Secretary of State Alexander Haig told French Foreign Minister Claude Cheysson that the deal was "a stab in the back." U.S. officials charged that France was doing the Soviets' job, and argued that the weapons would further "militarize the Nicaraguan regime, helping it export revolution and destabilize the region." Dissatisfaction with French policy in the Third World had been simmering for several months. In December, the outspoken U.S. ambassador to Paris, Evan Galbraith, had protested France's support for guerrillas in El Salvador and its recent decision to normalize relations with Libya. "Believe me," he said, "we are not naive about seeing Cubans everywhere for the fun of it. It is the French who are naive to take their desires for reality" (Financial times, Dec 15, 1981; Latin American Weekly Report, Jan. 15 1982; New York Times, Jan. 30, 1982).

U.S.-French relations over defense policy in Europe and Africa were the closest in 25 years, and Paris could not afford to ignore these stern protests. Many of France's Western allies also criticized the sale. Spain (another of Nicaragua's potential arms suppliers) condemned the French for "meddling in areas where they had no business." Even Mexico was unhappy. One French high-technology firm complained that "its markets in at least three countries had been cut off" as a result of the sale (Financial Times, March 10, 1982).

Mitterrand caved in. In a private meeting with Reagan in March, 1982, the French president informed Reagan that the delivery of the helicopters "would face indefinite delays." As late as September 1983 the Sandinistas were complaining that the rockets and armaments for the patrol boats had still not arrived. French officials conceded privately that they contemplated no new arms sales to Nicaragua (Financial Times, March 31, 1982; Jacobsen, 1984: 19; Washington Post, July 10, 1982).

France, with the world's third largest arms export industry, a popular new left-wing government, and a history of relative independence from Washington, proved unable to fulfill Nicaragua's hopes of Western arms supplies. For the Sandinistas, the lesson was clear. Henceforth, Nicaraguan diplomacy, trade, and aid initiatives would have to factor in the Soviet bloc's exclusive role as supplier of Nicaragua's defense needs—which escalated rapidly as Washington's preference for a .nilitary solution became ever more apparent.

By the beginning of 1982, Nicaragua's international course was set. Its twin priorities of securing continued military aid and economic support both became more critical as the *Contra* war escalated and took its toll on the country's resources. The Sandinistas' foreign policy also looked to build a diplomatic wall in the West that would raise the costs of U.S. aggression. This wall, made up of a network of relationships with Western governments, social democratic parties, and transnational bodies like the SI and the European Economic Community (EEC), admittedly had more than a few loose bricks. Yet many Sandinistas believe it has been a crucial deterrent to military intervention. As one senior Nicaraguan official told me, "The United States has not invaded Nicaragua, but not because it has not wanted to. It is because it has not been politically expedient" (Interview, Alejandro Beñdaña, Nicaraguan Vice-Minister of Foreign Affairs, February 19, 1985, Managua).

LATIN AMERICAN RELATIONS

From the beginning, the Sandinistas' program for spreading the risk has aimed at building a broad network of alliances in Latin America. They have probed the limits of this diplomatic space, especially around three key junctures: the Latin American-U.S. conflict produced by the Falklands/Malvinas War (Spring 1982); the Contadora peace process (January 1983 to present); and the redemocratization of the Southern Cone (1983 on). But support from Latin America has been hampered by the region's continuing debt crisis, its vulnerability to U.S. financial pressure, and the conservative tide that swept Central America and the Caribbean after 1979.

The governments of Michael Manley in Jamaica (1972-1980) and Carlos Andrés Pérez in Venezuela (1974-1979), which had been prominent supporters of the Sandinista struggle against Somoza, were replaced by administrations antagonistic to Nicaragua. After the death in 1981 of General Omar Torrijos, who personified Panamanian support for the Sandinistas, a conservative government there soon distanced itself from Managua. Relations with Costa Rica deteriorated, a circumstance encouraged by the United States, but largely due to historic antipathies. During the insurgency, these had been directed against Costa Rica's long-standing enemy, the Somoza dynasty; now they resurfaced as beligerence toward the Sandinistas, whose ideology at any rate was abhorrent to the Costa Rican bourgeoisie. And, of course, relations with Honduras—owing to that country's complicity in the subversion of the Sandinista government—have been at an all-time low. After Nicaragua's surprise signing of the draft Contadora treaty in September 1984, the United States has used the carefully engineered hostility of these last two countries to sabotage acceptance of the document.

Only Mexico, with its tradition of international independence, has proved a reliable backer. After Venezuela halted oil shipments to Nicaragua in 1982, Mexico filled the gap. From 1979-1984 Mexico provided Nicaragua with over $500 million in loans and credits, more than any other single nation (see Table 8.1). However, Mexican oil shipments have been intermittently suspended since 1983, ostensibly because of the Sandinistas' inability to keep up payments.

Oil-rich Mexico and Venezuela are the most powerful of the four countries involved in the Contadora peace initiative. But together, they

TABLE 8.1
Nicaragua: Loans and Lines of Credit Contracted,
July 1979-June 1984 (millions of dollars)

		Amount	*Percentage*
I.	Multilateral Organizations	$ 632.2	25.3
	CABEI (Central American Bank for Economic Integration)	125.9	
	World Bank	106.1	
	IDB (Interamerican Development Bank)	256.7	
	Others	143.5	
II.	Official Bilateral Loans and Lines of Credit	1,844.7	73.7
	North America:	83.0	3.3
	U.S.A.	72.6	
	Canada	10.4	
	Western Europe:	258.3	10.3
	West Germany	25.8	
	Holland	57.9	
	Italy	5.4	
	France	64.4	
	Finland	5.7	
	Spain	81.9	
	Austria	12.4	
	Sweden	4.8	
	Latin America:	758.0	30.3
	Mexico	519.0	
	Venezuela	64.2	
	Brazil	50.5	
	Argentina	47.8	
	Peru	10.0	
	Colombia	4.5	
	Costa Rica	37.0	
	Honduras	25.0	
	Socialist Countries:	605.6	24.2
	U.S.S.R.	262.2	
	German Democratic Republic	140.0	
	Yugoslavia	25.0	
	Bulgaria	60.0	
	Czechoslovakia	30.0	
	Hungary	5.0	
	Cuba	53.4	
	Korea	30.0	
	Africa and Asia:	139.8	5.6
	Libya	100.0	
	Taiwan	6.0	

(continued)

TABLE 8.1 Continued

	China	7.0	
	Iran	26.8	
III.	Suppliers Credit	24.6	1.0
	Italy	24.6	
	Grand Total	$2,501.5	100.0

SOURCE: Ministry of Foreign Cooperation, Managua. Cited in Berríos and Edelman (1986).

owe more than $100 billion to foreign creditors and are vulnerable to U.S. pressure. The other two members, Colombia and Panama, are limited in making their weight felt in Washington. In mid-1985, Argentina, Brazil, Peru, and Uruguay joined to form the "Lima Group" to provide added support for the Contadora process. However, the economic problems and political fragility of the recently elected governments in these countries will likely limit the group's assertiveness in the region. Costa Rica, Honduras, and El Salvador must agree to any negotiated settlement of the Central American conflict. Their foreign policies, however, are captive to U.S. designs in the Caribbean Basin. Thus, Washington's ability to sabotage Contadora diplomacy by manipulating these clients, remains very great. Inasmuch as every Contadora proposal has called for demilitarizing the region and has ultimately favored the survival of the Sandinistas, it is likely that any agreement acceptable to Nicaragua would continue to be blocked by the United States.

RELATIONS WITH WESTERN EUROPE AND THE MULTILATERALS

Western European backing has generally been a more positive and consistent part of the equation.[2] Social Democratic governments offer Nicaragua certain built-in advantages. First, they back the Sandinistas' stated goals of political pluralism and social justice, and subscribe as a matter of principle to the notion of self-determination. Second, even governments that see containment of the Soviet Union as the core of their foreign policy are worried that an escalating U.S.-Nicaraguan confrontation will divert Washington's attention from its NATO obligations. Third, many Europeans see support for the *Contras* and the violation of international statutes as weakening the United States' political prestige, thereby harming its ability to defend Europe. Last, governments that rely on good relations with Washington fear mass domestic unrest over Central America and the nuclear arms issue.

The Sandinistas have tried to capitalize on those sentiments in their effort to balance Soviet-bloc military and economic aid with diplomatic and financial support from Western Europe. Nicaragua saw trade and aid programs as its best means of cementing ties to Europe; they would also help to "diversify dependency" and compensate for what the Sandinistas initially felt was inadequate economic aid from socialist countries. As late as March 1985, Castro reportedly criticized Moscow for its meager support to Nicaragua (Washington Post, March 24, 1985).

From 1980-1984, 27.3% of Nicaraguan exports have gone to Western Europe; only 6.6% to the socialist countries. Western Europe has supplied 12.9% of Nicaragua's imports, the Socialist countries 11.2%. The bulk of aid has also come from the West. Latin America provided $758 million (30.3%), multilaterial institutions $632.2 million (25.3%), and Western Europe $258.3 million (11.3%) of loans and credit lines to Nicaragua from July 1979 to June 1984. The Socialist countries made available $605.6 million, or 24.2% of the total (see Table 8.2). In the face of U.S. efforts to discredit Nicaragua's nonaligned stance, the Sandinistas have shown considerable skill in their East-West balancing act. Yet there are severe constraints on the amount of economic and diplomatic support they can expect from the West. For one thing, Washington's ability to apply diplomatic and financial pressure on its allies is more than enough to neutralize any *political* clout they can bring to bear on the White House or Congress. Also, Europeans recognize that their hands are more than usually tied in the Caribbean Basin, an undisputed sphere of U.S. influence. France's chastening experience over Nicaragua has been instructive.

For Latin Americans, the need to maintain good relations with their powerful northern neighbor is especially strong. The debt-ridden countries of Mexico, Venezuela, and Argentina all have differences with the Reagan administration's Central American policy. But financial crisis and stagnating economies have considerably narrowed the latitude to assert their positions. Economic factors play a less visible, but far from unimportant role in Europe. As one scholar wrote at the beginning of Mitterrand's term: "Ultimately, not only the success or failure but the very nature of French foreign policy will be determined by the outcome of Prime Minister Pierre Maurroy's economic program"

TABLE 8.2
Nicaragua: Foreign Trade, 1980-1984 (millions of dollars)

	1980		1981		1982		1983		1984	
Exports										
U.S.A.	162.1	(36%)	134.7	(27%)	90.0	(22%)	74.9	(17%)	45.3	(12%)
CMEA countries*	12.2	(3%)	31.8	(6%)	20.5	(5%)	54.8	(13%)	22.8	(6%)
Central America	75.2	(17%)	70.7	(14%)	52.2	(13%)	33.5	(8%)	32.9	(9%)
Other Latin America**	0.5	(0%)	22.1	(4%)	25.0	(6%)	15.9	(4%)	6.7	(2%)
Western Europe	147.7	(33%)	98.6	(19%)	95.1	(23%)	111.4	(26%)	138.8	(37%)
Japan	12.6	(3%)	57.0	(11%)	45.0	(11%)	65.8	(15%)	93.5	(25%)
Other	40.1	(9%)	93.3	(18%)	77.7	(19%)	72.5	(17%)	34.0	(9%)
Total	450.4	(100%)	508.2	(100%)	405.5	(100%)	428.8	(100%)	374.0	(100%)
Imports										
U.S.A.	244.0	(28%)	262.9	(26%)	147.4	(19%)	156.7	(19%)	158.8	(20%)
CMEA countries*	1.8	(0%)	43.7	(4%)	87.4	(11%)	133.6	(17%)	209.0	(26%)
Central America	300.7	(34%)	210.5	(21%)	116.9	(15%)	123.6	(15%)	88.5	(11%)
Other Latin America**	179.2	(20%)	304.3	(30%)	244.1	(31%)	241.1	(30%)	111.4	(14%)
Western Europe	87.8	(10%)	103.0	(10%)	109.1	(14%)	78.4	(10%)	169.4	(21%)
Japan	28.4	(3%)	28.3	(3%)	18.5	(2%)	19.2	(2%)	26.0	(3%)
Other	45.3	(5%)	46.7	(5%)	52.2	(7%)	54.3	(7%)	26.9	(3%)
Total	887.2	(100%)	999.4	(100%)	775.6	(100%)	806.9	(100%)	790.0	(100%)
Trade Balance	−436.8		−491.2		−370.1		−378.1		−416.0	

SOURCE: Nicaraguan Central Bank, Managua. Cited in Edelman (1985: 49).
*Includes Cuba; **does not include Cuba.

(Moïsi, 1981-1982: 356). It has proven easier for the French to make a ringing defense of Nicaragua's right to self-determination when it had little to ask from North American bankers. Today, France's deficits, its economic woes, and the defensive political posture of the Socialists have compelled modesty in its Central American affairs.

Bully tactics are used to influence decisions in Western muiltilateral institutions as well. Over the last four years, the United States has coerced European and Latin American representatives to the International Monetary Fund (IMF), the World Bank, and the Inter-American Development Bank (IDB) into denying loans to Nicaragua. The Sandinistas have not received a cent from the IDB since 1982 because of their "macroeconomic policies." The repressive dictatorship of Augusto Pinochet in Chile, on the other hand, has been awared over a billion dollars in IDB credit since 1980. The bank's U.S. executive director, José Manuel Casanova, is a Cuban expatriot who professes a fierce anti-communism and "intrudes into bank affairs to an extent unknown in the past and decidedly unwelcome in the present." As one senior bank official told me, "I have never seen such political pressure on the bank as in the last four years" (Interview, Senior Official of Inter-American Development Bank, March 1, 1985, Miami; see also Gardenschwartz, 1985; Washington Report on the Hemisphere, March 19, 1985.)

Nicaragua's request for a $58 million loan to develop private-sector agriculture has been stalled for three years. Secretary of State George Schultz recently spearheaded another successful effort to derail it. A January letter from Schultz to IDB president Antonio Ortiz Mena asserted that "fungible" bank funds might "free up other monies that could be used to consolidate the Marxist regime and finance Nicaragua's aggression against its neighbors." Casanova had let it be known that if the loan came up for a vote, he would walk out of the Executive Board meeting, deying the meeting a quorum, and paralyzing bank operations (Bird and Holland, 1985; Center for International Policy 1985; Washington Post, March 19, 1985). Schultz's letter hinted ominously of a cut-off of U.S. funds to the IDB:

> We are all too well aware of the increasing difficulties involved in gaining Congressional appropriations for the international financial institutions, such as the Inter-American Development Bank. There is little doubt that Executive Board approval of the proposed credit loan for Nicaragua would make our efforts even more difficult [Schultz, 1985].

The EEC has been a victim of similar arm twisting. At the September 1984 meeting of EEC foreign ministers in San José, Costa Rica, Claude Cheysson made public a letter from Schultz to each of the delegates, urging that European assistance to Central America "not lead to increased economic aid or any political support for Nicaragua." The United States, with less power over this body than it has over the U.S.-dominated financial institutions, lost this fight. The incensed French foreign minister responded tartly: "Where does Mr. Reagan come in here? As far as I know, he is not a member of the European Economic Commission, unless it happened in the last few minutes" (Los Angeles Times, Sept. 30 1984).

In the second place, foreign policy agendas of Western nations may relegate Central America to a low priority, or may conflict with the FSLN's diverse diplomatic goals, especially its ties to Third World nations and movements. This is especially true with regard to Europe. Nicaragua's relations with the PLO and Libya, which has supplied the Sandinistas with $100 million in credits, (see Table 8.1) as well as arms and petroleum, have clashed with the Mitterrand government's agenda in Lebanon and in Chad, where Libya is challenging French control. The widespread belief in Spain that the Sandinistas have links to the Basque separatist group ETA, though not shared by Prime Minister González, has not helped the Nicaraguan case.

Most important, relations with Western democracies face the inherent dilemma of continuity. There are a few exceptions. Among the Scandinavian countries Sweden has provided the most prominent and consistent support for the Nicaraguan revolution. Despite conservative turnovers, elevation of Nicaragua (alone among Latin American nations) to "program status" has assured an unbroken flow of economic aid. Swedish government loans and donations have in fact increased every year to its present level of $12 million annually. The Swedes also distinguished themselves among the Europeans in their degree of support for the Nicaraguan electoral process in November 1984. Although the Dutch have maintained a lower political profile on Nicaragua, they consistently have been generous with low-interest credit lines. By mid-1984 Holland had granted Nicaragua some $58 million in loans, nearly as much as France and on better terms. Spain has provided $82 million more in trade credits than any other European nation, but at the highest interest rates. The Dutch and the Belgians are second only to West Germany in the category of nongovernmental—mainly private voluntary organizations—donations to Nicaragua. (Interview, Cesar Vega, director of the Cesar Augusto Sandino Foundation, February 22, 1985, Managua; also see Table 8.3).

Nevertheless, ties to other European governments are plagued by inconsistency. A friendly government may be voted out of office and a valuable aid package scrapped, as happened when West Germany's Social Democrats lost to Helmut Kohl's Christian Democrats in 1982.

The conservative Kohl government soon began to distance itself from the pro-Sandinista policies of its predecessor. Its anti-communism and alignment with the United States colored its perception of Soviet-bloc links to the Nicaraguan government. By 1983, government-to-government aid was virtually frozen. Although the West Germans allude to suppression of civil liberties, including press censorship, as prime factors in their disillusionment, they also admit that "their distaste for the Sandinistas" is a result of pressures from the United States. One official stated flatly: "We rely on the Americans for our defense and we are part of the Western alliance (Grabendorff, 1984: 285; New York Times, November 16, 1983).

Although Social Democratic politics and the Green-inspired popular opposition enter into the calculus of Kohl's foreign policy, many believe that Central America is simply not that important to the West Germans given more pressing needs for U.S. cooperation. As a U.S. official put it: "The Germans seem to be saying that they might as well go along with us on this one [Central America]—that it doesn't matter to them in order to get aboard later on something that is important." Echoing Washington's line, Bonn declared in 1984 that as long as Nicaragua continues its acts of destablization (defined as the "export of ideology" and the shipping of arms to El Salvador) West Germany will not extend aid to Nicaragua. The U.S. success in installing Duarte and the Christian Democrats in El Salvador was key in ensuring the continued convergence of the Reagan and Kohl lines on Nicaragua (Washington Post, Oct. 25, 1983; Washington Report on the Hemisphere, May 15, 1984).

Political shifts can also occur during the tenure of a friendly government. As we have seen, the Socialist government of France, beset by economic problems and in ideological disarray, has pulled back from its earlier commitment to Nicaragua. By 1983, Mitterrand's senior adviser on Latin America, Régis Debray, declared that he was "extremely disappointed with Nicaragua." A 1984 report stated that French interest and influence in Central America have "virtually disappeared" and according to Debray, French sympathy for anti-

TABLE 8.3

Nicaragua: Bilateral Loan and Lines of Credit with Terms,
July 1979-June 1984 (millions of dollars)

Country	Amount	Grace Period (years)	Payment Period (years)	Annual Interest (percentage)
U.S.A.	72.6	n.g.	n.g.	n.g.
Canada	10.4	n.g.	n.g.	n.g.
West Germany[+]	25.8	10	30	2-2.5
Holland	57.9	4-8	23-30	2.5*
Italy	5.4	2	12	4
France	64.4	7.5-10.5	10-30	3-10.6
Finland	5.7	7.5	25.5	.75
Spain	81.9		1-7	8.25-10
Austria	12.4	10	30	1
Sweden	4.8		7	1.25
Mexico	519.0	n.a.	1-8**	6-6.5
Venezuela	64.2	5	20	2
Brazil	50.2		2-10	6.5-8
Argentina	47.8		3-10	7.5-13.5
Peru	10.0		2-5	7
Colombia	4.5		5	LIBOR***
Costa Rica	37.0		2	LIBOR***
Honduras	25.0		3	6
U.S.S.R.	262.2	1-3	5-10	3-5
East Germany	140.0	0-2	2-10[++]	4.5-6
Yugoslavia	25.0	1-2	5-10	6.5-7
Bulgaria	60.0	1-2	2-10[+++]	3.5-7
Czechoslovakia	30.0	2-3	10-12	2.5-4
Hungary	5.0	1.5	6	7.25
Cuba	53.4	3	12	6[++++]
North Korea	30.0		3	5
Libya	100.0		5	6.3
Taiwan	6.0	2-2.25	10	7-7.5

SOURCE: Nicaraguan Ministry of Foreign Cooperation, Managua.
NOTE: n.g. = not given; n.a. = not available.
*$3 million financed for 8.5 years at 10.3%; **lines of credit only; ***London Inter-Bank rate (market rate); [+]no credits extended since 1980; [++]$28 million financed over 2 years, remainder over 10 years; [+++]$35 million financed at lowest rate over 10 years; [++++]terms listed are for a $49.9 million credit; $3.5 million financed at 7.5% over 7 years.

imperialist enterprises had been subordinated to "socialist realpolitik" (New York Times, November 16, 1983; December 25, 1984).

Sandinista nonalignment is reflected in the FSLN's relations with a variety of parties and supranational political organizations. Although it signed a party-to-party agreement with the Communist Party of the Soviet Union (CPSU) in 1980, it has also joined the Permanent Conference of Latin American Political Parties (COPPAL), founded in 1979 by the Mexican PRI and consisting of 23 centrist and leftist parties from Latin America. The FSLN's Tomás Borge serves as vice-president of the organization. The Sandinistas have also devoted considerable effort to cultivating good relations with the Socialist International, that loose-knit and heterogeneous grouping of European and Latin American social democratic parties.

There are political and ideological constraints on these party relationships. The Socialist International is a case in point. Its ongoing ambivalence toward the Sandinistas has prevented its reaching a clear consensus position toward Nicaragua. In the first place, given the broad ideological mix of the SI, it is not surprising that the Sandinistas would encounter difficulties. Moreover, Nicaragua's relationship with the Cuban and Soviet regimes did not sit well with the moderate and conservative parties in Europe and Latin America, who still subscribed to the anti-Communist principles of the 1951 Frankfurt declaration.

But second, and more to the point, SI-Nicaraguan relations are prey to the same forces that make diplomatic relations with Western European governments so problematic. When social democratic parties are not in power, their progressive wings tend to set their foreign policy agendas—particularly relating to the Third World. However, once in power, party leaders become heads of state sensitive to the kinds of internal and external influences described previously, and increasingly receptive to conservative views. The Sandinistas have expended great energy nurturing party-to-party relations, with mixed results.

For instance, there was great hope that with the election of Felipe González, a Spanish Socialist Prime Minister, in late 1982 Nicaragua's cause would be advanced before the European community. But even during the campaign critics noted a perceptible shift in González's support, having "softened his tone toward Washington" and concentrated on "cultivating an august international image rather than showing solidarity." Although González is clearly unhappy with Reagan's behavior toward Nicaragua, he has also been publicly critical of the Sandinistas. We have already seen how France's Socialists have modified their policy over the last three years. This attitude has also been reflected in the SI. In December 1984 the French representative was the only one not to sign the SI document validating the electoral process in Nicaragua (Interview, Vegard Bye, Norwegian journalist with

Arbeiderbladet, February 21, 1985, Managua). At the moment the SI's Committee for the Defense of the Nicaraguan Revolution is virtually defunct; nevertheless, the Sandinistas continue to attach great importance to the SI as a keystone of their "diplomatic wall."

In contrast to this tenuous solidarity shown by Western governments and parties, Nicaragua's Socialist-bloc friends have been more predictably consistent and dependable in their support—politically, and militarily. In this context Daniel Ortega's controversial trip to Moscow in May 1985 made more sense. Nicaragua's economy was in desperate shape; there was a critical shortage of petroleum and the U.S. trade embargo, imposed as Ortega left for Europe, was only the latest act in four years of unilateral trade reduction and economic sabotage by the Reagan Administration.

As a result of the visit the Soviets agreed to provide Nicaragua with some $200 million in economic aid, including 90% of its urgent oil requirements. The Western Europeans, on the other hand, although not supporting the trade embargo, have been unwilling to offer much in the way of economic compensation. After meeting with Ortega on the Western leg of his trip, Mitterrand said France was willing to broaden commercial relations with Nicaragua, but stopped short of committing any additional political or economic support. Ortega also met with Prime Minister González in Madrid. The Spanish Socialist leader's remarks are eloquent testimony to Western Europe's ambivalence toward the Nicaraguan revolution and to the dilemma posed by depending on the West to bolster Nicaragua's strategy of nonalignment. Although opposing the embargo, González privately criticized the trip to Moscow. He flatly declared that "Spain would not increase aid to make up for the losses to the Nicaraguan economy or sell arms to Nicaragua," and added, "What we are not going to be is hostile toward either Nicaragua or the United States. Our policies will not change" (New York Times, May 9, 12, 14, 1985).

CONCLUSION

Sandinista relations with the West have been conditioned by a global dynamic created and maintained by the United States. Powering this dynamic is the Reagan administration's belief that the very existence of Sandinismo is a threat to U.S. national security. Ronald Reagan's commitment to "change the present structure of the Nicaraguan government," publicly declared in early 1985, was in fact an article of faith of his Central American policy from the start. If nonalignment is, among other things, an immediate survival strategy for the Nicaraguan Revolution, then the United States had to undermine the ability of the Sandinistas to cleave to a nonaligned policy and delegitimize them in the eyes of the West. The Reagan administration has thus worked overtime to engineer the self-fulfilling prophecy of an inexorable drift into the Soviet orbit and isolate Nicaragua regionally and in the Western world.

This goal has been pursued with a three-pronged strategy of military, economic, and diplomatic pressures. Like a Chinese finger trap, U.S. policy is self-reinforcing, designed to tighten the bind the more Nicaragua tries to free itself. First, Washington has menaced the Sandinistas by conducting joint maneuvers with the Honduran army near the Nicaraguan border; the main purpose, however, is to prepare Honduras as a base for rapid deployment of U.S. troops against Nicaragua. Also, the administration has orchestrated support from Congress and a variety of private and international sources for CIA-backed counterrevolutionary forces. These *Contras*, acting as U.S. proxies and operating mainly from Honduras, have struck economic targets inside Nicaragua and committed well-documented atrocities against civilians in an attempt to deplete the resources of the country and demoralize the population. The strategy forces the Sandinista government to augment its military capacity in response to this threat by securing increasing military aid from the Socialist bloc—the only nations willing and able to provide such assistance. This in turn buttresses Washington's argument that Nicaragua is not truly non-aligned but is in fact a Soviet client, justifying ratcheting up the tension another notch.

Second, the current U.S. administration has waged an economic war against Nicaragua, suspending U.S. economic aid in 1981 and curtailing and finally embargoing U.S.-Nicaraguan trade in April 1985. The policy also includes diplomatic pressure on Western allies to reduce their aid and forcing U.S.-dominated multilateral lending institutions like the IMF, the World Bank, and the IDB to suspend credits to Nicaragua. As these measures, together with the economic destruction of the *Contra* war, inevitably compel Nicaragua to seek more economic aid from the Socialist bloc, they again strengthen Washington's efforts to discredit the Sandinistas' commitment to nonalignment. At the very least this policy has narrowed Managua's diplomatic space in the West. At most, it will produce economic chaos and political instability, causing the regime to collapse from within; failing that, it may ultimately set the stage for an invasion to counter a "Soviet threat in the hemisphere."

In the face of these contradictions imposed on their foreign policy, the Sandinistas have tenaciously sought to remain nonaligned. They have attempted to diversify economic and military dependency, both to encourage development and to defend national sovereignty. Although the overall statistics on trade and economic aid for the period July 1979-July 1984 are balanced, Nicaragua has been forced to rely increasingly on Soviet-bloc economic support. After 1982 it became empirically obvious that only the Soviet bloc could meet Nicaragua's military needs. However, as a matter of principle and practicality the Sandinistas would prefer to limit their dependency on the Soviet Union and its allies. They have no illusions about the willingness of the Soviet Union to underwrite the Nicaraguan Revolution as it has Fidel Castro's Cuba.

However, the West has not been the most useful or consistent ally the Sandinistas could have hoped for. Aid flows and diplomatic support from Western Europe, although important, have not matched the priority and intense effort Nicaragua has given to European relations. The vagaries of the French connection underscore both the possibilities and the limits of playing the European card. Mexican largess in the form of petroleum credits has been made more problematic in the wake of the devastation of the October 1985 earthquake. In general, Latin America's economic and financial woes will continue to inhibit its role in mediating the Central American conflict or influencing the discussion inside the United States.

Washington's confrontational stance is part of a high-risk game with global dimensions. Virtually all of the international actors involved agree that the United States will ultimately determine the outcome. Hence, Nicaragua has insisted on a return to the bilateral negotiations abandoned by Washington in January 1985. However, it is no longer reasonable to expect that the FSLN can directly influence the Reagan administration to modify its stance. It is more likely that Congress and the U.S. media may play a decisive role in determining Nicaragua's fate. Here, the attitude of Washington's Western allies could become an important factor in the public debate. Ultimately, the dilemma for Europe and Latin America is how to influence a U.S. administration as ideologically fixated as that of Ronald Reagan. To date, Washington has closed its ears to efforts by its allies to provide an alternative analysis of Nicaragua and it has actively subverted any initiative that might offer Nicaragua options in the West.

What can be achieved by Western opponents of Administration policy? As long as Washington remains able to continue a low-intensity war, designed to bleed Nicaragua slowly to death on the back pages of the world's newspapers, protests from Western Europe or the Latin American democracies will not deflect the Reagan Administration from its goal of removing the Sandinistas. Only if that option is removed, and Washington is confronted with a choice between negotiated coexistence or a direct invasion by U.S. troops, may Europe and Latin America find the space and the voice to influence the course of events more decisively.

The questions remain: Can the Sandinistas thwart Washington's strategy and remain nonaligned in the face of a major U.S. effort to foreclose Nicaragua's options in the West? Can Nicaragua rely on Soviet-bloc military aid to confront the war on its borders without risking a critical erosion of political and material support from Western nations—or worse, a U.S. invasion? How the Sandinistas manage these challenges in the current conjuncture of escalating U.S. beligerence presents Nicaraguan foreign policy with its most severe test yet.

NOTES

1. For a more detailed discussion of both the pressing need for the Sandinistas to create a security and defense establishment and their failure to secure U.S. and Western military aid in this period, see Matthews (1985: 24-27).
2. Wolf Grabendorff offers an interpretation of Western Europe interest in Central America that stresses its basic liberal attitudes, differences with the Reagan administration, and role in mediating the conflict (see, for example, Grabendorff, 1984, 1985). Michel Tatu, on the other hand, takes a less sanguine view, describing European convergences with Washington and the limits of European influence in the region (Tatu, 1985).

REFERENCES

ARMSTRONG, R. (1985) "Nicaragua: sovereignty and non-alignment." NACLA Report on the Americas (May-June): 15-21.
BERRIOS, R. and M. EDELMAN (1986) "Diversifying dependence: Nicaragua's new economic links with the Socialist Countries." Journal of Communist Studies II, 1.
BIRD, K. and M. HOLLAND (1985) "Nicaragua: no friend at the IDB." The Nation (March 2): 231.
BLACK, G. and R. MATTHEWS (1985) "Sandinistas' no-win choice: arms from the U.S.S.R. or from nobody." The Nation (August 31): 129, 148-149.
Center for International Policy (1985) Aid Memo. Washington, D.C. Author.
Central American Historical Institute (1984) U.S.-Honduran Relations: A Background Briefing. Washington, DC: Author.

Robert P. Matthews   215

Defense Monitor (1984) Center for Defense Information, Washington, DC.

EDELMAN, M. (1985) "Lifelines: Nicaragua and the Socialist countries." NACLA Report on the Americas (May/June): 33-53.

GARDENSCHWARTZ, M. (1985) "Has politics spoiled the IDB?" Institutional Investor (March): 97-100.

GOROSTIAGA, X. (1984) "Los dilemas de la revolución sandinista a los tres años del triunfo popular," pp. 213-239 in O. Pellicer and R. Fagen (eds.) Centroamérica: Futuro y opciones. Mexico: Fondo de Cultura Económica.

GRABENDORFF, W. (1984) "The role of Western Europe in the Caribbean Basin," pp. 277-293 in A. Adean and R. Reading (eds.) Confrontation in the Caribbean Basin. Pittsburgh, PA: University of Pittsburgh Press.

———(1985) "The Central American crisis: is there a role for Western Europe?" pp. 125-139 in J. Cirincione (ed.) Central America and the Western Alliance New York: Holmes and Meier.

JACOBSEN, C. (1984, June) "The Jacobsen report: Soviet attitudes toward aid to and contacts with Central American revolutions." Prepared for the Department of State, External Research Programs, Washington, DC.

JONAS, S. (1982) "The Nicaraguan Revolution and the emerging cold war," pp. 375-389 in T. Walker (ed.) Nicaragua in Revolution. New York: Praeger.

LeoGRANDE, W. (1982) "The United States and the Nicaraguan Revolution," pp. 63-77 in T. Walker (ed.) Nicaragua in Revolution. New York: Praeger.

MATTHEWS, R. (1985). "The limits of friendship: Nicaragua and the West." NACLA Report on the Americas (May/June): 22-23.

MOISI, D. (1981-1982) "Mitterrand foreign policy: the limits of continuity." Foreign Affairs (Winter): 347-357.

SCHULTZ, G. (1985) Letters from the Secretary of State to IDB President Antonio Ortiz Mena, January 30.

TATU, M. (1985) "Europe, the United States and Central America: a nest of misunderstandings," pp. 113-123 in J. Cirincione (ed.) Central America and the Western Alliance. New York: Holmes and Meier.

Chapter 9

RESTRATIFICATION AFTER REVOLUTION:
The Cuban Experience

Susan Eckstein
Boston University

The benefits of post-World War II economic growth have been shared unequally by rich and poor in Latin America. The urban and rural masses have been especially hard hit by the 1980 world recession. Latin American governments, partly under pressure from international lending institutions, have introduced austerity programs that have reduced subsidies to low-income groups and kept wages from rising commensurate with inflation. Cutbacks in government spending, plus a contraction in private investment, have contributed, in turn, to increased unemployment and underemployment.

To what extent has the Cuban Revolution enabled the island to escape the social and economic problems that plague the other countries in the region? It will be shown that the Cuban state has intervened on behalf of the groups that in market economies benefit least. However, the extent and nature of its intervention on behalf of low-income and economically marginal groups have varied over the years with its accumulation strategy and the success of the strategy. Over the years, revolutionary leadership has relied on different mixes of state/market and domestic/foreign sources of accumulation, each of which has had a somewhat distinctive effect on labor force experiences. Initially it permitted the continuation of some prerevolutionary market sources of accumulation while emphasizing "inwardly oriented" public sector-based growth (1959-1962), then an export-based growth strategy involving the complete suppression of domestic market features (1963-1970), and then the progressive reintroduction of market features and a combined emphasis on internally and externally rooted accumulation. The government shifted its accumulation strategy as economic and political problems arose.

The strategies and their effects on the island's economic performance are described in detail elsewhere (Eckstein, 1985, 1986) but their impact on property relations and labor force experiences are delineated in this chapter. In particular, their impact on property ownership, sectoral employment opportunities, and occupational and gender stratification will be traced. It will be shown that property relations and labor force experiences have varied with different accumulation strategies, based on distinctive mixes of state and market features, and the success of the strategies. Low-income groups *gained* most, *relative* to top income groups, when the state sector first impinged on the market. Property, wage, and occupational differences—as summarized below—were minimized when revolutionary leadership relied least on domestic and most on external market accumulation, because the strategy failed to generate necessary and anticipated revenue, and consumption options deteriorated. When the market and state-based growth features were combined, occupational, income, and consumption differentiation increased; nonetheless, all groups gained under the combined state/market strategy, at least as long as external market conditions contributed to a particularly robust economy.

| | | Growth | |
		High	Low
Domestic Market Emphasis	+	High inequality, extensive opportunity	Declining but remaining inequality, expanding opportunity
External Market Emphasis	−	−	Low inequality, limited opportunity

The various state/market and, in turn, property and labor force policies will be shown to be legitimated by different Marxist principles. Because the Communist Party and government control the ideological apparatus—through the media and organizations—the revolutionary leadership has been able to justify policy shifts in ways that have obscured underlying interests.

STATE-CLASS TRANSFORMATION

When Castro assumed power in 1959, global and domestic market dynamics largely shaped property relations and labor force opportunities. Foreign capital played a key role in agriculture and increasingly in industry. Employment opportunities varied both seasonally and cyclically with the sugar export economy. Even in "good times" unemployment and underemployment were high during the so-called dead season, when the demand for labor in the sugar sector was minimal.

Castro was not guided by a revolutionary blueprint. The new government came to assume an ever more central role in the accumulation process owing to a combination of economic and political considerations. As business interests on the part of both foreign and national capital, conflicted with newly defined national interests, and as business resisted labor demands for wage increases and other concessions, the government appropriated economic holdings. Within two years ownership of most of the economy, outside of agriculture and the retail trade, had passed into state hands (Table 9.1).

Although undermining the economic base of capital, the revolutionary government initially protected petty bourgeois property rights in the city and the countryside. During Castro's first years of rule he even extended rural and urban small-scale property rights, increasing the number of Cubans who owned the means of production and housing units.

Changes in the
Agrarian Class Structure

The 1959 agrarian reform increased the number of rural small-property owners, as it entitled sharecroppers, squatters, and tenant farmers to own the land they tilled. Nearly two-thirds of all current private farmers received land rights as a result of the 1959 reform, and the land they acquired is estimated to involve about one-fourth of the land that remains privately held. The main beneficiaries were in the

TABLE 9.1
Collectivization of Ownership of Means of
Production and Services (in percentages)

Sector	1961	1963	1968	1977
Agriculture	37	70	70	79
Industry	85	95	100	100
Construction	80	98	100	100
Transportation	92	95	98	98
Retail trade	52	75	100	100
Wholesale and foreign trade	100	100	100	100
Banking	100	100	100	100
Education	100	100	100	100

SOURCE: Mesa-Lago (1981: 15). Reprinted by permission of University of New Mexico Press.
NOTE: Figures refer to property, not to production. In 1976 the output of the private sector represented about 4% of national output (excluding trade) with the following shares by economic sector: 25% in agriculture, less than 7% in transportation, and less than 1% in communication. (The percentage in the latter statistics refers not to national output but to the private share of output in each economic sector.)

regions where pressure on the land had been intense, land security an issue, and peasant support for the Revolution great.

Although the "land to the tiller" program does not distinguish Cuba's land reform from other reforms in the region, Cuba was the first—and until Nicaragua, the only—Latin American country to transform large estates into state farms. The 1959 reform called for the nationalization of farms over 402 hectares at the same time as it extended land rights to peasants. Because large farms were capitalized, redistribution was not considered a pragmatic alternative. The sugar plantations initially were converted into cooperatives, but within a few years they too were turned into state farms. Workers on the newly created state farms were granted year-round employment, social benefits, and wage increases.

Yet the economic base of the agrarian bourgeosie was not fully destroyed until the government issued a second agrarian reform in 1963. This reform called for the nationalization of all holdings over 67 hectares (exceptions being made for very productive farms). The second reform left about 30% of the farm population and an even smaller percentage of the farm land in private hands. As a result of the reform, only about 5% of all private land and less than 1% of all private farms are in holdings larger than 67 hectares. The government continues to honor property rights that conform with the stipulations of the two reforms, although since the late 1970s it has encouraged farmers to organize production cooperatives.

Although land was less concentrated in Cuba than in most countries in the region before the Revolution, the two reforms reduced property inequities and changed the bases of property ownership to an extent that no other country in the region has. Prior to the Revolution, land ownership concentration was high (a Gini Index value of .79), but tied with two other countries as third lowest in the region (World Bank, 1978: 2).[1] As a consequence of the Revolution, though, Cuba has come to have Latin America's smallest percentage of private holdings and the least amount of land in large estates (Eckstein, 1986: 520). Moreover, no other Latin American country has implemented an agrarian reform that has benefited as large a percentage of the farm labor force or distributed as large a percentage of the land area as has Cuba. The agrarian reforms reflect the revolutionary leadership's anti-capitalist class bias on the one hand, and its commitment to the peasants who helped make the revolution on the other hand. However, the peculiarities of Cuban agriculture and the centrality of the capitalized sugar industry to the economy have also had an impact on how property relations and the organization of production have been restructured since 1959.

Although Castro maintained his promise to honor small farmer property rights, when state and private farmer interests conflicted, as they did in the late 1960s, the *significance* of private property changed in ways concealed by statistics on land ownership. During the latter half of Castro's first decade of rule, small farmers lost control over production and labor on their holdings. The government regulated what farmers produced, it pressured farmers to work part-time on state farms and to collaborate with state plans, and it discouraged farmers from hiring labor. Private farmers tended to produce crops that were domestically consumed because they were the most remunerative and suited to small-scale, labor-intensive farming.

Despite the productivity and profitability of private farming, the government restricted domestic market dynamics in agriculture to maximize sugar exports. The sugar was to be sold both to COMECON and Western countries. Although the government argued that it was hastening the transition to Communism by subordinating private to collective concerns, the policy shift addressed the government's material concern at the time. The sugar project was designed to improve the island's trade balance; its balance of payments had severely deteriorated by 1963 as a result of the government's initial "inwardly" oriented growth strategy. To promote global market integration the government tightened the belt on remaining domestic market features in agriculture. Private ownership persisted *de jure*, but it lost most of its historical meaning.

When the 10 million-ton sugar project failed to generate anticipated revenue and when its adverse effects on domestic consumption generated widespread discontent, the government reemphasized nonsugar production and accordingly reduced its controls over private farm activity. The government and the Party acknowledged that it had incorrectly tried to hasten the transition to communism; instead it would revert back to the socialist stage in which limited market features were tolerated. As of the late 1970s and early 1980s agriculturalists could, for the first time since the introduction of rationing in the early 1960s, legally sell whatever surplus they produced privately, at the price the market would bear. Production improved but farmers increasingly sold their best produce privately, to maximize their own profits. Meanwhile, the government encouraged farmers to form production cooperatives, a "higher" stage of organization permitting economies of scale. Private property thus resumed some of its former economic and social significance, although the government continues to regulate access to credit and capital inputs and it still prohibits property accumulation. In permitting the limited market opening the government hoped to stimulate production for domestic consumption.

In sum, agrarian class and property relations have been shaped over the years by economic and political considerations. The government continues to recognize small property rights, but the implications of private land claims hinge on which other market features operate. In the late 1960s agrarian class distinctions were minimal, as the state undermined landowners' ability to regulate production and pressured them to become part-time wage laborers.

Changes in Urban
Property and Class Relations

As in the countryside, in the cities the composition of classes and class relations have been shaped by the government's stance toward private property and market forces. Its stance has varied—as in agriculture—with changing economic and political concerns.

The government initially regulated urban real estate to consolidate its political base. It accordingly undermined the economic base of large propertied interests while extending small property claims. It forced the sale of vacant land, ended urban and suburban land speculation, limited rental earnings, regulated purchase and sales agreements, called for the expropriation without compensation of all tenement buildings, and conceled all mortgages and loans. The measures that eroded large private real estate interests expanded the government's revenue base and its power to shape urban class relations. Prerevolutionary tenants, who were allowed to purchase their dwellings, paid the government monthly fees. Prerevolutionary landlords were entitled to take in a maximum of $600 a month in rent.

Meanwhile, the government extended small property rights. Castro argued that just as each rural family should be able to own its own tract of land, so too should each urban family have the right to own a home or apartment. Castro first articulated this idea in his famous 1953 Moncada "History Will Absolve Me" speech that he delivered in his own defense as a revolutionary on trial for treason. In the spirit of the Moncada address two agencies—the National Institute for Savings and Housing (INAV) and the Self-Help Mutual Aid Program—helped subsidize private home construction. During its first year of operation INAV alone facilitated the construction of some 10,000 units (Schuman, 1975: 6). However, the programs were short lived, probably for both political and economic reasons. The housing made inefficient use of scarce resources and it isolated families.

Initially the government promoted small-propertied interests in the city, not only through private home construction but also through an Urban Reform Law. Promulgated in 1960, the reform legislation outlawed leasing and established procedures for home purchasing. It provided the bases for tenants to acquire the housing they inhabited, through monthly payments equal to no more than the rent they had paid, over 5-20 years. By 1970 all citizens were to enjoy housing free of charge.

Other measures protected small prerevolutionary urban property owners. Landlords who lived in the buildings they owned could continue to collect up to 150 pesos per rental unit a month, and homeowners benefited from tax exemptions (Eckstein, 1984).

Small urban-property ownership did not, however, have the same class implications as rural property ownership. The income-generating purposes to which the urban holdings could be put were more restricted. Also, the government limited urban property owners' ability to pass on their class privileges to their children. When an owner of a building dies, the next of kin of do not necessarily inherit the property. Whoever resides in the home at the time of the death is entitled to continue to live there.

Although the government continued to honor small urban property rights, it stopped promoting private home ownership in the mid-1960s. Instead, it began to construct large-scale low-cost prefabricated housing developments (with various community facilities) and it retracted its promise to allow all city dwellers to own their own home or apartment by 1970. The new housing was to be leased for no more than 10% of household income; it was not free, but available on an ability-to-pay basis. The shift in housing policy occurred at the same time that the government subordinated private to state interests in agriculture. The new housing policy, like the new agricultural policy, permitted a subordination of consumption to investment and it was consistent with, and justified in terms of, the rapid transition from socialism to communism. Although the publicly financed housing did not keep pace with demand, state regulation prevented the land speculation and massive land squatting so characteristic of the capitalist countries in the region.

The emphasis on tenancy continued in the 1970s, except that the government promoted a new building strategy that was asssumed to reduce the costs of construction. The government called on work centers to form "minibrigades" and build their own apartments. Enterprises were expected to maintain output despite the temporary loss of labor, and the workers who were released for the construction projects did not necessarily move into the new dwellings. Workers gained rights to housing through their work centers, purportedly on the basis of merit plus need. Thus housing allocations were linked to productivity, though not through market mechanisms.

In 1984, however, the government officially *reversed* its stance toward state-financed and state-owned housing. Instead of emphasizing large-scale developments built either by the state or by workers, the government once again promoted private housing. The minibrigade program proved to be more costly than assumed, as builders were inexperienced and work centers failed to maintain output levels with fewer employees. To address the housing problem, beginning in 1984 the government even allowed, for the first time, homeowners to use their property for *private* accumulation. According to the 1984 housing law, all remaining tenants are to become property owners, and to pay the government the assessed cost of their homes in small monthly installments. The law affects about half the population, the other half having acquired property ownership rights in conjunction with the 1960 Urban Reform Law (Boston Globe, 1985: 8). The 1984 law provided Cubans with incentives to build their own homes, and it permitted home owners to rent out space. It was "up to the people" to determine rental rates. The law was rescinded after one year.

The 1984 housing law had economic and social ramifications. It addressed Cubans' desire for home ownership and housing flexibility, at minimal cost to the state. If formalized a tendency toward private housing construction that evolved once the government began to permit, as detailed below, private contract work in the late 1970s. By early 1984 three times as many dwellings were constructed privately as in any year when worker brigades and the state assumed responsibility for housing (Brundenius, 1981: 110; Granma Weekly Review, 1984: 3). However, people got rich buying, selling, and trading homes.

The market opening had been designed to address city-dwellers' housing needs while allowing the government to tend to its global market concerns. Castró noted that Cuba then had to devote resources primarily to building industries that produce exports for Western countries (Boston Globe, 1985: 8). The island had a large hard-currency foreign debt, due to loans contracted when sugar prices had been high and interest rates low, in the mid-1970s. However, it remains to be seen whether both domestic demand and foreign exchange needs can be resolved simultaneously. There is some evidence that the demand for private housing may jeopardize the completion of major industrial and institutional works (Granma Weekly Review, 1984: 4); construction workers are tempted to devote time to, and probably pilfer state construction resources for, the more profitable domestic market. The domestic market opening may result in a greater resurgence of private activity than the government had intended. It is also likely to result in an increase in income-based housing stratification. Apparently, budgetary constraints and balance of payments problems rooted in the externally based growth strategy contributed to the reprivatization of housing construction.

Yet the government's stance toward private commerce probably had an even greater impact on domestic class and property relations than has its housing policy. Castro nationalized the wholesale trade soon after the Revolution, but continued until 1968 to permit considerable small private retail activity. The retail trade policy was consistent with the pro-small ownership stance in other economic sectors and with the demand-based accumulation strategy in the early 1960s. But when the government shifted from a domestically rooted to an export-based growth strategy private retail trade stood in the way. Thus, the 1968 "Revolutionary Offensive" to nationalize all commerce served the government's economic priorities and not merely—as was publicly portrayed—its ideological commitment to the "rapid transition to communism." The Revolutionary Offensive freed labor for the sugar maximization project.

The government permitted farmers to sell produce directly to consumers for a brief period in the early 1980s. However, this market opening as well generated consequences the state had not intended: it led to illegal vending, considerable profiteering, and economic activity not always consonant with state priorities. Consequently, the private urban markets were closed at the same time as the clamp down on private housing construction.

Meanwhile, as indicated in the discussion of housing, service activity was also reprivatized. Since 1976 the government permits individuals to offer such services as appliance and auto repair work, carpentry, plumbing, and gardening, provided that they register, pay a fee, and do it on a self-employed basis. The contained reprivatization of the service economy is designed to address consumer dissatisfaction with inefficiencies and inadequecies in the bureaucratized state sector, and probably also to absorb labor; the policy was introduced at a time of growing unemployment, owing to the entry of an early post-revolutionary "baby boom" into the labor market and a contraction in the economy. Yet here too evidence suggests that the market opening guaranteed unintended consequences. Many workers directed time and resources from their governmental jobs to more profitable private contract work.

In sum, the revolutionary government undermined the economic base first of the bourgeoisie and then of the independent petty bourgeoisie. More recently it has permitted a limited market opening, and in so doing provided the bases for a resurgence of private employment and private sector activity. As individuals take advantage of both state and market opportunities, the distinction between public and private sector work, and between classes rooted in the structure of production and distribution, became increasingly fuzzy. Distortions in the economy led the government to modify its accumulation strategy once again in the mid-1980s, in ways that will undoubtedly affect the distribution of wealth among socioeconomic groups.

THE IMPACT OF THE STATE-CLASS
TRANSFORMATION ON LABOR FORCE OPPORTUNITIES:
STATE/PRIVATE EMPLOYMENT,
THE SECTORAL DISTRIBUTION OF LABOR,
AND OCCUPATIONAL STRATIFICATION

The nationalization of ownership of the means of production has shaped labor force employment options. Most obviously, it has contributed to a decline in private employment. Despite considerable private moonlighting since the latter 1970s, as of 1980 about 94% of the employed labor force worked for the state (Brundenius, 1984: 138). Consequently, nearly all employed persons receive official wages and qualify for pension and unemployment insurance benefits. In other Latin American countries such economic security is reserved for the small fraction of the labor force who work in modern professional, industrial, and bureaucratic jobs. The advantages notwithstanding, state employment lacks the flexibility of informal-sector jobs; the inflexibility is probably most problematic for women with young children who prefer combining paid work with child rearing.

The little officially registered private employment is concentrated in agriculture. However, as new private opportunities opened up, agriculture's importance declined: from about 86% of total employment in 1970 to 81% in 1980 (Brundenius, 1984: 138). Agriculture's share of total private employment has undoubtedly declined even more in the 1980s with the expansion of private service work.

Nationalization of ownership has also resulted in some sectoral employment shifts. Under Castro employment dropped in agriculture and rose in manufacturing and especially services. Although such sectoral shifts have occurred throughout the region in recent decades, what distinguishes Cuba from the other countries is the extent of industrial employment and—interestingly—the relatively *low* growth of service sector employment. Cuba's regional ranking in the sectoral distribution of the labor force rose in industry and fell in service activity between 1960 and 1980 (see Table 9.2). Moreover, the nature of service employment differs in Cuba: More of the labor force is employed in social services and fewer in personal services and commerce than in other countries in the region. Employment in commerce contracted dramatically with the nationalization of the retail trade in 1968. A comparable crackdown on private commerce in the other Latin

TABLE 9.2

Cuban Sectoral Distribution of the Labor Force and Cuba's
Ranking Among Latin America's (LA) 20 Principal Countries
in the Sectoral Distribution of Labor

	1960		1970		1980	
	Percentage	LA Rank[c]	Percentage	LA Rank[c]	Percentage	LA Rank[c]
Agriculture	39	16	31	16	23	16
Industry	22	4[a]	27	4[b]	31	2
Service	39	5	43	5[b]	46	9[a]

SOURCES: World Bank, World Development Report (1979: 162-163; 1984: 258-259); World Bank, World Tables (1980: 462-465).
a. Tied with one other country.
b. Information for 19 countries; the one country with missing information is assumed to have a similar rank as in 1960.
c. The higher the rank, the larger the percentage.

American countries would result in massive unemployment that would be politically intolerable. In Cuba there was a general shortage of labor when the crackdown occurred; therefore, the 1968 Revolutionary Offensive freed labor for other economic activity.

Nationalization of the economy, in addition, has given rise to a state "managerial class" and to occupational upgrading of the labor force. Workers in the state civilian sector are grouped into five different occupational categories: (1) *workers*: unskilled, semi-skilled, and skilled blue-collar laborers; (2) (white collar) *service employees*; (3) *administrative employees*, such as clerical workers; (4) *technicians*: persons with a university or technological school education, and persons employed in the creative arts (e.g., physicians, engineers, agronomists, scientists, professors, experts in mechanics, and writers); and (5) *executives* (*dirigentes*): persons who plan, organize, coordinate, and direct activities in government agencies, the Communist Party, enterprises, and mass organizations. The occupational categories suggest that the government makes no effort to eliminate occupational distinctions among state employees and that it recognizes an internally differentiated "new middle class" made up of different types of white-collar workers who do not own the means of production. The government distinguishes *among* white-collar workers as well as between them and blue-collar workers (direct producers); it does so on the basis of job-related tasks and responsibilities.

Not only has the Revolutionary government's self-proclaimed "proletarian state" distinguished between "intellectuals" and "direct producers"—in status and, as will be shown later, in income—but it has also overseen the growth in the number of discretionary power of technicians, and most notably, administrators (*dirigentes*) over workers and low-level white-collar employees. Property is not the primary basis of work-based earning and power differentiation in contemporary Cuba.

Two organizational changes were introduced in the 1970s that increased administrators' and managers' discretionary power and possibly contributed to the growth of the "new middle class." One, the New System of Management and Planning (SPDE), reintroduces certain market features into the organization of production, which strengthens managerial prerogatives. Premised on self-financing and profit, the SPDE allows for decentralized management. As it gives enterprises material incentives to maximize efficiency, managers may respond by expanding supervisory personnel. The other organizational innovation, the Organs of Popular Power (OPP), involves the administrative decentralization of service activity as well as production. Local OPP officials, who are popularly elected, are responsible for overseeing economic activity within their territorial domain. Because they risk recall or electoral defeat if their constituencies are dissatisfied with the delivery of goods and services on the local level, the OPP may also contribute to the growth of the supervisory administrative stratum. However, in this instance, unlike in the case of the SPDE, the growth is not rooted in market dynamics.

Gender Stratification

The nationalization of the economy has also affected employment opportunities for women. Under Castro increasing number of women have entered the paid labor force and the government has made it easier for them to do so. However, the government has facilitated and indeed encouraged women's labor-force participation for its own material reasons, and not merely because of a moral commitment. Accordingly, as its economic needs and priorities have changed, so too has its institutional supports for and its public proclamations about working women shifted.

Women's labor-force participation has risen substantially under Castro. Although estimates differ, available evidence indicates that women did not enter the paid labor force in significant numbers until the 1970s. In 1958 they accounted for 13% of the labor force, a decade later for only 3% more (see Table 9.3). By 1984, however, 33% of the labor force was female. During the 1970s the number of employed women more than doubled. Women hold about 70% of the jobs created since 1970.

Cuba's ranking among Latin American countries in women's labor force participation (as a percentage of the total labor force) jumped dramatically in the 1970s—from sixteenth to fifth place between 1960 and 1975 (Agency for International Development, 1980: 11; Brundenius, 1984: 134). That is, women's labor force participation has been growing throughout the region but not as rapidly as in Cuba. Moreover, the nature of female employment is distinctive in Cuba. Most working Cuban women are employed by the state, and accordingly benefit from official wage and employment legislation. They make at least the minimum wage and qualify for unemployment insurance. By contrast, in the other Latin American countries most working women currently are privately employed, often in informal-sector jobs that offer no job security and pay poorly.[2] Before the Revolution, the same was true in Cuba. Many Cuban women, for example, used to be domestics.

Not only does the state, in employing women, free them from market discrimination; in addition, it lends them institutional and moral support to an extent that no other government in the region does. State day-care facilities nearly doubled between 1970 and 1983 (Gutiérrez Muñiz, 1984: 120), during which time women's labor force participation increased markedly. Workers and students also receive free meals at work and school, respectively. In assuming partial responsibility for unpaid work traditionally performed by wives, the government has helped to free women in order to work outside the home for pay. In the mid-1970s the government issued a family code that specified that men should help in housework, and a Maternity Law that guaranteed working women pregnancy and maternity rights. Working women were also spared cues at food stores. The various measures were designed to reduce further working women's home responsibilities and to minimize tension between family and work life. In addition, the government urged that certain new jobs be slotted for women. The Party, the workers' organizations, the mass organizations, and public administration were to see that women indeed filled the slots (Castro, 1981a: 65). Meanwhile,

TABLE 9.3
Female Labor Force Participation

Year	Percentage of Labor Force	Percentage of Unemployed	Female Unemployment Rate	Combined Male and Female Unemployment Rate	Occupied Labor Force as Percentage of Available Labor Force
1956	13	12	–	–	–
1960	13	35	32	12	–
1968	16	–	–	4[b]	–
1970	18	18	1	1	25
1972	21	42	6	3	28
1974	23	58	10	4	31
1976	26	74	14	5	36
1978	29	69	13	5	42
1980	31	59	8	4	48
1984	39	–	–	–	–

SOURCES: Brundenius (1984: 134-135); Mesa-Lago (1981: 111, 118).
a. Available labor force equals population of working age (17-54) minus full-time students.
b. Estimated by Mesa-Lago (1981).

the Communist Party, at its 1975 Congress, encouraged women to excel both at home and at work, by emphasizing that socialist emulation campaigns take women's dual role into account (Communist Party of Cuba, 1981: 87).

Other government policies not specifically targeted at women probably gave females added incentive to work in the 1970s. Government wage and consumer policies seem to have had such an effect. Women's paid labor-force participation had barely increased in the 1960s because women were given few material incentives to compensate for the strains the work imposed on family life. The government had depressed domestic consumption in conjunction with its emphasis on investment and export-based accumulation. Women were not motivated by the official moral incentives to join the labor force. The policies of the late 1960s had evoked such widespread discontent and they had such a negative effect on productivity that the government reemphasized material incentives in the 1970s. The material incentives, plus the institutional supports, induced many more women to work.

According to revolutionary leadership, the issue in the mid-1970s was not merely greater female labor force participation but full gender equality. Concern with gender equality is rare in Latin America. Castro claimed that both objective and subjective factors impeded gender equality. Although the government was committed to removing objective barriers by reducing women's "double burden," Castro called upon the people to overcome their prejudices and old habits. The battle had to be waged—as the 1975 Party Congress formalized—in the field of consciousness. Material conditions alone were not expected to erase the "backward ideas that we have dragged with us from the past" (Communist Party of Cuba, 1981: 80).

There were, as Castro himself acknowledged, material as well as moral reasons for the concern about women's labor force participation in the mid-1970s. It was a question of "elemental justice," but also an "imperative necessity" for economic development because "the male work force will not be enough" (Castro, 1981a: 65). Thus, as economic conditions changed so too did the government's and Party's emphasis on women's labor-force participation. The 1981-1985 Five Year Plan, for example, called for no increase in women's labor-force participation rate (Mesa-Lago, 1981: 120). An enlarged male labor pool (owing to an early post-revolutionary "baby boom" generation coming of work age) on the one hand, and a contraction in the economy plus a quest for economic efficiency on the other hand, were pushing unemployment upward. Moreover, as the demand for labor receded public concern about women's labor force participation became less frequent. The big push to get women into the labor force occurred during the Revolution's most buoyant period of economic growth, when demand for labor peaked. Women at the time were still a relatively untapped source of labor. Egalitarian socialist principles should not conceal the state's underlying material interests.

Nor should the egalitarian principles conceal the differing labor force experiences that women and men have had. Jobs tend to be sex-typed and women absorb the shocks of economic restructuring more than do men. Explicit discriminatory hiring policies account for some but not much of the sex-typing of jobs. In 1968 certain jobs were slotted specifically for women while jobs possibly hazardous to women's reproductive role were reserved for men; the government and Party at the time sought to rationalize the work force so that all jobs would be filled in a period of full employment. Although the number of jobs from which women are barred is purportedly diminishing as technical advancements reduce work risks, women continue to be clustered in low-status jobs. In 1974 Castro noted that women held only 15% of the leadership posts in production, services, and administration (Castro, 1981a: 57). Women, moreover, are concentrated in the service sector, whereas men are employed primarily in agriculture and secondly in industry (Mesa-Lago, 1981: 119; National Research Council, 1983: 144). Although sectoral gender typing diminished in the 1970s, as of 1979 women still accounted for nearly two-thirds of all workers in the social services (e.g., education, public health, social security) but less than 15% of the workforce in agriculture/mining, construction, and transportation/communication.

Opportunities for women are confined largely to expanding sectors of the economy. Women who entered the labor force in the 1970s mainly were absorbed into the expanding service sector (Brundenius, 1984: 136). They are concentrated in expanding sectors because job competition and entrenched interests are undoubtedly less there. Also, as noted above, the Revolutionary leadership specified that new places of employment reserve slots for women. Although there is no evidence that job slotting is legally enforced, employers may make some effort to abide by the affirmative action measure.

Meanwhile, when sectors contract, women bear the dislocative costs disproportionally. Accordingly, when commerce was consolidated women's employment in the sector dropped off more than did men's.

Unemployment data also suggest that women disproportionally bear the brunt of contractions in the economy and economic restructuring. Although the open unemployment rate for both men and women dropped dramatically after the Revolution—from 12% in 1958 to a low of 1% in 1970—the rate has always been higher among women (Brundenius, 1984: 73; Mesa-Lago, 1981: 122). The rate among women dropped from 32% in 1960 to 1% in 1970, after which it rose again, to a high of 14% in 1976. Women's unemployment rate rose at the same time that their labor force participation expanded. Moreover, whereas women's share of the unemployed dropped from 35% to 18% during Castro's first decade of rule, since 1973 women account for the majority of the unemployed and still the minority of the employed. Their share of the unemployed peaked at 74% in 1976 during an economic recession caused by a major drop in world sugar prices. However, in 1980 they still accounted for 59% of the unemployed (Brundenius, 1984: 135).

Women bear the brunt of unemployment even though they are, on average, more educated and therefore in principle more qualified for work than men. In 1979 22% of working men compared to 37% of working women had at least 12 years of schooling (Brundenius, 1984: 137). The gender educational gap reflects, in part, the younger average age of the female labor force. Cuban youth—of both sexes—are becoming ever more educated. Yet reflecting working women's commitment to education, more employed women than men study part-time (in 1980 31% versus 25%) (Castro, 1981b: 108).

Women bear the brunt of unemployment even though they are increasingly inclined to work during childbearing years. As institutional supports have improved and material incentives increased, female job stability has picked up.

In light of women's job qualifications and increased job commitment, either women are subject to more employment discrimination than men, or employment security comes with longevity of work. Women may suffer from being the last hired and the first fired in employment cutbacks. The decentralization of production and administration may also work to their disadvantage. Local managers may be more inclined than the centralized administration to fire female workers, both because they may be less committed to gender equality and because they may see men as more dependable. The SPDE, as previously indicated, encourages enterprises to streamline operations to maximize efficiency and profit. Castro hinted in his 1980 speech to the Federation of Cuban Women (FMC) that the decentralization of hiring may jeopardize women's employment prospects. Said he:

> Direct hiring of workers means that there be no more centralized allocation of work force, but it doesn't mean that the manager is accordingly given complete free rein.... I think we must be very careful in that certain situations do not lead us to retrace our steps in what we have gained for women [Castro, 1981b: 119].

Whatever the reason, women more than men serve as a pool of labor that is absorbed during periods of economic expansion and let go during periods of economic contraction and restructuring.

Yet it should not be forgotten that the impact of unemployment differs in present-day Cuba from other Latin American countries. Unemployed Cuban women qualify for generous unemployment compensation benefits; by contrast, in the other countries in the region only the fraction of women employed in modern industry and bureaucracies qualify for such unemployment compensation. Moreover, unemployed Cuban women need not fall back on stigmatized welfare as in the United States.

Earnings and Income Distribution

Wage policies, like employment policies, have varied with accumulation strategies. The official wage schema served to equalize earnings among workers during the first revolutionary decade and to increase earnings differentials thereafter. Unlike other Latin American countries, in Cuba most labor force participants work for the state and are subject to official wage policies.

Initially official policy improved the absolute and relative earning capacity of the groups that benefited least before the Revolution. During Castro's first years of rule the real wage of the poorest 40%, in both the nationalized and the remaining private sector, apparently doubled (Brundenius, 1984: 108). Castro raised the minimum wage and guaranteed all workers year-round employment and therefore year-round earnings. Farm workers in general and canecutters in particular benefited. Not only wage but other economic policies improved the earning power of low-income groups. The 1959 agrarian reform, for example, enabled land beneficiaries to appropriate the full product of their labor, while the expansion of free social services and rent reductions increased the disposable income of urban and rural poor. The various redistributive measures helped Castro consolidate a "mass base" in the city and countryside as well as stimulate demand-based domestic accumulation.

Not surprisingly, the policies of the 1960s reduced earnings differentials. Available evidence, which is piecemeal, suggests that the ratio between the highest- and lowest-paid workers dropped from more than 1000 to 1 in 1958 to 10 to 1 in the mid-1960s (Mesa-Lago, 1981: 148). Similarly, the difference between the *average* earning of the highest- and lowest-paid sectors declined from 4.1 to 1.0 in 1962 to 3.6 to 1.0 four years later (Mesa-Lago, 1981: 153).

In the late 1960s, when the government shifted to an export-based accumulation strategy and pressed for the rapid transition from socialism to communism, earnings differentials declined even more. The differential between average earnings of the highest- and lowest-paid sector dropped to 2.6 to 1 in 1971. Indicative of the egalitarian emphasis at the time, the average wage of low-paid occupations—such as agriculture and fishing—rose whereas the average wage of high-paid occupations, such as electric power, petroleum, and communications, declined. Workers were encouraged to work for society, not individual gain. Inspired by moral incentives, they were to be paid according to need, not work. Yet wage policies reflected accumulation and not merely moral considerations. As wages for most workers declined, more revenue could be allocated to investment. And in line with the externally rooted accumulation strategy, workers in the trade sector were paid comparatively well. The average wage of the foreign trade sector, for example, was 60% higher than that of the domestic retail trade sector (Mesa-Lago, 1981: 153).

The political and economic failure of the late 1960s strategy led not merely to greater tolerance of private-sector activity but also to a reintroduction of certain market-based wage and consumer policies. Officially, the socialist principle of distribution according to work, rather than need, was reinstituted. Earnings were increasingly linked to productivity and to export earning potential. Jobs were "normed," with wages tied to work output. Workers who overfulfilled their work quotas received bonuses, and the bonuses were set higher than they had been before they were eliminated in the late 1960s (Mesa-Lago, 1981: 151).

In addition to monetary remuneration, exemplary workers now qualified for privileged rights to purchase scarce, coveted consumer durables and to acquire new housing. Workers, at work-center assemblies, participated in the allocation process.

The reemphasis on material incentives resulted in a widening of the average wage earnings between the lowest- and highest-paid economic sectors to 2.02: 1.0 in 1975 (Mesa-Lago, 1981: 153). However, estimates differ considerably on the net effect of the 1970s policies on the *range* of earnings among state civilian employees from about 10:1 to 3.5:1 (Mesa-Lago, 1981: 155, 225). Reflecting continued state concern with export revenue, in 1978 cane cutters earned about six times the average farm wage. Cane cutters were then among the highest-paid workers; they received—according to data compiled by Mesa-Lago (1981: 154)—more even than cabinet ministers. With the successful mechanization of cane harvesting the government has opted for a small well-paid dependable work force. Private tobacco farmers, who also produced a valued export crop, were another well-paid group; because they are self-employed but must sell their crop to the state procurement agency, the government improved their earning power by raising the procurement price.

The domestic "market opening" seems also to be contributing to new income inequalities. In particular, the new decentralized economic system (SPDE) includes an incentive fund. The fund is based on enterprise profits and is distributed primarily to employees individually in accordance with their productivity, but secondarily collectively in the form of social services (Mesa-Lago, 1981: 151). The new peasant markets also provide new channels for profit for private farmers and vendors.

A wage schema introduced in 1980s is also likely to increase earnings differentials. Under the new payment schema (see Table 9.4) the salary

TABLE 9.4
Wage Range Among Different Occupational Groupings
According to Initial (1963-1979) and
Revised (1980+) Wage Scale

Occupational Grouping	1963-1979	1980
Farm worker	71-170	82-128
Nonfarm worker	82-250	93-254
Administrative and service personnel	75-211	85-231
Technical personnel	118-350+	128-450
Executives	100-350+	111-450

SOURCE: Brundenius (1984: 115).

of high-level technical personnel and executives improved the most and the *range* of possible earnings diminished among agricultural and nonagricultural workers, increased somewhat among administrative and service personnel, and increased significantly among technical personnel and executives.[3] Actual earnings depend on adjustments made for productivity, overtime, and "historical wages" (wages that exceeded the rate set when the wage-scale system first went into effect).

An increase in wage-based inequality will therefore be contingent on an expansion of highly skilled over medium- and low-skilled jobs, and on differences in workers efficiency. The new wage schema rewards disproportionally the "new managerial class." Moreover, it heightens income distinctions between "intellectual" (or, in U.S. terminology, "white collar") and "manual" labor and among different types of white-collar workers, while reducing differences among manual workers.[4] Since the labor force has been upgrading, moving from low-skilled jobs in the poorly paid agricultural sector into better-paid jobs in other sectors, average earnings have risen at the same time that income disparities have widened.

Yet the range of income disparities remains minimal by Latin American standards, even with the new basis for disparities beginning in the mid-1970s. There are, unfortunately, no official income distribution figures, but rough unofficial estimates indicate that since the Revolution Cuba has equalized earnings more than any other country in the region. In the most recent year of available data, the poorest 20% of the population earned proportionally more and the wealthiest 10% proportionally less in Cuba than anywhere else in Latin America (Eckstein, forthcoming: Table 6). Moreover, data on income distribution more accurately reflect the actual distribution of wealth in Castro's Cuba than in the other countries, for the nationalization of ownership of the economy prevents Cubans from holding assets. Since most people work for the state, the percentage of the labor force whose earnings can go unreported is minimal. Income redistribution under Castro has been dramatic. In the latest prerevolutionary year with income data the poorest fifth of the population received only about one-fourth as much whereas the wealthiest 16% received more than twice as much of the national income as in 1976 (Eckstein, 1986).[5] The greatest redistribution occurred shortly after the Revolution.

Cuba stands out among Latin American countries not just in the equality of its income distribution but also in the significance attached to income. Under Castro, nonwage policies eroded much of the historical significance of income, to the extent that income is a much less adequate indicator of overall living standards on the island than in other Latin American countries. On the one hand, technicians, executives, military staff members, and other persons in high-ranking positions enjoy such work-linked benefits as free use of automobiles and opportunities to travel abroad. On the other hand, manual workers enjoy free benefits that their counterparts in other Latin American countries do not. Cuba, for example, is the only nation in the region to provide free and near-universal health care, primary school education, retirement pensions, and unemployment insurance, as well as free or low-cost housing to the entire populace. It also has regulated the price of many consumer goods and access to such goods through rationing. Although scarcities kept living standards low in the 1960s, material goods consumption increased in the 1970s. As the supply of goods has improved more items have become available off the ration system (see Eckstein, 1986: 523, 524). Income, in turn, is coming to have a greater bearing on consumption. Yet because the income spread remains small by regional standards, low-income groups in Cuba undoubtedly continue to live better and more like upper-income groups than do their counterparts in other Latin American countries. Meanwhile, upper-income groups live less well than their counterparts elsewhere in the region.

CONCLUSION

Under Castro, property relations have changed and in the process the class structure has been transformed. As state-class relations have been altered and the state's role in the economy has changed, most of the labor force has come to be state-employed and subject to state employment practices. The labor force has been upgraded occupationally, and state policies have resulted in new opportunities for women and a more egalitarian distribution of wealth. Nevertheless, opportunities for different socioeconomic groups have varied over the years, with changing accumulation strategies and the success of the strategies. Low-income groups gained most, relative to other socioeconomic groups, when the revolutionary government first consolidated power and relied on a demand-based growth strategy.

Although Cuba's continued dependence on foreign trade subjects the island to world economic conditions, government control of the economy has limited the impact that the 1980s economic recession and even its own foreign-debt crisis have had on the citizenry. As a result, low-income groups have been less hard hit than have their equivalents in other Latin American countries. Cuban socialism, in essence, does not permit the island to escape the fiscal and economic problems that plague the region, but it enables the island to modify and minimize their adverse affects.

NOTES

1. Information is available for 17 of Latin America's principal countries for years between 1930 and 1961. The other countries with which Cuba is compared in this study, and ranked in the tables, are Argentina, Bolivia, Brazil, Chile, Colombia, Costa Rica, the Dominican Republic, Ecuador, El Salvador, Guatemala, Haiti, Honduras, Mexico, Nicaragua, Panama, Paraguay, Peru, Uruguay, and Venezuela.

2. However, women's employment in formal-sector jobs has increased in recent decades in the capitalist countries in the region as well.

3. Although the wage-scale system had not been fully revamped between 1963 and 1980, some modifications had been introduced over the years, affecting the range in wage earnings. The modifications account for differences in the wage-scale information presented by Mesa-Lago (1981: 147) and Brundenius (1984: 115).

4. The income "homogenizing" effects of the 1980 wage reform among the proletariat furthers a trend in force since Castro's first years of rule, when trade unions yielded income and fringe benefit privileges enjoyed by the "labor aristocracy" and the Ministry of Labor set wages for state workers. Worker wage differentials were further reduced in the late 1960s during the "push toward Communism." The government then argued that the benefits of productivity and profitability should be shared collectively, and that all workers performing the same job should be paid equally, regardless of enterprise profit.

5. Inasmuch as the rich had assests in 1953 that they lost in the revolution, the equalizing effect of the class transformation is even greater than available information suggests.

REFERENCES

Agency for International Development (1980) Keeping Women Out: A Structural Analysis of Women's Employment in Developing Countries. Report OTR-C-[80]. Washington, DC: Office of Women in Development, Bureau of Program and Policy Coordination, Agency for International Development.

Boston Globe (1985) (February 3): 8.

BRUNDENIUS, C. (1981) Economic Growth, Basic Needs and Income Distribution in Revolutionary Cuba. Lund, Sweden: Research Policy Institute, University of Lund.

———(1984) Revolutionary Cuba: The Challenge of Economic Growth with Equity Boulder, CO: Westview.

CASTRO, F. (1981a) "The struggle for women's equality," pp. 55-73 in Elizabeth Stone (ed.) Women and the Cuban Revolution. New York: Pathfinder Press.

———(1981b) "Into the third decade," pp. 107-132 in Elizabeth Stone (ed.) Women and the Cuban Revolution. New York: Pathfinder Press.

Communist Party of Cuba (1981) "Thesis: on the full exercise of women's equality," pp. 74-106 in Elizabeth Stone (ed.) Women and the Cuban Revolution. New York: Pathfinder Press.

ECKSTEIN, S. (1984) "The debourgeiosement of Cuban cities," pp. 91-112 in Irving L. Horowitz (ed.) Cuban Communism. New Brunswick, NJ: Transaction Books.

———(1985) "State and market dynamics in Castro's Cuba," in Peter Evans et al. (eds.) States Versus Markets in the World Capitalist System. Beverly Hills, CA: Sage.

———(1986) "The Cuban Revolution in comparative perspective." Comparative Studies in Society and History 28: 502-534.

Granma Weekly Review (1984) (March 11): 3.

GUTIERREZ MUÑIZ, J. (1984) La economía Cubana y la atención infantil: aspectos básicos (1959-1983). Havana: Congresos de Pediatría.

MESA-LAGO, C. (1981) The Economy of Socialist Cuba: A Two-Decade Appraisal. Albuquerque: University of New Mexico Press.

National Research Council (1983) Fertility Determinants in Cuba. Washington, DC: Committee on Population and Demography, National Research Council.

RODRÍGUEZ CERVANTES, M. and A. FARNOS MOREJON (1985) "Política de población en Cuba en el contexto de la estrategía para el desarollo." University of Havana, Centro de Estudios Demografícos.

SCHUMAN, T. (1975) "Housing: a challenge met." Cuba Review 5 (March): 8.

World Bank (1978) Land Reform in Latin America: Bolivia, Chile, Mexico, Peru and Venezuela. Staff Working Paper 275. Washington, DC: Author.

———(1979) World Development Report. New York: Oxford University Press.

———(1980) World Development Report. Baltimore, MD: Johns Hopkins University Press.

———(1984) World Tables. Baltimore, MD: Johns Hopkins University Press.

———(1984) World Development Report. New York: Oxford University Press.

Chapter 10

THE INTERNATIONAL MONETARY FUND AND CONTEMPORARY CRISIS IN THE DOMINICAN REPUBLIC

Martin F. Murphy
University of Notre Dame

The Dominican Republic seems to come to the forefront of international news only when something dramatic occurs. The Caribbean's second largest country in both land area and population is usually dwarfed in the international press and even more so in the scholarly literature by reports on Cuba, Haiti, Puerto Rico, Jamaica, Grenada, and Trinidad and Tobago. Nonetheless, in April 1984 the former fiefdom of the Trujillo family made front-page news as 86 people were killed during street protests over drastic price increases. The Dominican Republic became another case study of what has happened and what could happen in other countries when International Monetary Fund (IMF) "stand-by" measures are put into effect.

This chapter begins by outlining briefly the role of the IMF in the international economic order, and proceeds to review the history of the Dominican Republic's international debt crisis. It then focuses on the

AUTHOR'S NOTE: Much of the information presented in this chapter comes from fieldwork performed in the Dominican Republic from 1980 to 1984. The original version of this chapter was current as of February 1985. Subsequent fieldwork was undertaken in the Dominican Republic during July and August 1985 to update the analysis for the present version.

dynamics of the present-day crisis, emphasizing the economic, political, and social consequences of the IMF accords. It concludes that the contemporary problems the Dominican Republic faces are to be found in its traditional role within the international economic order; the various economic "development" schemes that previously have been implemented; and the consequences of the recent demands of the IMF.

BRIEF DESCRIPTION AND
DISCUSSION OF THE IMF

Some authors claim that the historical roots of the International Monetary Fund are to be found in an effort in the 1920s to restore the gold standard (Horsefield, 1969: 4). Others state that its origins are to be found later in the Great Depression with attempts by various countries to competitively devalue their currencies and initiate exchange and trade restrictions (Hooke, 1981: 1). Regardless of this discrepancy of one decade we can safely state that the IMF developed out of a period of crisis in the generally expanding world capitalist economy of the early twentieth century, and that the clarification of currency values and international trade relations in the progressively more sophisticated world economic system were the basic ingredients of the scenario.

During the years of World War II international debates and fora addressed the desirability and possible design of a more stable and open international monetary system. The International Monetary Fund was conceived at the United Nations Monetary and Financial Conference at Bretton Woods, New Hampshire, in July 1944. In December of the following year the IMF was born.

As of June 1981 there were 141 member nations, including all industrial capitalist economies—except Switzerland—and most dependent or Third World economies, capitalist and socialist. Notable exceptions to the membership roll of the IMF are the Soviet Union and Cuba.

The principal raison d'être of the Fund is the maintenance of supposedly coherent exchange rates for the currencies of member countries. On the operational level the IMF's financial and technical resources may be called on by member countries to resolve international payment deficits. The Fund's loan conditionality is, of course, directly related to the organization's orientation and philosophy. In 1979 the Executive Board of the IMF approved a set of 12 guidelines for conditionality that notes that "stand-by" agreements should not disrupt the social and political fabric of the borrowing society. Nonetheless, recent examples—such as the crisis in the Dominican Republic—have demonstrated very different results. The basic philosophy of the IMF is found in its demands for general fiscal conservatism; equilibrium in a country's balance of payments through reductions of imports and increased exports; increased public sector production per worker; increased tax bases and rates and improved methods of capturing taxes; wage freezes; liberalization of currency exchange rates and the creation of a floating exchange value; and the stimulation of both foreign and national private sector investment and production.

THE DOMINICAN REPUBLIC
AND THE INTERNATIONAL ECONOMIC ORDER

The Dominican Republic's true entry into the international economic order is placed in the 1870s with the development of the modern sugar industry. Growing through transnational capital investment, imported technology and labor, and sales on international markets, the sugar industry was the economy's major link with the international system. The subsequent debt crisis of the country at the turn of the century was the major cause of the United States military invasion and occupation from 1916 to 1924. Fearing that European creditors would encourage their governments to take control of the Dominican economic and political mechanisms, the United States acted first and seized the Customs Houses in 1907 in order to "help" the Dominicans collect duties and pay off creditors.

The Era of Trujillo

Rafael Leonidas Trujillo Molina rose to power after the retreat of the North American forces using his position and expertise achieved in the U.S.-trained National Guard. The 31-year dictatorship of Trujillo (1930-1961) employed a dynamic policy of economic development through strict controls on imports, and industrial and agricultural import substitution, especially during and after World War II.

By the late 1950s Trujillo and his family controlled the majority of the sugar mills in the country, employed a full 75% of the economically active population, owned vast tracts of land, livestock, banks, insurance and other financial institutions, import-export concerns, and mines. Prior to the country's economic crisis in the mid-1950s (caused by excessive government spending and low commodity prices for traditional exports), Trujillo had completely paid off the foreign debt and stimulated the value of the Dominican peso to the point that one peso was worth US$1.04.

Capital accumulation under Trujillo was based on a confused definition of the state (Trujillo was the state and the state was Trujillo), strong reliance on foreign investment, and little appreciable investment by the national bourgeoisie. As Roberto Cassá (1978: 57) notes, at the time of Trujillo's assassination in 1961 "fifty-one percent of the industrial investment was that of the Trujillo family and the State, forty-two percent foreign, and as little as seven percent that of the national bourgeoisie."

Political and Economic Chaos (1961-1966)

After a very brief attempt to maintain the status quo by Trujillo's son Ramfis and his chosen President, Joaquín Balaguer, Dominican politics and economics entered a period of chaos from 1962 to 1966. The nation's traditionally weak elite briefly held power through the second Consejo de Estado (State Council) for 13 months (1962-1963). Policies of custom duty exemptions for large importers and exporters, many intimately associated with the Consejo, and attempts to sell many of the Trujillo business interests inherited by the state to national and foreign concerns proved most unpopular.

In February 1963, Juan Bosch assumed the presidency after winning the national election on the Partido Revolucionario Dominicano (PRD; Dominican Revolutionary Party) ticket. Bosch's short-lived government was faced on the economic front with little confidence by national and foreign investors because of his supposed leftist orientations, as evidenced by his attempts to prohibit land ownership by foreigners and to actively and effectively redistribute land. Regardless, Bosch accomplished little before he was toppled by a coup d'état in September 1963. As U.S. Ambassador to the Dominican Republic, John Barlow Martin (1975: 351) wrote: "While everyone was nervous because they thought Bosch had moved too far to the left, I was worried that he had not moved at all."

From the overthrow of Bosch on September 25, 1963 until the inauguration of Joaquin Balaguer in July 1966, the Dominican Republic experienced tremendous political turmoil—12 governments, a civil war, and a military invasion by the Organization of American States and United States. The Dominican economic scene during this period can best be described as that of attempts to divide the Trujillo pie among the dominant classes, wholesale corruption, and a catch-as-catch-can survival strategy.

The Industrial Import-Substitution Model (1966-1978)

When Joaquín Balaguer of the Partido Reformista (Reformist Party) again came to power in 1966 he applied, as the title of his party signifies, reforms rather than revolutionary changes to the society. On entering the National Palace he was faced with a virtually bankrupt economy, ineffective state administration, and a divided Armed Forces and national bourgeoisie. To Balaguer's benefit, a traditionally uncontrollable variable—commodity prices for major Dominican exports—started an upward climb and generally remained high during his three administrations (1966-1978).

The basic economic policies of Balaguer during his 12-year tenure were as follows:

(1) large-scale foreign investment, especially in mining;
(2) increased reliance on foreign loans;
(3) emphasis on industrial import substitution aided by the enactment of Law 299, which granted tax exemptions for reinvested capital and either lowered or completely eliminated duties on imported capital, raw materials, and semimanufactured goods;
(4) an exchange policy that offered U.S. dollars at preferential rates to foreign and national capitalists for the purchase of imported goods used in national industry;
(5) protection of Dominican-based producers through import bans and extremely high tariffs;
(6) state-sponsored infrastructural development through construction projects in highways, housing, irrigation, and communication;
(7) personal management, through the Office of the Presidency, of more than 45% of the national budget in the last four-year administration; and
(8) an austerity plan that virtually froze agricultural prices through the measures taken by the Instituto Nacional de Establización de Precios (INESPRE) (National Institute of Price Stabilization), and froze wages through edict and repression of the labor movement (Ceara Hatton, 1984; Díaz Santana and Murphy, 1983).

The results of these policies were a tremendous increase in economic activities, especially in the industrial sector; dramatic growth of the

construction industry; reduced prices for nonexport agricultural products; marked increase in rural-urban migration; the development of a
dynamic national bourgeoisie and middle class; reduced real wages for
workers; one of the world's highest economic growth rates; and, a
300+% increase in the foreign debt. The Dominican Republic, like many
non-oil-producing dependent economies, embarked on a model of
industrial import-substitution "just in time" for the oil crisis of the
1970s. Given the fact that virtually all energy sources for Dominican
industry are petroleum products, the Dominican Republic's "economic
miracle" was, of course, short lived.

Economic Collapse and Incoherence (1978-1982)

Inheriting an outstanding national debt of US$967 million on
assuming the presidency in 1978, Antonio Guzmán of the now-moderate
PRD found his country's traditional export prices at abysmal levels and
import volume and prices at astronomical rates, resulting in a trade
deficit of over US$170 million. His administration soon faced incal-
culable losses due to hurricanes David and Frederick and an epidemic of
African swine fever that resulted in the total elimination of the country's
porcine population.

The orientation of Guzmán's economic policies was based on a
Keynesian model of increased public expenditures to stimulate the
private sector. For example, the administration increased the rolls of
public employees in four major branches of the government between
1980 and 1981 by 54.9%. This increase in personnel, together with
augmented employee salaries and benefits, resulted in a 159% increase in
state expenditures in these areas.

The Guzmán emphasis on public spending initially generated distrust
expressed through reduced investment by national and foreign interest.
However, as Ceara Hatton (1984: chap. 3) cogently argues, the
capitalist classes generally misread Guzmán's actions as an affront to the
the private sector; though in fact, Guzmán wished to continue with the
Dominican Republic's mixed economy, stimulate consumption, and
thereby stimulate private sector growth and profits.

Regardless of its basic Keynesian orientation, on the ground level this
administration is best characterized as one without a coherent economic
policy. The Guzmán government tended simply to react to pressures by
divergent and conflicting sectors: It failed to define its class orientation
and tried to please everyone at once. The result was a four-year
succession of presidential decrees and countermands while the inter-

national debt and the deficit column of the trade balance grew to record proportions.

On July 4, 1982 when the Dominican president committed suicide for unknown reasons, the economic system was truly in shambles: Import payments in arrears amounted to some US$350 million, the foreign debt due in 1982 was over US$458 million, and the balance of payments deficit was projected at over US$400 million. Vice-President Jacobo Majluta Azar succeeded the late President for the 42-day period before the inauguration of President-elect Salvador Jorge Blanco, also of the Partido Revolucionario Dominicano (PRD). Immediately, Majluta started his own campaign for the 1986 elections by further draining public coffers through augmented price subsidies for basic foodstuffs sold primarily to the urban poor through INESPRE and the disbursement of multimillion peso government payments, which were in arrears, to both the private sector suppliers and contractors and government employees.

TESTING THE WATERS WITH
THE IMF AND OTHER LENDERS (1982-Present)

Even before taking office in August 1982, President Salvador Jorge Blanco had decided to follow most of the austerity guidelines suggested by the World Bank, United States Agency for International Development, and the International Monetary Fund; however, he refused to enter into formal negotiations with the latter. In his inaugural address, the new president informed the Dominican people of the proposed drastic economic changes. The basic measures of the government of "Concentración Nacional" would be the following:

(1) salary reductions for all government employees who earn more than RD$375.00 per month, with reductions of up to 23% per month for those in the highest pay categories—more than RD$1,200.00 per month;[1]
(2) wage freezes for all employees in the private sector;
(3) strict controls on all government spending;
(4) prohibition on the importation of numerous "nonessential" items;
(5) price freezes on basic foodstuffs;
(6) increased income taxes; and
(7) increased custom duties (see Díaz Santana and Murphy, 1983: 73).

The major suggestions by these international agencies with which Jorge Blanco would not comply were increases in the prices of basic foodstuffs, to be discussed later, and a devaluation of the Dominican peso. Briefly, since Balaguer's administration one peso had since been valued on the preferential market at the official exchange rate of one U.S. dollar. However, only certain types of importers could buy dollars at this rate. There also existed a free-floating parallel market for the purchase of dollars at exchange houses and through "gray market" money changers on the streets, with the value of the dollar for this period at approximately RD$1.50. The official exchange rate, or preferential market rate, was to be used to provide U.S. dollars for the importation of petroleum products, basic raw materials and semifinished products for industry, pharmaceuticals, and by the state and its dependencies.

Jorge Blanco vehemently and repeatedly stated that his administration would never devalue the Dominican peso. In other words, the administration supposedly would never reduce the volume or the value of the peso on the preferential exchange market, although for non-privileged purchasers of U.S. dollars there was an almost daily devaluation on the parallel market.

On the ground level, the Central Bank processed all receipts from the sale of traditional exports (sugar, gold, coffee, cacao, ferronickel, etc.) in dollars and gave the seller pesos at a US$1.00 = RD$1.00 exchange rate, less a small commission. In this manner, the central government hoped to capture the lion's share of the foreign currency. These monies were then to be used to subsidize the purchase of petroleum, raw materials, and other "essential" imports, and assist in the payment of the public and private foreign debt. For two major reasons the system never worked according to plan. First, many major exporters never processed a large portion of their sales through the Central Bank; instead they traded directly with the commodity brokers and retained the dollars. The case of the Grupo Vicini, a major sugar producer, is an excellent example. In 1983 the state charged the corporation with illegally trading over US$40 million worth of products. When the dollars were demanded, Grupo Vicini simply stated that it no longer had the money and that if the government wanted compensation it would have to embargo the corporation. The second major flaw in the system was the extremely high prices for imported products at a time when prices for traditional exports, especially sugar, were close to the century's all-time lows.

Other economic measures taken by the Jorge administration included the stimulation of and incentives for the tourist industry, nontraditional agro-industry for domestic consumption and export, and foreign-owned duty-free manufacturing zones. All of these new industries were to generate employment primarily for unskilled and poorly paid labor, and to capture U.S. dollars for the economy. In fact, these industries have done very little to ameliorate the economic crisis of the Dominican Republic.

Enter the IMF

To borrow the necessary U.S. dollars (in actual loans or credits) to make payments on the foreign debt and keep the government, agriculture, and industry afloat, the Jorge administration formally turned to the IMF. After more than a year of publicized negotiations, the Dominican Republic put into effect the first stages of its monetary and economic reforms during the Easter holiday weekend of 1984. The measures demanded by the IMF and agreed upon by the presidency centered on, first, the partial or complete transfer of many imported products—most important, pharmaceuticals, petroleum products, and agricultural and industrial input and component products (fertilizers, pesticides, machinery, etc.)—from the preferential exchange market (US\$1.00 = RD\$1.00) to the parallel market (US\$1.00 = ±RD\$3.00); and second, reduced subsidies for many basic foodstuffs.

These measures were to take effect immediately for all such products imported after the date of enactment. Nevertheless, merchants raised the prices of the products they had in stock. Thus, products previously purchased at the preferential market rate were sold at prices as much as 200% higher the following day, and the profits were held by the merchants and intermediaries. Merchants argued that by selling the products at their pre-Easter holiday prices they would become "decapitalized" and therefore unable to purchase the necessary merchandise to restock their warehouses and stores at the higher prices. What occurred, then, was that the wholesalers and retailers of these products temporarily increased their profit margins astronomically, and other speculators took advantage of the confusion to augment the prices of nationally produced items, such as plantains and vegetables grown on peasant garden plots.

On Monday morning, April 23, cries of discontent were heard in the poorest neighborhoods of the nation. The poorest citizens make their daily purchases in small urban stores (*colmados*) for lack of both refrigeration and sufficient money to make weekly or monthly shopping trips. The basic scenario—repeated thousands of times that Monday morning in urban neighborhoods and squatter settlements around the country—was that consumers went to local *colmados* to purchase the ingredients for their mid-day meals or to pharmacies to buy the medication that an ill member of the family would need that day. What they found was that prices had increased dramatically "overnight." The consumers' first reaction was that the *colmado* or pharmacy owners were cheating them. Verbal assaults were launched directly at the owners or employees and generally in the neighborhoods about the "*abusadores*" (abusers) who were sellings merchandise at inflated prices. The response of the store owners was: "It's not me. It's the government. It's the IMF."

For the first time the acronym IMF began to assume a somewhat concrete meaning for the majority of the population. No longer was the IMF a group of faceless "*gringos*" who were making demands on the president of the republic. Now this previously little-known entity was somehow taking advantage of the consumers, radically altering their lives.

Spontaneous protests began in the streets of Santo Domingo, but with no concrete target. People were furious, but at whom? The store owners said that they had nothing to do with the increases; they themselves claimed to be victims. The *barrio* residents tended to mill around and shout obscenities at unknown and absent perpetrators, and discarded tires were placed in the streets and ignited. National Police troops then arrived with tear gas grenades, thereby supplying the necessary catalyst for violent confrontation. The presence and actions of the troops offered the protestors a vicarious vent for their emotions: The police became the convenient and concrete enemy.

Rocks were answered with automatic weapons. Protests soon spread to virtually all squatter settlements, poor and working-class neighborhoods in the nation's cities. After the first day of rioting fewer than 10 people were killed; however, the administration then called out the Armed Forces. When a forced calm returned after 72 hours of disturbances, the official National Police spokesman announced that 47 people had been killed; however, the Dominican Committee of Human Rights later claimed to have the names and addresses of 86 victims, ranging in age from 16 days to 84 years, as well as documented eye-witness accounts of their deaths.

The president, members of his Partido Revolucionario Dominicano, and the National Police and Armed Forces claimed that the riots were the result of a conspiracy by the extreme Left, Right, and labor unions with designs to topple the government. My own participant observation in many of the poorest *barrios* of Santo Domingo shortly before and during the disturbances contradicts this conspiracy theory. True, some youths had gathered discarded tires during the preceding Easter holiday, and for months before the Comités de Luchas Populares (Committees of Popular Struggles) had coordinated "consciousness-raising" activities in the neighborhoods. Nonetheless, and unfortunately, those who took to the streets from April 23 through April 25 were simply reacting to the price increases and subsequently to the repressive tactics of the police and military. The poor were, and still are, unaware of the structural causes of the crisis.

As evidence of the lack of planning one must note that leftist, rightist, and labor leaders are both politically and physically isolated from the daily lives of the poorest of the country and the violence. Not until almost 12 hours after the protests began did a coalition of labor unions call a 24-hour national strike; and this announcement was made when the country had already come to a complete standstill, with no hope for return to normalcy for days. Most national opposition leaders, regardless of ideology, were shocked by the magnitude of the disturbances, although they later claimed to understand the poor's frustration and anger, and promptly condemned the PRD administration.

The Second Round

On August 30, 1984, President Jorge Blanco was to announce the measures to be taken as a result of the second round of negotiations with the IMF. The principal result of these talks was that the administration had agreed to subsidize less of the price of petroleum products through the preferential exchange market. On August 27, three days before the planned presidential address, a joint communique from the National Police and Armed Forces was read to the president and broadcast nationally. The communique claimed that political parties and labor unions from the extreme Left were planning "destablizing violent acts." Capricious house searches and jailings of known leftists began immediately. The labor coalitions, which had for weeks been calling for a national strike if petroleum product prices were increased, called off their threat after "secret" meetings with National Palace personnel.

On August 29, while everyone anxiously awaited the presidential speech scheduled for the following day, all urban areas were "secured" by mixed patrols of National Police and Armed Forces and an undeclared state of seige took effect. The next day President Jorge

Blanco announced that the price of diesel oil would almost double (96% increase) and the prices of gasoline and propane gas would be raised by almost one-third, and that customs duties would be increased dramatically as well.

Many analysts expected renewed disturbances in the *barrios* of Santo Domingo, and most believed that the transport sector would definitely launch a nationwide strike. Neither of these events came to pass. In the former case street protests were made impossible because of the police and military control over the neighborhoods. In the latter case most analysts misinterpreted the class interests of the majority of the transport sector. Transport sector interest groups, erroneously called labor unions (*sindicatos*), have a reputation for effectively and often violently opposing increases in petroleum product prices. They do not, however, represent the interests of the working class or unemployed; rather, these federations are numerically and politically dominated by medium-sized owners and owner-operators, a petit bourgeoisie. Their interest was to raise fares and charges to cover increased fuel costs and maintain profits. On August 30, the trucking companies and cab owners simply raised their prices, apparently without government authorization but with no objection either (see Garrido Ramírez, 1984).

The Third Round

The latest phase of price increases, which primarily affected petroleum products and cement, was implemented in January 1985. Sporadic neighborhood strikes and later a national strike were coordinated, primarily by the Comités de Luchas Populares. Again, the National Police and Armed Forces entered the *barrios*, the press was banned from reporting on the strikes, and union and opposition party leaders were jailed. Meanwhile, the police and military vowed allegiance to democracy and the transport sector raised fares.

Using his by now traditional "carrot and stick" approach, Salvador Jorge Blanco in his national address not only announced the price increases, but also proposed to raise the nonagricultural minimum wage from RD$175 to RD$225 per month. Nevertheless, we must note that more than 40% of the economically active urban population is in the informal sector, which is not covered by minimum wage regulation; and for the first time the minimum wage earner will have to pay income tax, as the cutoff point is RD$200 per month. Hence, for a worker with no dependents the increase in social security deductions and payment of income tax will result in the loss of almost half the wage increase. In other words, as much as half of the raise will go to the state.[2]

THE POLITICAL, ECONOMIC, AND
SOCIAL CONSEQUENCES OF IMF REFORMS

With the mass demonstrations and the violent, repressive tactics employed by the police and military during the period from April 23-25, 1984, the Dominican Republic reembarked on a political course that most Dominicans hoped had ended in 1978. To be sure, balance of payment deficits, mounting foreign debts, inappropriate economic measures, and administrative corruption during the PRD presidencies of Antonio Guzmán and Jorge Blanco had pushed the nation into economic disaster. However, the fact remained that a clear pattern of greater respect for civil liberties had been emerging. At no time in Dominican history had the populace enjoyed a more open national election than that of 1982 in which all political parties were allowed to participate. For the first time in recent memory there were no political prisoners or exiles. The military and police had been controlled to a significant degree and the active role of these forces in civilian and political affairs had been reduced. Progressively, Army officers had been replaced by civilians in nonmilitary positions, the civil rights of detainees had more often been respected and a program of prison reforms was planned.

However, the political climate has changed dramatically since April 23, 1984. After 5½ years of movement toward greater political freedoms, Salvador Jorge Blanco in a period of three days returned much of the power that these forces had previously wielded. Through a kind of self-inflicted *golpe de estado*, President Jorge Blanco relinquished much of his control when he first permitted the police and military to enter neighborhoods and shoot at will. A striking visual representation of Jorge Blanco's loss of power came on April 24. That evening he appeared on national television with over 25 field and general-grade officers as a backdrop, and the president of the republic spoke only after party leaders, cabinet members, and Lt. Gen. Cuervo Gómez stated their commitment to him, Dominican democracy, and the need to effectively put down the protests.

Since April 1984 there is room to question the President's power vis-à-vis the National Police and armed forces, regardless of their repeated public statements and open letters published in the press as to

their unfaltering loyalty to both the president and Dominican democracy. Commonplace since the spring of 1984 are roundups and
detentions of union leaders and leftist opposition party officials without
formal charges being filed, house raids, street corner document checks,
and the almost constant police or military presence in the *barrios*.

For a variety of reasons—a central one being the austerity programs—the ruling party is in complete turmoil. Most of the major
figures in the PRD are generally trying to disassociate themselves from
Jorge Blanco and his programs in order to gain support for their
candidacies on the party's presidential ticket in 1986. In 1982 the PRD
held, for the first time, a majority in both the Chamber of Representatives and Senate; however, the administration now finds almost as
many enemies among its fellow party members as it does in the
opposition parties within these legislative bodies.

The extreme division within the party was clearly evidenced late last
year when two presidents of the Senate were elected, one from the Jorge
camp of the PRD and the other, ex-President Majluta, also of the PRD,
and neither they nor their followers would acknowledge the other's legal
right to lead the Senate. Not until Pope John Paul II visited the country
was the situation resolved through mediation.

The macroeconomic ingredients of the crisis are fourfold. First,
imports have been reduced substantially and greater revenues are filling
the government coffers through new and increased import duties and
taxes. Nevertheless, the world market prices for traditional Dominican
exports—sugar, gold, coffee, cacao, tobacco, and ferronickel—generally
continue downward, and the Dominican Republic will not be able to
resolve the current balance of payments deficit until the values of these
products raise substantially.

Second, from the spring of 1984 until the summer of 1985 the value of
the Dominican peso relative to the United States dollar fluctuated
between RD$3.00 and RD$3.40 = US$1.00. The major causes of this
reduced value are to be found in the accelerated demand for dollars on
the parallel market caused by the reduction in the volume of the United
States currency available at the preferential exchange rate, capital flight,
and speculation in currency. This reduction in the value of the local
currency relative to the U.S. dollar has brought about a 200% inflation
rate in the prices of many imported products and, some say, a general
inflation rate for this period of almost 100%.

Third, before the April 1984 crisis the capital city of Santo Domingo
exhibited an unemployment rate of 25% and an underemployment rate
of more than 40%. Now, with proposed increases in the minimum wage

and inability to purchase many imported raw materials, many firms are laying off workers and the ranks of the unemployed and underemployed are growing even larger.

Fourth, the most important macroeconomic consequence of the implementation of the IMF demands is an accelerated opening of the Dominican economy to exports and foreign investment. Since the reign of Trujillo the country has exhibited a mixed economy, with emphasis on agro-industrial and extractive industry exports and attempts to attract private foreign capital in all sectors of the economy. Since negotiations with the IMF this general trend has been intensified by expansion and diversification of the agro-industrial export sector and attempts to attract more foreign capital.

The major question in the Dominican Republic today is: "How are the poor surviving?" The answer is that many are not. Prices of most basic ingredients in the Dominican diet are being further subsidized, contrary to IMF recommendations, through INESPRE and its Ventas Populares (Popular Sales) program, and the average poor person finds some way to keep body and soul intact. However, hardest hit are infants and young children. With present prices for infant formula being over 200% higher than a year ago, the price of the daily subsistence portion is now equivalent to almost half a minimum wage earner's daily salary. With respect to juvenile and adult needs, public hospitals are generally without disposable surgical equipment and most common medicines, and when a family is told to purchase a prescribed daily dose of medicine at a local pharmacy, they often find it costs more than their daily collective wage. No study has examined the rise in infant mortality during the last year, but my own informal interviews with medical personnel indicate that deaths among infants and young children from malnutrition, dehydration, and common viruses may be twice as high as before April 1984. The incidence of tuberculosis in the adult population is considered to be at epidemic proportions.

In 1985 there prevades in the Dominican Republic a marked somber and expectant mood. What appears to concern all social classes is not so much what has happened, nor what is happening, but what will happen. A common retort to one's complaints about the present economic, political, and social crisis is: "Things are going to get worse." Most Dominicans believe that the only hope lies in the planned elections of May 1986. Some believe that they will find a savior (but not *Salvador* Jorge Blanco) in their next president—one who will redeem them from their present situation.

PROSPECTS FOR THE FUTURE

All three PRD Presidents (Bosch, 1963; Guzmán, 1978; and Jorge Blanco, 1982) were elected through tremendous support from the urban poor and working classes. These groups, however, have been hardest hit by price increases and political repression. Recent polls have noted the electorate's preference for ex-President Joaquín Balaguer, despite his advanced age, extremely poor health, and record of brutal repression during his association with Trujillo and 12-year tenure as President (1966-1978). According to such polls, ex-President Juan Bosch—who split with the PRD in 1973 to form his own left-leaning Partido de la Liberación Dominicana (Dominican Liberation Party), and who finished a distant third in the 1982 national elections—runs far ahead of any PRD candidate (Moya Pons, 1984).

By supporting Balaguer and even claiming in a recent survey that Trujillo's record was not that bad (Vega, 1984, cited in Oviedo, 1984: 50), many Dominicans are apparently demonstrating their desire for economic well-being over civil liberties. Although these trends demonstrate the electorate's short memory, they also demonstrate the seriousness of the crisis. When asked how they could favor these repressive regimes, many people answer: "We ate better, and besides they didn't kill anyone in my family."

A simultaneous and quite different development is the apparent emergence of a popular political movement in the *barrios*. Many analysts had noted that the Comités de Luchas Populares were demonstrating an uncanny ability to mobilize the urban masses. Working clandestinely and in opposition to government economic measures, the Comités have organized numerous isolated neighborhood strikes and one successful national strike. Supported by the Central General de Trabajadores and Juan Bosch's Partido de la Liberación Dominicana, many observers believe that the Comités exhibit two essential ingredients that no Dominican national political party possesses: active leadership and participation by the poor, and a true comprehension of the plight of the poor.

On closer examination and through participant observation in the *barrios*, however, it is evident that the Comités have not been very successful in organizing the masses and effectively representing them in the long run. True, the Comités have called neighborhood and national strikes and the populace has responded at particular times. However, more often than not the organizing and coordinating efforts of the

Comités have been futile. Generally, this urban-based national network announces strikes at specific times when the necessary ingredients are in place for collective action. If the strike occurs the Comités take credit for its coordination. Basically, these groups take advantage of the unrest rather than direct it. More important, residents of the neighborhoods where the Comités are supposedly most active do not seem to know what the Comités de Luchas Populares are and who the representatives of these groups are. Nor do they see the Comités as valid vehicles for the expression of their interests.

Nonetheless, the Comités, or future like organizations, may eventually develop into viable political movements and fill a crucial void in the Dominican Left. Presently, the nation's leftist parties and leftist labor federations are politically and socially distant from the poor. The leftist parties tend to be dominated by a university-educated petit bourgeoisie that neither experiences the hunger of the poor nor lives in their neighborhoods; and the leftist labor federations visualize the world in terms of worker versus owner, even though the Dominican Republic is at best a semi-industrialized society. A "grass roots" political movement, in contrast, would suffer from neither of these faults. Its political focus would be *limited* neither to esoteric discourses on United States imperialism—as in the present case of many leftist parties—nor to wage increases and benefits for a somewhat privileged group, industrial workers, as in the case of most labor federations. Rather it would address concrete issues—food prices, housing, lack of water and sewage systems, education, medical services, public transportation fares, and political repression—that are essential to the lives of citizens.[3]

To many, the present and future political scenes seem quite confusing, with two apparently conflicting trends: on the one hand a shift to the Right in the opinion polls, on the other popular protest. Many observers have tried to explain away the simultaneous existence of these two trends by claiming that different ideological groups and social classes are associated with each movement, or by stating that "the average Dominican doesn't know what he wants." Both arguments are incorrect.

An appropriate explanation of the political actions and preferences of the Dominican people, especially the poor (the majority of the population), is found in an understanding of the political consciousness of many Dominicans. For the average citizen, there exist socioculturally defined and accepted relations and levels of exploitation; when the rules are violated—as in the case of drastic price increases—individual or mass protest occurs. The same participants of the protests often go into the streets days later to receive and cheer moderate and rightist politicans. There is no contradiction in their actions. Protests, for the majority of the population, are immediate responses to what are socioculturally defined as unjust actions against their interests. For the participants, protests are not considered as essential steps in a revolutionary process or directed actions to change the relations or levels of exploitation; rather they are attempts to maintain the traditional relations and levels of exploitation within acceptable limits (Centro de Investigación y Documentación Social, 1984: 27-32).

The question remains: Can any political movement, party, president, or even military junta resolve the present crisis? Actors from virtually all points along the ideological spectrum blame only the International Monetary Fund for the present plight of the Dominican Republic. These strategists, however, are missing the essential point. True, the IMF has made many onerous demands on the Dominican economy and the implementation of its recommendations have had drastic and immediate effects for the population; nevertheless, the problem is much greater than the IMF and its demands. Outside of academic circles, few are examining the structural roots of the crisis: the causes of Dominican public and private sector indebtedness; the factors resulting in the present trade deficit; the abysmal failures of past "development" schemes; and the country's dependent role in the international economic order. By overlooking these structural roots, no viable solutions to these problems are forthcoming.

Now, without thorough evaluation of Balaguer's previously applied industrial import-substitution model, or Guzmán's Keynesian approach, the Dominican Republic is opting for another economic policy. Based on recommendations from the World Bank, U.S. Agency for International Development, and the IMF, the economy is presently being partially retooled for nontraditional agro-industrial and light manufacture for export. The Reagan administration's Caribbean Basin Initiative is being taken seriously by many quarters with little concrete planning for the time when this preferential import plan expires, and little analysis of its present and future impact on agricultural and manufacturing production for the domestic market. Despite certain immediate gains for specific sectors of the Dominican society, this variation on the traditional export model will not alter the Dominican Republic's subservience to its principal trading partners, the United States and Western Europe.

NOTES

1. In August 1982 the parallel market exchange rate was approximately: US$1.00 = RD$1.50.

2. In the spring of 1985 the Dominican Congress called for a more substantial increase in the minimium wage—RD$350 per month. However, President Jorge refused to acknowledge the congressional bill and unilaterally and apparently without constitutional authority again raised the monthly minimum wage from RD$225 to only RD$250. This presidential decree took effect in July 1985.

3. It is, of course, recognized that "grass roots" or popular political movements are not without their problems, as has been repeatedly demonstrated in Latin American and Caribbean history.

REFERENCES

CASSA, R. (1978) Modos de producción, clases sociales y luchas políticas. Santo Domingo: Alfa y Omega.

CEARA HATTON, M. (1984) Tendencias estructurales y coyuntura de la economía dominicana, 1968-1983. Santo Domingo: Nuevas Rutas.

Centro de Investigación y Documentación Social (1984) Crisis y movimientos populares en República Dominicana. Santo Domingo: Buho.

DÍAZ SANTANA, M. and M. MURPHY (1983) The 1982 National Elections in the Dominican Republic: A Sociological and Historical Interpretation. Caribbean Occasional Series 3. Río Piedras: University of Puerto Rico.

GARRIDO RAMÍREZ, R. (1984) "Army gives the hungry a taste of repression." The Guardian (September 19).

HOOKE, A. (1981) The International Monetary Fund: Its Evolution, Organization, and Activities. Washington, DC: International Monetary Fund.

HORSEFIELD, J. (1969) The International Monetary Fund, 1945-1965: Vol. I. Washington, DC: International Monetary Fund.

MARTIN, J. B. (1975) El destino dominicano. Santo Domingo: Editora de Santo Domingo.

MOYA PONS, F. (1984) "La política dominicana." Latin American Studies Association Forum XV, 3: 19-21.

OVIEDO, J. (1984) "La estabilidad del equilibrio inestable: el Partido Revolucionario Dominicano como partido popular o gobernante." Nueva Sociedad 74: 43-50.

VEGA, B. (1984) "Menos de la mitad de los dominicanos creen que Trujillo fue un mal gobernante." Listin Diario (Santo Domingo) (June 9).

NOTES ON THE CONTRIBUTORS

DAVID BRAY received his Ph.D. in anthropology from Brown University. He has taught at Tufts, was project manager for the Caribbean Migration Program at the Center for Latin American Studies, University of Florida, and from 1983-1986 was Assistant Director and Visiting Assistant Professor at the Roger Thayer Stone Center for Latin American Studies at Tulane University. He has published studies in Caribbean Basin export agriculture, migration, and industrialization. He is currently Foundation Representative for Paraguay and northern Argentina with the Inter-American Foundation in Arlington, VA.

SUSAN ECKSTEIN is professor of Sociology at Boston University. Her publications include *The Poverty of Revolution* (Princeton University Press, 1977), *The Impact of Revolution: A Comparative Analysis of Mexico and Bolivia* (Sage, 1976), and numerous articles on Latin America. She currently is writing a book on the Cuban Revolution.

ROBERT P. MATTHEWS has a Ph.D. in history from New York University. He is a staff researcher with the North American Congress on Latin America (NACLA) and teaches Latin American history and politics at New York University's Center for Latin American and Caribbean Studies. His publications include a book on nineteenth-century rural violence in Venezuela and various articles on contemporary Venezuela and Central America.

SIDNEY W. MINTZ is William L. Straus Jr. Professor of Anthropology at the Johns Hopkins University. He specializes in the anthropology of the Caribbean region, and has worked with sugarcane cutters in Puerto Rico, peasant cultivators in Jamaica, and market women in Haiti. He has also done fieldwork in Iran. His publications include *The People of Puerto Rico* (1956), *Worker in the Cane* (1960), *Slavery, Colonialism and Racism* (1975), *Esclave-facteur de production* (1980), and three new books in 1985, including *Sweetness and Power*, a cultural history of sugar consumption in the West.

MARTIN F. MURPHY is Assistant Professor of Anthropology at the University of Notre Dame. He received his Licenciatura degree from Universidad de las Americas, Mexico, his M.A. from Syracuse University, and his Ph.D. from Colombia University. He formerly held positions as Visiting Assistant Professor, Center for Latin American Studies, University of Florida, and Profesor Especial, Universidad Autónoma de Santo Domingo. He has written on various aspects of Dominican and Haitian society, including the plantation economy, labor practices on sugarcane plantations, migration patterns, the urban informal sector, and Dominican politics. Most pertinent to his contribution to this volume is *The 1982 National Elections in the Dominican Republic: A Sociological and Historical Interpretation*, coauthored with Miriam Díaz Santana.

JEFFERY M. PAIGE is Professor of Sociology and Research Associate in the Center for Research on Social Organization at the University of Michigan. He is author of *Agrarian Revolution* and (with Karen Ericksen) *The Politics of Reproductive Ritual*. He currently is engaged in a comparative study of the political consequences of the rise of the coffee, banana, and cotton export sectors in Central America. "Cotton and Revolution in Nicaragua," a companion piece to his analysis of coffee and politics in this volume, appears in Peter Evans et al. (eds.) *States versus Markets in the Capitalist World Economy*, Vol. 8, Political Economy of the World-System Annuals (Sage, 1985).

RICHARD TARDANICO is a Sociologist in the Latin American and Carribean Center, Florida International University, and is spending 1985-1987 as Fulbright Professor, Escuela de Historia y Geografía, Universidad de Costa Rica, and Visiting Professor, Facultad Latinoamericana de Ciencias Sociales (FLACSO), San José. His articles on state making during the Mexican Revolution and on international urban political economy have appeared in such journals as *Comparative Studies in Society and History, Revista Mexicana de Sociología, Revista Occidental, Anthropologie et Sociétés,* and *Theory and Society*. In addition to his continuing work on comparative state making in Mexico and Colombia, he currently is conducting research on socioeconomic networks and collective action in low-income districts of San José.

DALE W. TOMICH is Associate Professor of Sociology, SUNY-Binghamton. His research has focused on the changing place of slavery in the historical development of the capitalist world-economy. He is completing a book on the decline of slavery in the French West Indian colony of Martinique during the nineteenth century.

CYNTHIA TRUELOVE is an independent consultant to small-scale development agencies working in Latin America and a doctoral student in the Program for Comparative International Development at Johns Hopkins University. Her primary research interests include the Latin American informal sector, policy dimensions of Latin American development, and women's labor participation in the periphery. She currently is working on research for her dissertation, "Gender and Labor Market Segmentation in Rural Colombia."

RALPH LEE WOODWARD, Jr., is Professor of Latin American History at Tulane University. He is author of *Central America: A Nation Divided* (Oxford University Press, 1985), as well as numerous other books and articles on Latin American history. He is on the Board of Editors of *Latin American Research Review* and editor of the Central American section of the *Research Guide to Central America and the Caribbean* (University of Wisconsin Press, 1985).